CONTENTS

WHY DO YOGA?

Yoga has been practised for thousands of years. It is believed to unite the mind, the body and the spirit. Yoga helps you become more aware of your body's posture, alignment and movement.

Yoga is a great way to get fit. It makes the body more **flexible** and helps you to relax. Practising yoga can make you happier and feel peaceful, too. Yoga is thought to help improve your memory and concentration. Many schools now start the day with a yoga session to help concentrate their student's minds. Yoga is also believed to help with anxiety and depression, and help lower your blood pressure and your pulse rate.

Yoga is fun and great exercise.

In a yoga class, the students usually place their mats facing the front. Leave a little space around your mat so you have space to do the poses. The students often sit cross-legged waiting for the class to start, or they do some gentle stretches. The teacher may start the class with a breathing exercise or **meditation**. This is followed by warm-up poses, more vigorous poses, then stretches and then final relaxation exercises.

Yoga classes may use blankets to roll up and use as props for some poses. Some classes use blocks and straps (below) as well. The blocks act as props and the straps help in poses where you need to hold your feet, for example, but can't quite reach.

Wear stretchy exercise trousers or shorts. A fitted T-shirt is best. Baggy T-shirts can slide up when you are upside down. You can usually rent yoga mats to start with. Yoga is usually done barefoot.

TRY THIS

Most yoga classes end a session by saying 'namaste', which means 'I bow to you' in Hindi.

MEDITATION

Meditation is an important part of learning yoga. You don't have to learn to meditate to enjoy yoga, but it is generally considered to be part of the experience.

Yoga means union. Meditation is a way for people doing yoga to unite their body and mind. Meditation improves your ability to focus on things, including your yoga. Benefits of meditation include a decrease in blood pressure, improved breathing and a slower resting heart rate. Chemicals in the body that are associated with stress may get lower as well.

You can meditate in any still position. Sitting is the most common posture. A simple cross-legged pose is good for beginners.

Many people like to meditate near the calming presence of water.

To try to meditate, create a peaceful atmosphere and wear comfortable clothing. Concentrate on one thing, such as your breathing, a word or sensations you feel in your body. If your thoughts start to wander, take them back to your object of focus. To prevent other thoughts coming into your mind, try looking at an object such as a candle. Once your mind is clear of thought, you will feel calm, yet aware. People say this feeling cannot be described by words.

This child's pose is physically relaxing and one of the best yoga poses for mental relaxation.

BREATHING

Controlling your breathing is important during yoga. Breathing correctly brings more oxygen to the blood and the brain.

Yoga breathing techniques help increase your lung **capacity**. Just as with meditation, concentrating on your breathing develops your focus, too. It fights away stress and relaxes the body. Breathing correctly during a pose is important. If your breathing isn't relaxed, your body can't relax into the pose. If your body isn't relaxed, your mind can't relax. And if your mind isn't relaxed, you can't draw the full benefits from your yoga.

Yoga breathing control is called pranayama. The breath sets the rhythm for the practice. When you **inhale**, move into pose. When you **exhale**, move out of it. Your movements should match your breath.

The following yoga breathing exercises can make you feel dizzy, so make sure you're with a trained adult when you try out these techniques. Kapalabhati is a cleaning breath. Breaths are short, rapid and strong. The lungs work as a pump, creating pressure as they expel the air and remove waste from the air passages.

Take two normal breaths. Breathe in.

Breathe out, pulling in your **abdomen**. Repeat twenty times, emphasising breathing out. Finally, breathe in fully and hold your breath for as long as you can. Slowly breathe out.

TRY THIS

Alternate nostril breathing helps some people to settle the mind and the body. Only try this under the supervision of a trained expert.

Hold your hand as shown in the picture. Inhale through your left nostril, closing the right with your thumb. Count to four. Hold your breath, closing both nostrils. Count to sixteen. Exhale through the right nostril, closing the left with the ring and little fingers. Count to eight. Inhale using the right nostril, keeping the left nostril closed with the ring and little fingers. Count to four. Hold your breath, closing both nostrils, and count to sixteen. Exhale using the left nostril, keeping the right closed with the thumb. Count to eight.

Relaxing Breathing

You can help get rid of stress using these yogic breathing techniques.

Sit comfortably in a chair. Close your eyes and picture a swan gliding peacefully across a crystal-clear lake. Now, like the swan, let your breath flow along in a long, smooth, peaceful movement. Inhale and exhale through your nose. If your nose is blocked, use your nose and mouth, or just your mouth. Inhale and exhale as deeply as you can, and repeat this 20 times. Then, gradually let your breath return to normal. Take a few moments to sit with your eyes closed and notice how different you feel overall.

One method of breathing used in yoga is called ujjayi breathing. The breathing is quite noisy, which helps focus your attention on each breath. The breath is done through the nose. First fill your lower abdomen, then your lower rib cage and finally your upper chest and throat. As the throat passage is narrowed the passage of air creates a 'rushing' sound.

Ujjayi breathing should sound like the ocean. The 'ocean sound' is created by moving the **glottis** as the air passes in and out.

SEATED EXERCISES

Yoga isn't all about tying yourself in complicated knots. There are some simpler seated poses that are very good at improving your strength and flexibility.

This seated twist pose stretches your shoulders, hips and back. It helps increase circulation and tones the abdomen. If you find this too hard, make it easier by keeping your bottom leg straight and place both hands on your raised knee. If your lower back rounds forwards sit on a folded blanket.

Seated twist

- Sit on the floor with your legs extended.
- Cross your right foot over the outside of your left thigh. Bend your left knee. Keep your right knee pointed toward the ceiling.
- Place your left elbow to the outside of your right knee and your right hand on the floor behind you.
- Twist right as far as you can, moving from your abdomen. Keep both sides of your bottom on the floor. Stay for one minute.
- Switch sides and repeat.

This boat pose is great at exercising your stomach muscles and helps your balance.

Boat pose

Sit with your legs out in front of you. Lean back and bend your knees, lifting your legs off the floor. Lean back further. Hold your thighs with your hands and pull in your lower back. Stretch your arms to the front, with your palms facing your body. After 5 to 10 breaths, slowly straighten your legs. Your feet should be higher than your head. Hold the pose for 5 to 10 breaths, then slowly release.

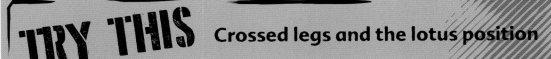

TRY THIS
Crossed legs and the lotus position

1

A cross-legged position is a good way to meditate, and is a good way to sit in between poses in class.

2

To do a lotus, start cross-legged. Place one foot on the thigh, sole upwards. Slowly try to lift the other foot and place it on the other thigh.

STANDING POSES

Standing poses help open up your chest and shoulders and help you build long, lean, strong arms and legs.

Doing a tree pose helps you with your balance and focus. Try it on both legs.

1. Stand with your arms at your sides.

2. Shift your weight onto your right leg and place the sole of your left foot inside your right thigh, keeping your hips facing forwards.

3. Once balanced, bring your hands in front of you in a prayer position, with your palms together.

4. On an inhalation, extend your arms over your shoulders, palms separated and facing each other. Stay for 30 seconds.

5. Repeat the pose using the other leg.

The warrior pose is great for leg strength. It's important to keep your body straight over your hips.

1 Start by doing a low lunge, with your feet far apart. Bend your front knee.

2 Roll your back heel to the ground. Drop your shoulders and turn them parallel to your mat.

3 Reach your arms out, palms down, parallel to the ground. Keep your body vertical over your hips, with your front knee directly over your ankle.

Gaze out over your right hand. Hold the pose for one minute. Then try doing it on the other side.

Warrior and Triangle

Yoga doesn't just involve separate poses. Part of the workout you get is from moving from one pose to another.

There are several different warrior poses. You can try moving through them all. The pose on the right is called warrior I. Remember to inhale as you move into a pose, and exhale as you move out of it.

TRY THIS

Try this variation of warrior pose, warrior III.

Start from warrior pose, then hold both arms up, palms together. Lean forwards and exhale. Lift your back foot and straighten your leg.

The triangle pose will help expand your shoulders and chest. This pose increases flexibility in your hip and neck joints. It also stretches the muscles in your spine, your **calves** and your thighs.

Start from a warrior position.

Straighten your front leg, and follow your front hand forwards, down to your shin or the floor.

Reach your top arm straight up, and bring your body and legs in the same line.

17

ARM BALANCES

This pose is called the downward dog. It is usually one of the first poses you will learn in a yoga class.

Downward dog uses the strength of your arms and legs to evenly stretch your spine. It stretches your hips, **hamstrings** and calves. It opens your chest and shoulders and tones your arms and abdomen. It even tones your hands and feet, preparing you for standing poses and arm balances.

Start on your hands and knees, with your shoulders over your wrists and your toes tucked.

Make a tall 'V' shape by lifting your hips straight up, sinking upper chest and shoulders, and relaxing down the backs of your legs into your heels.

The plank builds arm and abdomen strength. You might find your arms shaking as you practise it at first.

The plank
Start on your hands and knees, shoulders directly over your wrists.

Tuck your toes, extend your legs, and walk your feet back until your shoulders, hips and ankles form a straight line.

TRY THIS

Stop your plank from sagging by inhaling to pull your abdomen in and straighten your lower back.

The sideways plank
From a plank, lift your hips up and shift your weight onto one hand. Roll your whole body to that side. Your shoulders, hips and ankles should be in one straight line. Reach your top arm straight up.

19

The Crow

The crow builds strength in your arms, inner thighs and abdomen. It looks really cool, too!

The crow posture can be painful for the wrists at first. To make it easier, try shifting your weight forwards until you feel some pressure on your wrists, and then practise lifting one foot and then the other off the ground until your wrists build up strength to lift both feet off the ground together.

1 Squat with your feet apart. Put your palms on the ground under your shoulders. Bend your arms slightly, and squeeze your knees firmly around your elbows or upper arms.

2 Rock your weight forwards into your hands, coming up high on your toes. Lift your feet off the ground.

3

Your feet will lift easily off the ground when your weight is more in front of your hands than behind them. Lean your shoulders out past your wrists to shift your weight forwards.

Try doing a half crow if you find the crow too difficult.

From a downward dog, lift one leg and bend your knee, pressing your calf into the back of your thigh. Roll your shoulders forwards over your wrists and bring your knee to the outside of your upper arm. Bend your elbows slightly and shift your shoulders forwards to bring your back foot off the ground.

FLOOR POSES

Floor poses can be a great opportunity to leave any stresses you have behind. One of them simply involves lying down!

It's called the corpse pose for a reason. It gives your body and mind a rest, surrendering and letting go of control. The corpse pose relaxes your central nervous system and calms your mind.

The corpse pose

Lie on your back with your knees bent. Lift your hips off the floor and lengthen your spine along the floor. Then drop your hips down again. Straighten your legs and let your feet fall out naturally to the sides. Slide your shoulders away from your ears and tuck your shoulder blades under you. Stretch out your arms and rest them loosely away from your body.

Let your head feel heavy. Breathe naturally in and out through the nose. Fill your throat, chest and abdomen with every inhale. Exhale fully. Relax your eyes and focus on the inside of your forehead between your eyebrows. Feel a sense of stillness and calm. Stay for 5 to 30 minutes.

In child's pose you can hold your arms out to the front, like this, or drape them alongside your legs.

TRY THIS

Meditate!

The child's pose is not only physically relaxing. It's mentally relaxing, too. Try meditating in child pose.

The child's pose

Kneel on the floor, knees slightly apart and big toes touching. Lean forwards until your forehead touches the floor. Let your face, neck and shoulders relax. Breathe deeply into the abdomen. Release all tension away from the body as you sink deeper into the pose with each breath. Let your arms drape along your sides, palms up, or place them palms down in front of you.

The pigeon

Begin in a push-up position, with your palms under your shoulders. Place your right knee on the floor near your shoulder with your right heel by your left hip. Lower down to your forearms. Bring your left leg down with the top of your foot on the floor. Stay on your forearms, or, if you're more flexible, lower to floor and extend your arms in front of you, like in this picture.

Cobras and Bridges

Both of these poses exercise your spine and chest. The bridge strengthens your legs. The cobra is great for building arm strength, too.

The cobra
Lie face down on the floor with your hands just in front of your shoulders. Your legs should be extended with the tops of your feet on the floor. Push strongly down with your pelvis and push up using your thumbs and index fingers. Raise your chest. Feel the power and stretch in your lower back.

TRY THIS

Is it a cobra or an upward facing dog?

These two yoga poses look identical. The difference is where the power is coming from. In upward facing dog, the strength is in the shoulders and the rest of body falls away. In cobra, the power is in the lower back; the arms are merely props.

To do a king cobra, try to raise your legs to touch your head.

The bridge is called Chatush Padasana, which means 'four foot pose'. Your weight should be distributed evenly between your feet and shoulders, as if you had four feet.

1 Lie flat on your back. Bend your knees straight up, bringing your heels just behind your hips. Exhale and lift your hips up to knee height.

2 Grasp your ankles or **interlace** your fingers with your arms straight. Squeeze your shoulder blades together.

TRY THIS

If you find a bridge difficult, try using straps and blocks to help you achieve this pose.

THE HARD STUFF

Although the main mission of yoga is balance, it can seriously challenge your strength and flexibility, too.

Headstands can be very challenging. They require great core strength and courage. Headstands are great for focus and calming the mind. Muscular bodies can find headstands hard. Some very fit people have tight hamstrings, shoulders and backs.

1 Make sure the space around you is safe if you fall. Get on your hands and knees.

2 Lower your forearms to the ground. Position your elbows under your shoulders.

3 Clasp your fingers together behind your head. Put the top of your head on the ground.

4 Walk your feet towards you until your hips are over your head. Lift one leg, then the other until both are straight up in the air.

> Getting up is the tricky part. Try just lifting one leg at first and bending your knee so your calf is touching your thigh.

The aim of a wide-legged standing forward bend is to fold forwards from the hips so you stretch your hamstrings without straining your back.

Stand with your feet apart, hands on your hips. Lift up tall and then fold slowly over your legs. Place your hands flat on the floor, shoulder-width apart. Bring your head towards the floor. Bend your elbows.

TRY THIS

If you get flexible enough, try this standing forward bend. Stand with feet slightly apart. Exhale and bend forwards from the hip joints, not the waist. Try and touch your palms to the floor. Press your heels firmly into the floor.

If this is too difficult, you can try a half forward bend instead. Bend from the hips and touch the floor by your toes with your fingertips.

This pose is called the side extended hand to big toe pose! The pose helps with steadiness and poise.

Keeping your right leg straight, grasp your left big toe with your left first two fingers. Extend your left leg straight out to the side. Extend your right arm to the side for balance. Straighten both legs. Level your hips. Keep your body upright, lift and broaden your chest. Exhale and bend the left leg to bring the leg down. Repeat on the other side.

To help you, try using yoga straps and a chair to support your leg once you raise it.

TRY THIS

If you can't manage the yoga pose, try the hand position. It is called gyan mudra, and is thought to bring peace and spiritual progress. Connect your thumb and forefinger tip to tip. The other fingers are straight but relaxed.

Pressure between the thumb and forefinger should be light.

If you managed to do the lotus position on page 13, you could try this elevated lotus.

Once you are in the lotus position, place your palms on the ground next to your hips. Gradually and smoothly, raise your body above ground level so that your entire body weight rests on the palms of your hands. Lower your body and exhale. Your arms may tremble at first, but keep practising and this will stop.

Be careful as this position requires flexible hips and legs. Don't over-strain yourself.

This scorpion pose is a very advanced yoga pose. It can only be achieved after years of practice and discipline. Do not attempt this pose until your yoga teacher tells you that you are ready for it! The scorpion pose needs perfect balance and flexibility.

the scorpion pose

29

GLOSSARY

abdomen The part of the body between the chest and the hips

alignment The proper adjustment of parts in relation to each other

calves Fleshy part of the back of the lower leg

capacity The ability to hold or contain

exhale To breathe out

flexible Capable of being bent

hamstrings Muscles found at the back of the upper leg

incense Material used to produce a fragrant odour when burned

inhale To breathe in

interlace To unite or cross as if you are lacing your fingers together

meditation To spend time in quiet thinking

oxygen A colourless, odourless gas which forms about 21 percent of the atmosphere

oxygenate To combine or supply with oxygen

posture The position of one part of the body with relation to other parts. The general way of holding the body

FOR MORE INFORMATION

Books

Hoffman, Susannah, *Yoga For Kids: Simple First Steps in Yoga and Mindfulness* (DK Children, 2018)

Vinay, Shobana, R, *100 Yoga Activities for Children: Easy-to-follow Poses and Meditation for the Whole Family* (Skyhorse Publishing, 2017)

Websites

BBC Get Inspired: How to get into Yoga
www.bbc.co.uk/sport/get-inspired/32380383
Gives information and advice about getting into yoga.

NHS: Exercise: A Guide to Yoga
www.nhs.uk/live-well/exercise/guide-to-yoga/
All you need to know to get started with yoga, including the health benefits, yoga styles for beginners and finding a yoga class.

INDEX

All sports can be dangerous. Do not attempt any of the skills in this book without supervision from a trained adult expert.

Wayland
First Published in Great Britain in 2019 by Wayland.

Published by permission of Gareth Stevens Publishing, New York, NY, USA.

HB ISBN: 978 1 5263 1174 0
PB ISBN: 978 1 5263 1175 7

Produced for Wayland by Alix Wood
Art direction and content research: I
Editor: Eloise Macgregor
Editor for Gareth Stevens: Kerri O'D
Consultant: Molly Robertson

Photo credits:
Cover, 1, 3, 4, 5, 6 top, 8, 9, 10, 11, 13, 16, 18 top, 22, 23 top, 27 bottom, 28, 29, 30 © Shutterstock; all other images © Greg Dennis.

Acknowledgments
With grateful thanks to James Latus, Josh Latus, Storm Brennon, Kieron Turk, Will Ferris, Corie Stubbs and Ellena Harrison.

Printed in China

Wayland
An imprint of
Hachette Children's Group
Part of Hodder & Stoughton
Carmelite House
50 Victoria Embankment
London EC4Y 0DZ

An Hachette UK Comany
www.hachette.co.uk
www.hachettechildrens.co.uk

GET ACTIVE!

YOGA

Alix Wood

CONTENTS

NAMES AND ADDRESSES OF THE EXAM BOARDS

Associated Examining Board (AEB)
Stag Hill House
Guildford
Surrey GU2 5XJ

University of Cambridge Local Examinations Syndicate (UCLES)
Syndicate Buildings
1 Hills Road
Cambridge CB1 1YB

Joint Matriculation Board (JMB)
Devas St
Manchester M15 6EU

University of London Schools Examination Board (ULSEB)
Stewart House
32 Russell Square
London WC1B 5DN

Northern Ireland Schools Examination Council (NISEC)
Beechill House
42 Beechill Road
Belfast BT8 4RS

Oxford and Cambridge Schools Examination Board (OCSEB)
10 Trumpington Street
Cambridge CB2 1QB

Oxford Delegacy of Local Examinations (ODLE)
Ewert Place
Summertown
Oxford OX2 7BX

Scottish Examination Board (SEB)
Ironmills Road
Dalkeith
Midlothian EH22 1BR

Welsh Joint Education Committee (WJEC)
245 Western Avenue
Cardiff CF5 2YX

EXAMINATION TECHNIQUES

GETTING STARTED

As you will realise when you run through the list of chapter headings of this book, the A-level or AS-level French examination tests both different types of *knowledge* and a variety of language *skills*. The A-level candidate may be required to take as many as five written papers and an oral examination which test on the one hand knowledge and understanding of 'content' (literature or background studies) and on the other hand skills such as essay-writing in French, translation into French or English, aural comprehension, reading comprehension and competence in spoken French. It is therefore essential at the outset to make yourself fully aware of exactly what is required by the particular Examination Board whose papers you are going to take, since the boards vary somewhat in their requirements and in the options that they offer. You can do this by checking the examination syllabus and by asking your course tutor. There is a full listing of the addresses of the Examination Boards at the front of the book.

You should also find out from the syllabus the percentage mark carried by each of the papers that you are preparing for. You will not find it necessary to allocate your time in exactly the same way but you should, for example, guard against devoting too little time to preparing for a paper which carries a very significant proportion of the marks.

SKILLS TO BE TESTED

REVISION

ESSAY WRITING

IN THE EXAMINATION

ESSENTIAL PRINCIPLES

Once you have identified the types of 'content' paper that you are going to take, and the different skills that are to be tested, you should study the corresponding chapters of this book. They will help you avoid false assumptions concerning various parts of the examination, such as the notion held by many candidates that translation into English, one's own language, requires less attention than other tests. They will also help you to be aware of the work that you will need to get through in order to reach A-level or AS-level standard, and to form an understanding of what the examiner will be looking for and of how examinations are marked. Take note of this information and make certain that you know from the beginning of your course exactly what you are aiming at and the ground that you personally will need to cover.

Once you have established these *longer-term objectives*, it is important that you organise more *immediate tasks* according to a weekly and daily timetable. Keep to it but make it realistic and divide your study time into periods of manageable length. Make good use of your time and remember that there are many useful language-learning activities that fit comfortably into the odd half an hour, such as reading a few pages of French to build vocabulary or listening to a comprehension tape or a news bulletin. With language work in particular, keep a record of what you have covered – grammatical structures, vocabulary areas, etc. This will serve to indicate what you have achieved and to check that you are in fact acquiring a sufficient grammatical competence and vocabulary to cope with the essay in French, prose translation and indeed all other language exercises.

The key to success in any examination is *adequate preparation* and the language student, perhaps more than the student of any other subject, must lose no time in getting the preparation under way. It needs to be understood that the learning of new material or revision cannot be left to a late stage and certainly not to the last minute. What is learnt hurriedly will not be properly digested. Learning a language is not unlike learning to play a musical instrument: in addition to understanding the rules or theory it is necessary to be able to perform a skill. Successful performance requires practice and that practice should be constant and spread over a period of time. The structures and vocabulary of the language must be used and reused until the rules have been internalised, so that they are followed spontaneously. It is only in this way that you will be able to produce written or spoken French effortlessly and accurately enough to achieve the highest level in the examination.

❝ Newly revised syllabuses. ❞

From the beginning and throughout the course make the most of classes. Try to *participate actively in discussions* of set texts or background topics and take every opportunity to use and practise your French. It will help if you think ahead and come to your class prepared. If you attend a literature or language class having prepared the ground and having tried to anticipate the content of the discussion or the lesson, you will have a sense of purpose which will make your learning more interesting and efficient. Prepare some questions you might ask and take a critical interest in the subject area to be discussed. Try to take notes which do not have to be copied out neatly later (it wastes time) and be rigorously accurate when you take notes in a language class. It is clearly counter-productive to first record and then diligently learn misspelt items of vocabulary or grammatically incorrect examples.

❝ Reviewing the material. ❞

After the lesson you should spend time *reviewing* the material. Check your notes and add to them by following up references and prescribed reading. Reviewing the material you have covered should be an active period of study. Spend time thinking about the new material you have learnt and try to relate it to the rest of your knowledge of the subject. Evaluate the new ideas or the new language structures with your longer-term examination goals in mind. Ask yourself how the ideas which have emerged from a discussion could be developed to form an examination answer or part of one. Extract from any language text that you have worked on in class those expressions and structures which you can identify as being useful for a 'narrative' essay or a 'discussion' essay or for your translation work. Make a conscious effort to think and write about those aspects of your set texts or background topics which have been explained and discussed in class. Also make a point of practising and reusing any new items of language.

❝ Complete the work. ❞

You should, of course, *complete all the work* set by your tutors. Remember, however, that doing a piece of course-work, such as handing in a language essay or a translation, is only half of the exercise. There is equal value in looking critically at your performance and in devising means of improving it. Always go through marked work when it has been returned in order to analyse your strengths and weaknesses. This is particularly important in your language work where you must be prepared to learn from your mistakes. Tackle them without delay, classify them and keep track of them. Examination scripts show only too clearly that language errors may cover a wide range of categories and that many of these are easily neglected. Therefore identify your errors and make sure that you understand why they have occurred. Knowing what you are doing wrong and why is the first step to putting it right.

REVISION

" Critical review. "

It is unwise, particularly as far as your language work is concerned, to think solely in terms of a revision period which occupies the few weeks which precede the examination. In language learning it is necessary to carry out *continual short-term revisions* throughout the course in order to ensure that what you have learnt in the early stages can be carried forward as part of your active stock of vocabulary and structures. Remember that a weak performance at A-level in those parts of the examination which test written or spoken French, is nearly always caused by a lack of elementary knowledge. It is not too much of an exaggeration to say that A-level candidates fail because they have forgotten what they once knew well in the second or third year of the GCSE course. Make sure that this does not happen to you by frequently submitting your work to a critical review.

Language Revision

By the time you reach the weeks before the examination, language revision should have been reduced to a minimum and should consist of a final review of troublesome points that have already been worked on, or a review of vocabulary notebooks, grammatical examples and sections of the course-book which are already familiar. Immediately before the examination it is a good idea to read texts you know well or an undemanding novel, and to listen to tapes, simply to have French going through your mind.

Literature/Background Revision

Revision of literature or background material should begin early so that there is still time to fill any gaps which you may discover in your knowledge. Your revision will be most effective if, instead of merely running through past notes, you *do* something with them. Reduce them to lists of main ideas and summaries that can be memorised. Organise your notes to form the basis of an examination answer and devote plenty of practice to answering and to framing answers in the time allowed. Take questions from past papers and prepare outline answers. Devise your own questions. Go through your material and imagine that you are giving a lecture on it or explaining it to a friend. If you make revision a part of active study you will be better able to remember and use your material creatively in the examination.

ESSAY-WRITING

A number of the papers included in the examination will test specialised skills such as listening comprehension, reading comprehension, or translation. You will find advice on preparing for these tests in the chapters which follow. Essay-writing occupies a rather different position. You may be required to write essays in *English* in those papers which examine set literary texts or topics related to contemporary France; you may be called upon to write an essay in *French* which is a test both of command of the language and of literary appreciation or knowledge of contemporary France; you will also be required to write an essay in *French* which is primarily a linguistic test and not a test of knowledge. (It is essential to check the syllabus to be certain of what is required.) The remarks which follow concern mainly the essay in English which features in the literature or background paper but the general principles apply to the French essay (discussed in detail in Ch.4).

Course-work Essays

There is first of all a distinction to be made between the essays that you write as part of your course-work and those which are produced as examination answers. The course-work essay is an important part of the learning process and you can use it to establish a dialogue with your tutor in order to experiment with your ideas and measure your progress. The thinking, reading and planning which it requires are an essential part of active study and a means of making the subject your own. If you make full use of this opportunity throughout the course you will master the knowledge and the writing skills which are essential in a first-rate examination answer.

When an essay is set it is preferable, even if you have a week to complete it, to begin thinking about it immediately. The first step is to *interpret the title* so that you understand exactly what you are being asked to do. Acquaint yourself (by studying past exam questions) with the terminology which examiners use. At an advanced level it is unlikely that you will be asked simply to *describe*, to *give an account of*, to *relate* or to *outline*: the key terms are more likely to be *analyse, compare and contrast, define, discuss, examine critically*, or *explain*. Ensure that you understand what such terms imply and that when asked to analyse, discuss or explain, you do not simply describe.

Examination questions are carefully worded. You should therefore give attention to every word and identify every part of the question. A question such as the following on Molière's *L'Ecole des Femmes* contains a number of keywords, each of which should be responded to: 'It is not difficult to sympathise with Arnolphe: he is resilient, witty on occasions and, above all, the victim of bad luck.' Discuss the character of Arnolphe in the light of this opinion. The answer should discuss Arnolphe's character to decide whether he is resilient and witty; examine the situations to see whether he is a victim of bad luck and decide whether these elements (or any others) make it possible to sympathise with him. The question may be in two parts: 'Contrast the characters of Burrhus and Narcisse and examine the influence which they have on Néron.' Both parts must be dealt with. Remember that in considering carefully the working and arrangement of the question you will be anticipating what the examiner will do when he draws up the mark-scheme.

When it comes to the more demanding operation of *thinking out what should go into the essay*, many students find it helpful to put their ideas down in diagrammatic form. The main element or idea in the question is written down and circled in the middle of the page. Then as ideas begin to flow they are jotted down around the central idea and shown as connected to, or branching off, from it. Thinking with this visual 'map' in front of you may suggest further ideas which can then be plotted to show their linkage with the central idea. Such a diagram will enable you to see your essay as a whole before you attempt to express your argument in a discursive form and can usefully be referred to as you write up the essay.

When you begin to *write* avoid the mistake of adopting a plan which is a plan in name only. The least satisfactory essay is the one which has a shape only because it is possible to discern a disjointed discussion sandwiched between a pointless introduction and a false conclusion.

The poor *introduction* does little more than tell the reader that it is an introduction. Often it will introduce something general and irrelevant. You should guard against such faults. If you are writing an answer on the way in which Maupassant uses surprise endings in his short stories, the introduction should not contain generalities about the author's life and upbringing. You are not writing an introduction to a book on Maupassant; you are engaged in leading the reader directly to a specific argument. Be brief therefore. Define the terms of the question if they need to be made clear. Make your introductory paragraph strictly relevant to the points which follow and use it to arouse the interest of the reader. The often repeated advice that the introduction should be left until last is sound. You cannot focus the spotlight on the argument that you are going to develop until you are clear in your mind about what you are going to say.

> **Take special care with the introduction.**

Be equally careful over the *conclusion*. Avoid the rather meaningless phrases which do no more than announce that you are about to stop writing. Do not put yourself in the position of having to 'tack on' a false conclusion, one which claims that the question has been answered when it clearly has not. Avoid the following approach, only too familiar to examiners. The question is 'It is the tragedy of Néron, rather than of Britannicus which is the main theme of this play.' Discuss. The main body of the essay contains what is really an outline of the plot which is followed by a final paragraph which claims: 'Therefore it can be seen that the tragedy of Britannicus is the main theme of the play.' It is a false conclusion because it has not been demonstrated by the preceding discussion and it convinces nobody.

A conclusion should be logically related and necessary to the argument. It should not introduce any new points or afterthoughts. It serves no purpose if it simply repeats what has been discussed in the first part of the essay. A brief summary of preceding points is useful only if it genuinely concludes the argument, for example, by assembling points 'for' and 'against' in order to make a final considered judgement.

In the main body of the essay concentrate on making your points; make them clearly and develop them fully. Do not leave it to the reader to extract an argument from what is simply implicit. It is here that many candidates are not thorough enough and do not do themselves justice. They identify relevant points but fail to explore them in detail or to elaborate upon them and therefore they have not responded fully to the question which has asked for discussion, analysis, evaluation or critical examination. You should use the writing of course-work essays as an opportunity to practise thinking and to develop your techniques for presenting ideas on paper. Make yourself familiar with the set text or the background topic so that you have a personal response to it, one which you can then discuss and analyse. Discuss ideas in class, ask questions, read your primary sources critically, extract from secondary sources (e.g. works of criticism) those ideas which you can make your own, and construct your 'mind map' and essay plan. You will not have time to do all this when you write your *examination* answer but it is a form of training which, when the time comes, will enable you to produce a discussion of real substance and interest.

> **Learn ... by reading your *own work*.**

Endeavour to deal with points in *logical order* so that for the reader there is a progression which is easy to follow. Ordering an argument coherently requires practice and although your argument may seem clear in your own mind, its clarity may not be so evident to the reader. It is therefore a good idea to reread a course-work essay a day or two after writing it, trying to put yourself into the reader's position. If your idea is a valid one then spelling it out simply and completely will do it no harm. And above all, do not throw away good ideas and insights by expressing yourself inadequately.

Your argument should not only be well expressed it should be supported by appropriate *facts, examples and specific references* to the set text or other primary source. This is necessary if you are to make your discussion convincing and it is the way in which you display your knowledge and grasp of the subject. That is why it is usual for examination questions to ask specifically for examples and precise references to set texts and quotations. However when you provide these, remember that their function is to illustrate points that you are making; supplying quotations and examples is not an end in itself. You should guard against overloading an essay with quotations which are not really apt and against allowing textual references or factual examples to develop into a purely descriptive account. At A-level you are not asked to describe your knowledge but to *use* it.

The essay should be written in good, standard English. Avoid colloquial expressions and remember that the language of an essay is rather more formal than that of a classroom discussion. If you are interested in your subject and in your own ideas, you will be anxious to express them accurately. Strive for clarity and precision. Poor use of English, inaccurate spelling and an inappropriate style are self-penalising. They are faults which prevent the examiner from following the flow of your ideas, and if you fail to communicate effectively your performance can only suffer.

Before you hand in your course-work essay read it once more, asking yourself those critical questions that the examiner will ask:

- Have you answered the question/all parts of the question?
- Is the introduction useful?
- Are the points clearly made and thoroughly discussed?
- Is evidence provided to support them?
- How many good points are there?
- Could any other points be added?
- Is all of the essay relevant to the discussion?
- Is there any repetition or rambling?
- Have you used and displayed your knowledge of the subject well?
- Is the conclusion effective?

IN THE EXAMINATION

Well before the examination it is advisable to obtain a complete set of the most recent examination papers so that you are familiar with the instructions, the layout and the look of each. You will be better prepared to observe the following points when you take the examination:

1 *Follow the instructions* at the beginning of the paper which indicate how many questions should be answered and from which sections of the paper they may be chosen. Watch for alternative questions (either . . . or), and do not answer both.

2 If there is a *choice* of questions, allow yourself time to read them all and let them sink in before making your choice. Make sure (by turning each page over) that you have in fact read them all.

3 *Divide the time* allowed for the examination according to the number of questions to be answered. If each answer carries an equal proportion of marks, divide the time equally, allowing time for checking at the end. Remember that it is preferable, if you run short of time, to devote your last 15 minutes to starting your final answer (even in note-form) rather than add finishing touches to a previous answer. On any question marked, for example, out of 20, it is much easier to score the first marks (1–5) than the last 5 (16–20).

4 *When you tackle a question*:

a) Ensure that you have interpreted it correctly. Underline all the keywords and if you are unsure of the meaning of any of them, consider turning to another question. Pay particular attention to terms such as *discuss critically, explain, comment on, give reasons for*, etc.

b) Identify all the parts of a question and deal with all the parts in your answer. If you are asked to give *reasons for* or to discuss *ways in which*, deal with more than *one* reason or way.

c) Be wary of the question which is very similar to one that you have already practised. If you rush into the answer you may overlook the fact that the exam question implies a different angle or contains an additional part. Always answer the question set.

5 Spend sufficient time *planning* your answer. Use the methods which you have practised when writing course-work essays but adapt them to the shorter time available in examination conditions. Have in mind the check-list of questions which you have learned to ask yourself about a course-work essay before handing it in.

6 When you begin to write, *be purposeful and relevant from the first line*. Make your introduction useful. Try to capture the examiner's attention from the start and convince him that he has picked up the script of a candidate who really has something to say.

7 Organise your time so that you have 10 minutes left at the end for reading through and *checking your answers*. Check for legibility, incidental errors, the names of characters in novels and plays, the accuracy of quotations in French, punctuation and the numbering of questions.

8 Finally, *the examiner*. Remember that examiners are likely to be experienced, practising teachers who are fully conscious of the stress which many students undergo when taking examinations. They will be understanding and only too willing to reward your work highly as long as you give them the opportunity. Keep the examiner in mind when you write. Express yourself clearly, keep your handwriting legible, present the work as neatly as possible and set out to show that you have made a conscientious effort to do what the question asks.

Chapter	AEB	AEB (AS)	Cambridge	Cambridge (AS)–Cossec	JMB	JMB (AS)	London Syllabus A	London Syllabus B	London (AS)	NISEC	Oxford	Oxford (AS)	Oxford and Cambridge	WJEC	WJEC and NISEC (AS)	Scottish Higher Grade
2 Grammatical accuracy	●	●	●	●	●	●	●	●	●	●	●	●	●	●	●	●
3 Vocabulary	●	●	●	●	●	●	●	●	●	●	●	●	●	●	●	●
4 Essay in French	●		●		●		●	●		●	●		●	●		●
5 Discussion essay	●		●		●		●	●		●	●		●	●		●
6 Narrative essay			●		●		●			●			●	●		●
7 Guided composition	●		●					●		●	●			●		●
8 Letter writing			●	●	●		●	●	●	●			●	●		●
9 The dialogue essay			●		●		●	●		●			●	●		●
10 Translation into French	●		●		●		●	●		●			●	●		●
11 Reading comprehension	●	●	●	●	●	●	●	●	●	●	●	●	●	●	●	●
12 Listening comprehension	●	●	●	●	●	●	●	●	●	●	●	●	●	●	●	●
13 Translation into English	●		●		●		●	●		●	●		●			●
14 Oral work	●	●	●	●	●	●	●	●	●	●	●	●	●	●	●	●
15 Literature			●		●		●			●	●		●	●		●

NB The table does not represent an exhaustive list of the elements in each examination. Check with current syllabus.

Table 1.1

GRAMMATICAL ACCURACY

WAYS OF LEARNING GRAMMAR

COURSE-BOOK AND GRAMMAR-BOOK

GRAMMATICAL ACCURACY AND EXAMINATIONS

GETTING STARTED

You are probably well aware of the need to have a sound understanding of the grammar of French and of being able to apply that knowledge accurately. Most students look on 'learning grammar' as the main part of their language learning and identify it as the chief cause of difficulty when their progress in French is not very satisfactory. Examining Boards and teachers put heavy emphasis on grammatical accuracy, and examiners' reports complain with unfailing regularity about 'basic grammatical incompetence' or 'widespread inaccuracy'. It may seem to the struggling learner that they are obsessed with this particular problem and that they are never going to be satisfied with the candidates' efforts to write and speak French. However, it is better to find a more positive lesson in what examiners have to say. Remind yourself that because of the way in which examinations are assessed, grammatical accuracy is very important and that every bit of progress that you can make in this area is going to improve your final result.

It is inevitable, nevertheless, that you will make grammatical mistakes. It could even be argued that making *some* mistakes is a necessary part of learning the language but you should, of course, aim at minimising the chance of error by ensuring that your learning and practice of the structures of French are as efficient as possible from the outset. Some errors may be 'useful' but others are not and prevention is always better than cure!

ESSENTIAL PRINCIPLES

**WAYS OF
LEARNING
GRAMMAR**

There is much controversy about how the grammar of a foreign language is most effectively learnt. In recent years there has been a move away from the idea that the learner should concentrate on learning how to manipulate the rules and a move towards the notion that the emphasis should be on practising the language as a means of communication, i.e. on learning it through using it. Which is the best approach for the student preparing for an A-level examination? Most teachers would agree that there is a need for both approaches and that at A-level the student who is already able to handle a good deal of French which has been acquired by a process of induction based on pattern practice and on seeing language in use, will now benefit from a more formal insight into the structures of French and from a measure of grammatical description. There is a need for consciously learning the rule that pulls things together and provides short-cuts and there is a need for meaningful practice. You should therefore make sure that you have the means to learn the rule and apply it in useful writing and speaking activities.

**COURSE-BOOK
AND GRAMMAR-
BOOK**

❝Obtain a grammar
book.❞

Look critically at your course-book to see whether it gives you sufficient exercises of the right sort. Do the grammar exercises lead you to write the kind of sentences that you would want to reproduce in your essays in French or in your prose translations? If not, then supplement your work with exercises from a more suitable course-book.

If you have not done so already, you should obtain a grammar-book which you can understand and learn to find your way around so that reference becomes quick and easy. Get used to consulting it. Students sometimes complain that this is difficult because, as they have not learned basic grammatical terminology (e.g. terms such as demonstrative pronoun, possessive adjective, present participle etc.), they are not sure what to look for. You will find however that you are often able to look up the French word which is causing difficulty and then find the sections where it is treated grammatically. If you start by using the grammar- book in this way you will begin to learn the basic terms and above all you will get used to looking things up.

For much of the time you will use the grammar-book for reference, to find out how to correct an error or to look for clarification of a rule, but you should also use it to revise or learn the basic forms of French. You should give this area of grammar priority because errors involving the forms of regular and irregular verbs, the government of verbs, the feminine or plural forms of adjectives and nouns, the form of adverbs, pronouns and personal pronouns will be considered by the examiner as elementary and will therefore rank with the more serious types of error.

There are errors which are more 'excusable' than others. The correct choice between the past historic tense and the imperfect, or the decision to use a subjunctive in certain contexts or even the choice between *des* or *de* often requires considerable judgement and sometimes there may be no clearly right or wrong answer. Obviously, there is no difficult judgement to be made as far as grammatical *forms* are concerned. The plural of *cheval* is *chevaux* and the past participle of *lire* is *lu* and therefore *des chevals* or *j'ai lisé* would be considered to be serious errors.

Many students find that learning grammar is not a very interesting activity. Sometimes the rules themselves do not seem to be very helpful: some of them appear to be rather illogical while others, affecting perhaps just one letter or sound, may seem irritating to the student who wants to get on with saying something worthwhile in French. Even worse, the rules do not always do the job you had expected them to do. They are not always watertight; they do not always explain fully the examples which you hear or read and there always seem to be numerous exceptions which also have to be learnt.

Making your own discoveries

The point to be made is that you should not treat the grammar-book as an end in itself. You will find that studying the language becomes more interesting if you use the grammar-book to help you make your own discoveries about the French that you may read in newspapers or that you hear on the radio, or while talking to French people. Train yourself to be observant, try to find useful examples of structures and make a point of using them.

It is likely that the grammar in your course-book will be presented through texts which show structures working as they should in a context of authentic written or spoken French. The exercises which follow will be designed to give you practice in using the structure so that you can make it your own. It is important that you should realise what the teaching method of the course-book is so that you can make full use of it and continue the learning process.

- Make sure that you understand the point of the exercises.
- Ask yourself whether the exercises are going to help you to express what it is that you want to say in your essays or prose translations.
- When you have practised an important new structure ask yourself what you are going to do to keep it in circulation.
- Collect further examples from the grammar-book, the dictionary or your own reading.

Such language study can also be carried out on passages of your own choosing, such as those that you study intensively for vocabulary-building. Try to identify useful structures for study and devise your own exercises for practising them. It is possible to do this by making up simple substitution exercises. For example, assume that you had selected the following structures:

a) Nous sommes plusieurs à poser cette question.
b) Il a interdit à tous les élèves de revenir avant trois heures.

Build up further sentences on the same pattern:
a) Nous sommes plusieurs à poser cette question.
                  à vouloir partir.
                  à étudier le français.
                  à suivre ce cours.
Nous sommes plusieurs à poser cette question.
Nous sommes cinq à poser cette question.
Nous sommes nombreux à poser cette question.
b) Il a interdit à tous les élèves de revenir avant trois heures.
              à tout le monde
              à tous les clients
              à tous les spectateurs

" Practising with a partner. "

Some structures can be written into a mini-dialogue which can be practised with a partner. In order to use *celui-ci, celles-ci*, etc. you could put together a simple dialogue.

- Est-ce que ces places sont libres?
- Non, pas celles-ci, mais prenez celles d'à côté.
- Celles d'à côté sont prises aussi.
- Ah! C'est dommage!

and then for *ces places*, substitute *cette salle, cette cabine, ces fauteuils*, etc. and make the appropriate changes to the rest of the sentence.

If you do something with the grammatical structures that you hope to learn, something which involves making an active contribution of your own, then you will increase your chances of making the structure 'your own'. Explanation alone of a grammatical point will not ensure that you will be able to reproduce it spontaneously. Remember that in order to assimilate the rule, the following three elements should be present: an understanding of the rule, some form of practice and the opportunity to use the structure to express some personal meaning.

GRAMMATICAL ACCURACY AND EXAMINATIONS

How vital is grammatical accuracy when you write French in the examination? The answer, of course, is that it is very important since grammatical *inaccuracy* can be a major cause of failure in the prose, essay or use of French papers. However, it must be said that it is possible to make errors, even quite numerous errors, and still be awarded a pass in the examination. This is because examiners are realistic enough not to set standards of absolute accuracy which are taken into consideration when assessing the candidates' ability to produce French. Imagine that candidate A writes an essay which, overall, a native speaker would find agreeable to read. It is reasonably fluent, parts of it have an idiomatic flavour, the vocabulary is apt and the candidate has attempted to use a variety of structures. However, there are a dozen grammatical errors (a few wrong prepositions, some adjective agreements overlooked and occasional misuse of the partitive). Candidate B on the other hand produces an essay which has hardly any inaccuracies but it contains only a few common structural patterns which it tends to repeat and uses only a small range of vocabulary. Candidate A's essay is certain to gain the higher mark.

This should enable you to understand that you will not be assessed *solely* on the mistakes that you make and that it does not follow that the best strategy (at least when writing an essay) is to be over-cautious and defensive about making mistakes as this may seriously inhibit other qualities of expression.

DEGREES OF ERROR

> **Just how bad are your errors?**

It is also helpful to understand that there are degrees of error and that some errors may be considered by the examiner to be more serious than others. For example, those errors which are clearly the result of *elementary misunderstanding* of the rule (e.g. the structure was incorrectly learned in the first place or was not learned at all, are more serious than oversights caused perhaps by *lack of attention*, which may show that a candidate has learned a pattern but is inconsistent in the way he uses it. Errors involving *common forms* are among the more serious and the error which *obscures the meaning* of the whole sentence or causes ambiguity is less tolerable than the errors which would cause a native speaker 'irritation' without stopping his comprehension.

The lesson is that it will always pay dividends to work hard to eliminate errors involving common forms, and that you should try to distinguish those errors which interfere with communication and learn to avoid them.

Teachers and examiners recognise that grammatical and other errors are inevitable as it is not within the capacity of the human mind to retain everything it has learned. Mistakes can even be seen as a necessary part of learning: getting it right is a gradual process and you learn from your mistakes. This is a useful attitude to adopt to grammatical accuracy as you work towards the examination. It may be disappointing to have a piece of written French returned to you containing many underlinings in red but it does not follow that you have not achieved anything. The errors may show that you have learned a good deal but that there is still some way to go. Adopt a positive attitude towards your mistakes.

Nature of the error

Always make sure in the first instance that you understand exactly what has gone wrong. What should you have written? Has your teacher understood what you were trying to express? If he or she uses a marking code is it clear to you? Why has one error been treated as more serious than another? If you ask yourself questions like these you will begin to think through your mistakes.

Cause of the error

When it is clear to you what has gone wrong and what type of mistake you have made, try to understand what caused it. If you can identify the cause, you are more likely to be able to work out an effective strategy for dealing with the error.

- Was it a total misunderstanding? E.g. you were unaware that vouloir que is followed by the subjunctive.
- Was it caused by a partial misunderstanding? E.g. you were aware of the rule that a preceding direct object agrees with the past participle but were not able to distinguish direct object and indirect object.
- Was it perhaps the result of a guess based on English structure? E.g. il est arrivé *sur* le train de Paris.
- Was it a mistaken analogy? E.g. il est *mouru* à l'âge de 50 ans.

Of course, it may have been a careless mistake; you were perhaps in too much of a hurry or were tired or simply not sufficiently motivated to check through your work before handing it in for marking.

Seriousness of the error

The more serious errors which will lose you marks in the examination, should be given priority. Your teacher will point the serious errors out. They are:

- Those which involve a major rather than a minor rule or an exception.
- Those which show that basic forms have not been learnt.
- Those which really stand in the way of successful communication.

However, you yourself are best placed to know whether an error is a serious one for you, in the sense that it is one which you make frequently.

Categories of error

You should note your errors and classify them so that you have an overall view of the state of your knowledge. There will be errors which occur more frequently in essays than in proses, and vice versa. If there is a type of error which you are inclined to make in both exercises it obviously needs priority treatment. Patterns of error are often clear to see when a candidate's overall examination performance is analysed. For example, in a recent A-level examination one candidate's errors in French were distributed as follows:

	Vocabulary	Article/ partitive	Verbs	Tenses	Prepositions	Past participle/ adjective agreement
Essay in French	13	7	2	7	2	4
Prose	17	5	3	1	–	3
Guided Writing	8	7	2	6	–	4

Even this limited analysis produces enough evidence to show that the use of the article and partitive has not been fully understood and that adjective agreement is inconsistently observed. Tenses seem to be more inaccurate when the candidate does not have the English as a guide. Insufficient knowledge of vocabulary is a major problem. If the candidate had been in the habit of making his own error analysis he may well have realised which items of grammar needed most urgent attention and have avoided the loss of marks through inaccuracy. It may seem over-ambitious to hope to eliminate *all* errors from your work but it is realistic to identify and do something about priority areas. It could easily be the difference between failure and success in the examination.

Identify and prioritise.

When you work on your errors try to find an activity which is going to involve you intellectually and personally. It is more helpful to use the corrected grammatical form in new sentences of your own invention than to copy out mechanically the corrected sentences from your prose or essay. Imagine how you would teach the point in question to somebody else, or better still, work with a partner when going over corrected work. You could practise a grammar point by constructing a mini-dialogue.

It is easy to produce your own tests for grammatical points such as the distinction between *des/les*, *des/de* etc., verb forms and tenses and the choice of prepositions. Take a passage from a newspaper or novel, blank out the prepositions or articles and after a lapse of time use the passage as a 'fill-in' exercise.

Finding new strategies.

It is always more effective when you are doing remedial work to find an alternative strategy and different exercises from those that you used to learn the grammar point in the first place. Rather than repeat the exercises in your course-book, find something else. It is likely that your teacher will have a battery of exercises to cover troublesome points. There are also a number of self-correcting exercise books on the market which may also be of use.

Further Reading

Grammar-books

H. Ferrar. *A French Reference Grammar*, OUP
J. E. Mansion. *A Grammar of Present-day French*, 2nd edition, Harrap
L. S. R. Byrne and E. L. Churchill. *A Comprehensive French Grammar*, 3rd edition, Blackwell

French Verbs

G. Brereton. *The Concise French Verb Book*, Hodder and Stoughton
Le Nouveau Bescherelle – l'Art de Conjuguer, Hatier

Exercise/workbooks

B. Job. *Comment Dire. Exercices de Grammaire Auto-Correctifs*, Clé International
C. Grabner et M. Hague. *Ecrire sans fautes*, Hatier
G. D. de Salins et S. Dupré la Tour. *Nouveaux Exercices de Grammaire*, Hatier (has answers to the exercises)

CHAPTER

3

VOCABULARY

GETTING STARTED

It may seem unnecessary to point out to the student preparing for advanced examinations in French that a fundamental requirement is the acquisition of an adequate vocabulary and that this requirement is often not met. Students are generally aware of the problems and indeed many identify vocabulary-building as the most difficult aspect of learning a new language. This is probably partly due to the fact that the task seems endless. If you read the 'avant-propos' to the *Dictionnaire du français contemporain*, you will see that although it excludes much specialist vocabulary and concerns itself only with language which is in everyday use, the total number of terms recorded is in the order of 25,000. The student embarking on an A-level or similar course might well ask 'How many of these terms do I need to know to succeed in the examination? Where do I begin and how do I go about it?' It is the purpose of this chapter to suggest answers to these and other questions that the examinee may ask.

AN EXAMINER'S VIEW OF VOCABULARY

LEARNING VOCABULARY

LINGUISTIC SITUATIONS

VOCABULARY IN CONTEXT

REVISION AND SELF-TESTING

ESSENTIAL PRINCIPLES

AN EXAMINER'S
VIEW OF
VOCABULARY

It soon becomes clear on reading examiners' reports on the performance of candidates that they expect a wider range of accurately used, correctly spelled vocabulary than most examinees are able to produce. The main criticisms of the examiners may be summarised as follows:

a) When the candidate is attempting to produce French in the language essay, prose translation or oral examination, a too limited knowledge of vocabulary leads to anglicised invention (examples given are *abilité, capabilité, malcontent, dépriver, incentif, la publique,* etc.), to paraphrase and to undue repetition of terms.

b) Candidates have insufficient knowledge of common lexical areas (examples given are school life, the home, travel and transport, politics, clothing, the weather, etc.).

c) Too much vocabulary appears to be only half-learned with the result that nouns frequently appear with the wrong gender, terms are misspelt or are used in a way which indicates that their meaning has not been fully understood. Too often 'vocabulary appears to have been dredged up from the memory in imperfect shape'.

d) When there is evidence that candidates *have* made an effort to learn vocabulary it is unfortunately often clear that terms have not been learnt in context and that learning has not been extended to include the closely associated terms and the structures which are necessary if the item in question is to be correctly used in a sentence.

e) Many candidates do not see the need to push beyond a GCSE core, with the result that they are not able to express themselves with freedom and in idiomatic French on a sufficiently wide number of topics.

These comments and the evidence in A- and AS-level scripts show that insufficient knowledge of vocabulary is the most important single factor which determines a poorer grade or failure in those papers where candidates are asked to write in, or translate from, French. There are candidates who display range and depth of knowledge but too few, it seems, have applied themselves seriously to the business of learning a reasonably rich and varied vocabulary. It may be that they have not seen the need for a systematic approach to this aspect of learning a language. They may have felt that vocabulary learning presented no great problems or have assumed that the sum of words that they are required to know are all contained between the covers of the course-book and are 'just picked up as you go along'. There are certainly those who neglect the question of learning vocabulary because they feel that the real difficulty in learning French lies elsewhere, in grasping the use of the subjunctive or in learning irregular verbs. It is true to say that many teachers and courses give priority to the teaching of grammatical structures. There is nothing wrong with such an emphasis provided, of course, that it does not result in neglect of vocabulary-building. You should make sure that you do not neglect it.

> **Vocabulary is the key to better grades.**

LEARNING VOCABULARY

The acquisition of vocabulary demands a conscious effort and a *systematic approach*. There are no satisfactory short-cuts. Vocabulary is not efficiently learnt through the use of hastily memorised word-lists. The evidence is that the assimilation of words to the point where they have become part of the learner's *active* vocabulary, takes place gradually and over a period of time. The conclusion to be drawn from this is evident: if you are embarking on a course of advanced French study you must waste no time in organising this aspect of your preparation. It is not just a question of learning six new words a day for two years (although the number of new words which you should aim to learn to use by the end of a two- year course should be close to that sum); you must give yourself time to 'forget' them, recognise them again in different contexts, use them and reuse them before you can be confident that they have been fully assimilated.

If you set about it in the right way the task of learning vocabulary is not a difficult or a disheartening one. It is also an area of language study where the learner can do a great deal of useful work on his own. You should therefore make sure that that personal input is taking place by getting organised and by doing it now. If you are successful in building your vocabulary it will help you to build your confidence.

> **Get organised.**

THE GROUND TO BE COVERED

When you set yourself the task of learning new words systematically you will probably ask yourself how much vocabulary you will need to know in order to be certain of success in the examination. It is not a question which can be answered with any great precision. The examination syllabus will not prescribe a list of lexical items to be learnt by the candidate, and in any case this would not be a very satisfactory way of acquiring new vocabulary. You should, however, extract what information you can from the syllabus regulations. There may be an indication of the *general areas* of vocabulary or of *broad language functions* which candidates are expected to cover.

" Literary . . . "

" . . . and non-literary language. "

Read the descriptions given in the syllabus regulations of the various tests which make up the examination (e.g. prose, translation into English, reading comprehension, listening comprehension, etc.) to see what *type* of language you must be familiar with. Certain tests or even the whole syllabus may be based on what is described as 'non-literary' language. This implies that the sources used will include works of non-fiction, newspapers, periodicals and indeed the modern media in general. The material in a 'literary' syllabus, on the other hand, is more likely to be drawn from novels, plays, short stories and other works of fiction. Common sense will tell you that such information must guide your preparation and the selection of your reading material. You would not prepare yourself for writing an essay in French on, let us say, road accidents, the Channel tunnel or the problems of unemployment if your language and vocabulary study were based exclusively on novels by Georges Simenon or Françoise Sagan. On the other hand, such reading would be very useful preparation for the type of prose or translation passage which are set by certain of the Examination Boards.

For further guidance (and sometimes this will be the only source of guidance available) it is important to get hold of recent examination papers. Although the lexical content is not very clearly defined in syllabus regulations, there are always *unwritten conventions* which control the choice of passages which examiners set for prose, translation into French, listening comprehension and so on. Even though the regulations state no more than 'a passage of modern French or English will be set', it does not follow that there is no limit to the obscurity or specialisation of the vocabulary which the test requires the candidate to know or use. You can reassure yourself that the level of difficulty and the nature of the lexis will be controlled by the experience of the examiner and of those whose job it is (usually practising teachers) to moderate the papers.

However, knowing this will still not tell you what to learn and what to discard. You should therefore study as many recent papers as you can in order to reach as clear an idea as possible of the 'style' of setting for each of the papers that you are going to take. You will be able to decide broadly on the type of texts you should begin working on for the purpose of vocabulary-building. If, for example a typical prose passage is one which asks you to translate not just terms such as 'trade union', 'to go on strike', 'to ask for higher wages' but also terms such as 'free collective bargaining', 'picket' and 'blackleg', then obviously you are expected to know the semi-specialised as well as the 'everyday' terms which relate to aspects of modern life and institutions.

When you have found out 'where you are going' in your vocabulary study, then make sure that the texts that you select for intensive reading from newspapers, magazines or novels, as well as the material in your course-book are appropriate to the lexical requirements of *all* the papers that you have to take. If, for example, your course-book is based mainly on texts dealing with contemporary socio-political issues, you will not be able to rely on it to help you prepare for a prose paper which assumes knowledge of the type of language which belongs to the narrative-descriptive passage to be found in a novel. You must allow for this when planning your reading programme.

LINGUISTIC SITUATIONS

If you follow the advice given later in this chapter on extensive reading and the close study of selected passages for vocabulary-building purposes, you will in fact be taking practical steps to cover the main vocabulary areas. However, it is also useful to be able to refer to a framework of linguistic situations to guide your reading and study. Note that the following list of topics is not a vocabulary list. It is not a question of looking the items up in a dictionary, translating them and trying to learn them. The list is intended as a guide to the type of passage that you should work on when learning vocabulary in order to cover a basic range of language situations and functions. If you aim at acquiring the vocabulary necessary for expressing yourself adequately in these areas it will help you to acquire that common core of lexis which is necessary when learning French at an advanced level.

You can also use the list to help you to analyse past papers and to organise your vocabulary notebook. You will find for example, that the situations contained in most prose translations papers correspond very closely to the topics in the list. Passages which are narrative-descriptive in nature will very frequently involve the topics listed under "People", "Daily routine", "Home and family". A good working knowledge of the vocabulary relating to those areas alone would enable the candidate to deal efficiently with many of the prose passages set by A-level Boards in recent years.

Use the list as a guide to the common ground which you should cover and be prepared to supplement it in order to meet the particular requirements of the examination (or of certain papers in it) which you are going to take.

Topics	Sub-topics and examples	Topics	Sub-topics and examples
People		Special clothing	Sports gear
Age	Children		Uniforms
	Adults	Appearance	Colour
	Old people		Size
	Ages	Material	e.g. wool
	Date of birth		Fashion
Identity	Title	Accessories	e.g. handbag
	Name	Adornments	e.g. rings
	Sex		
	Address	*Days of the week, months, seasons*	
	Place of birth	Time and date	Asking time
	Introductions		Asking date
	Nationalities		Stating time
Appearance	Size		Stating date
	Colouring		Time at which
	Physical difference		Dates on which
	Comparisons		Approximate time
Care of personal appearance	e.g. make-up		Approximate date
			Sequence of events
Postures	e.g. standing		Duration
Movement	e.g. running		Frequency
The senses (verbs rather than nouns)	e.g. seeing		Reference to present
			Reference to past
Actions	Physical, e.g. hitting		Reference to future
	Visual, e.g. looking		Being early
	Vocal, e.g. shouting		Being late
Display of emotions	e.g. crying	*Daily routine*	Waking (up)
Bodily states	e.g. hungry		Getting up
Disabilities	e.g. deaf		Washing
Health	e.g. ill		Shaving
Common ailments	e.g. colds		Brushing
Accidents (usually verbs)	e.g. to cut oneself		Dressing
			Undressing
Treatment	Doctor		Changing
	Hospital		Going out
	Chemist		Setting off
	Dentist		Getting to school
	Dressings		Getting to work
	Remedies		Meals
Character	e.g. lazy		Coming home
Emotions	e.g. love		Evening activities
Qualities and virtues (usually adjectives)	e.g. kind		Clubs
			Organisations
Vices and addictions	e.g. smoking		Bedtime
Mental processes	e.g. thinking		
Clothing		*Leisure and weekend activities*	
Everyday clothing	Male		Meeting friends
	Female		Sports
	Indoor		Hobbies
	Outdoor		Excursions
	Summer		TV
	Winter		Radio
	Putting on		Cinema
	Taking off		Disco
	Choosing		Jobs
	Trying on		Do it yourself
	Buying		Church
	Making	*Weather*	
	Care of	Everyday weather conditions	

Topics	Sub-topics and examples	Topics	Sub-topics and examples
Light and darkness		Quarrels and disputes	Family
Sky			Neighbours
Extremes	Heat	*School*	Appearance
	Cold	Buildings	Layout
	Storm	Classrooms	Furniture
	Flood		Equipment
	Drought		Pupils' equipment
Forecasts		Playground	Games
Home and family	Address	Pupils and staff	
Houses and flats	Situation	The school day	Subjects
	Types		Timetable
	Appearance		Classes
	Built of. . .		Activities
	Layout		Outings
	Rooms		Breaks
	Furniture		Meals
	Furnishings	Behaviour in school	Attitudes
	Equipment		Discipline
	Heat		Praise
	Light		Blame
	New houses	Examinations	
	Old houses	*Travel*	
	Buying houses	Vehicles	Land
	Selling houses		Sea
	Renting		Air
	Cleaning		Shipped
	Removal		Common parts
Kitchen	Cooking	Journeys	Planning
	Equipment		Routes
	Utensils		Maps
	Washing up		Tickets
	Chores		Booking
	Washing		Travel agents
	Ironing		Catching
Bedroom	Bedding		Missing
	Bedclothes		Departure
	Sleeping		Stops
	Waking		Arrival
	Furniture		Hitch-hiking
Bathroom	Washing		Hostelling
	Toilet articles		Stations
	WC		Ports
Living/dining-room	Leisure		Airports
	Meals		Service stations
	Laying the table		Traffic noises
	Clearing up		Outings
Garden	Layout		Excursions
	Common flowers		Picnics
	Common fruits		Going abroad
	Common vegetables		Countries
	Equipment		Customs
Family and social relationships			Passports
Family relationships	e.g. mother		Exhange visits
Family celebrations	Birthday	Hazards	Accident
	Christmas		Breakdown
	Wedding		Delays
Meeting, visiting,	Visits		Help in difficulties
staying with,	Parties	Luggage	e.g. cases
looking after	Dances		
family friends	Introductions	*Hotel, restaurant, café, inn, bar*	
	Greetings	Buildings	Appearance
	Goodbyes		Layout
Social courtesies	Asking for	Staff	
	Thanking	Procedures	Booking
	Apologising		Cancellation
	Inviting		Arrival
	Accepting		Departure
	Declining		Bills
Social correspondence	Postcards		Tips
	Informal letters	Rooms	Comforts
	Formal letters		Facilities

Topics	Sub-topics and examples	Topics	Sub-topics and examples
Meals, snacks	Menu	Outdoor pursuits	e.g. camping
	Courses	Personal likes and	
	Dishes	dislikes, with	
	Drinks	reasons	
	Ordering		
	Paying for	*Town and village life*	
	Serving	Urban and rural	
	Common methods of	environments	Description
	cooking, e.g. roasting		Advantages and
Incidents	Accidents		disadvantages
	Deficiencies		Pollution
	Complaints		
		Streets and traffic	
Shops and shopping		Public buildings	
Types of shop	Common shops	Visit to a city	
Goods for sale	Food	Visit to a village	
	Drink	Visit to the countryside	Common birds
	Clothes		Common animals
	Consumer goods, e.g.		Common flowers
	record-player		Common trees
	Shop windows		Common insects
Quantities	Weight	Visit to the zoo	Common wild animals
	Length	Visit to a farm or	Common farm animals
	Containers, e.g. tin	vineyard	Animals noises
	of. . .		Common buildings
	Money		Common crops
	Prices		Activities e.g.
	Counting		ploughing
	Buying		Equipment
	Selling		
	Delivering		
Markets	Street markets	*Trades and professions*	
	Supermarkets	Manual trades	Most common (with
	Hypermarkets		associated verbs)
Advertising, display	Posters	Professions	Most common (with
	Advertisements		associated verbs)
Banks	Obtaining cash	Places of work	Factory
	Changing currency		Workshop
Post office	e.g. stamps		Office
		Common tools	e.g. hammer
Cinema, theatre, circus, fairground		Getting a job	
A visit	Seating	Losing a job	
	Tickets	Unemployment	
	Performers	Future career	
Types of film, play	Sets		
concert		*Holidays and festivals*	
Audience reactions		Seaside	Features, e.g. beach
Personal tastes			Beach activities
			Ports
Radio and television			Boats
Use of			Islands
Channels and stations	Of own country		
	Of foreign country	Countryside	Features, e.g. beach
Types of programme	e.g. news	Mountains	Features, e.g. summits
Personal tastes		Going on holiday	Britain
			Abroad
Sports, amusements, hobbies		Holiday	e.g. postcards
Major sports and	Matches	correspondence	
games	Prizes	Camping and	
Places for sport	e.g. swimming pool	caravanning	
		Festivals	e.g. Easter
Children's games		National days	e.g. 14th July
Toys			
Parlour games	Cards		
	Chess	*Events*	
Hobbies	Photography	*Faits divers*	Home and abroad
	Model-making	War	Army, Navy, Air Force
	Dancing		Spying
	Pets		Escape
	Collecting		

Topics	Sub-topics and examples	Topics	Sub-topics and examples
Rescue operations	Disasters: flood earthquakes fire avalanche famine explosion air sea road rail	Art Books	e.g. drawing Libraries Types of literature, e.g. novels
		Exhibitions	Museum Art gallery
The law	Police Crimes	*Fantasy and imagination* Dreams Ghosts Magic Legends	
Personal incidents	Misunderstanding Disappearance Forgetting Losing and finding Losing one's way Mistaken identity Coincidence Accidents Amusing experiences Helping and being helped	*Names of natural features and products* Common geographical features Very common geographical proper names	Regions Towns Mountains Rivers Seas
		Points of compass	Directions
Reactions	Bravery Fear	Basic products and industries	e.g. coal Common minerals, e.g. iron
Mystery and adventure	Treasure Disguise Plots		Common materials, e.g. wood
Communications Correspondence	Materials Postal service	*Government* Local government services	Fire Police Ambulance Taxation Refuse collection Town Hall
Telephone Telegram The press	e.g. newspapers		
Arts Music	Playing common instruments Playing/listening to e.g. records Types of music	Central government names	President, Republic
Drama	Plays Actors		*(Recommended Basic Requirements for Examinations in French.* Scottish Examination Board)

(Recommended Basic Requirements for Examinations in French. Scottish Examination Board)

VOCABULARY IN CONTEXT

Even when you have established the areas of vocabulary that you will need to be familiar with (e.g. the terms required when describing people involved in daily routines, terms which occur in any exchange of information on social issues such as unemployment, the cost of living, human rights, etc.), you will still need to know *where* you are going to find this vocabulary presented in a way which will enable you to study it meaningfully and learn it. It would not be advisable to go straight to the dictionary or to attempt to learn ready-made lists of words. Words do not occur in isolation: their meaning is always partly determined by *context* and it is when words are presented in context that their function, and the way they relate to and associate with other words, is most clearly shown. The most efficient way to learn what words mean and how they work is to meet them and study them in context.

It is therefore advisable to begin by basing your vocabulary study on a *collection of texts* which include the language situations which you need to cover. A very useful selection of literary and non-literary passages for study is contained in the *Penguin French Reader* (for further suggestions see the Further Reading section at the end of the chapter). An anthology of this type, chosen to extend your vocabulary in a planned fashion, should be regarded as an essential supplement to your course-book. At the beginning of your course it will be wiser and more convenient to use a collection of passages chosen by an experienced editor or tutor but eventually you should aim at making your own selection from your wider reading.

ASPECTS INVOLVED IN BUILDING VOCABULARY

Before you embark on your programme of vocabulary-building it is as well to understand exactly what learning an item of vocabulary means. It will help you when studying new words and when recording them in a learnable form. It is clear from the way that many students record vocabulary to be learnt that knowing a word in the foreign language is a more complex process than they realise.

What is involved will differ slightly according to whether the word is intended to become part of your *active* and your *passive* vocabulary. Nevertheless if you have successfully learnt a new word it will imply that you have mastered a number of aspects:

a) You will be able to *recognise* its spoken or written form.
b) You will be able to *recall* it from your memory, *pronounce* it acceptably and, in writing, be able to *spell* it correctly.
c) You will be able to *relate* the word correctly to an idea or object.
d) You will have learned the *grammatical elements* which belong to the word and enable you to fit it correctly into a sentence. For example, if it is a noun you will know its gender *le* problème *du* chômage; if it is a verb you will know which preposition follows it: cet enfant risque *de* tomber, elle apprend *à* nager, and so on.
e) You will know whether the word is *appropriate* in a given situation or context, that is to say whether it is formal or familiar.
f) You will know which other items of vocabulary the word may *collocate* with (i.e. which it will 'go with'). For example:

   ■ Le terrain de camping se couvre de *caravanes*, (not roulottes).

   ■ Le tracteur s'arrêta devant la *barrière* du champ (not la grille).

   ■ Cet enfant *apporte* beaucoup de satisfaction à ses parents (not amène).

   ■ Il faut faire attention en *traversant* la rue (not franchissant).

g) You will understand the *connotation* of a word and will therefore know whether it has overtones of approval or disapproval. In the following sentences, for example, the words underlined in pairs are similar in meaning but have different connotations:

   ■ Tous les élèves ont ricané/ri

   ■ Assis à la terrasse d'un café, il lorgnait/regardait toutes les femmes qui passaient.

Although points a) to f) might suggest that *knowing* a new word involves perhaps more than you realised, it by no means follows that *remembering* it is going to be that much more difficult. Experiments on the learning of vocabulary have shown that asking yourself meaningful questions about a word and processing it actually help you to remember it.

> **Get things into context.**

Points e) to f) further underline the importance of learning vocabulary in a meaningful context. It is the context which really presents in a learnable, recallable form those aspects of a new item of vocabulary described in e) to f). Instead, therefore, of recording lists of new words to be learnt it is more effective to ensure that the new material is contained in continuous passages or at least complete sentences. Your vocabulary notebook should be not so much a list of words (only very elementary vocabulary can be safely learned in this way) but rather a collection of extracts and illustrative examples.

USING A SHORT PASSAGE FOR VOCABULARY-BUILDING — AN ILLUSTRATION

A major part of your vocabulary-building should be based on the study of *short written passages*. The following passage has been worked as an example of how a text may be studied intensively in order to extend knowledge of vocabulary. It is advisable that when studying such a text that you go further than underlining the new words and looking them up in a French–English dictionary. It is very important *to do something* with new material to be learnt, to process it and if you can, become actively involved with it. Experience shows that if material to be learnt not only means something, but means something to the *learner* then the material is more effectively stored in, and recalled from, the memory.

You must first of all choose a text for study with some care, asking yourself whether it is relevant to the lexical areas which you will be required to cover. If it is too obscure, too technical or too specialised or if it is top-heavy with terms that you do not recognise, then turn to something else. The following passage is suitable because the vocabulary and subject-matter are typical of the French which you might be asked to recognise or use in an A-level translation or essay paper.

Remember that it is important to study and learn vocabulary in context. You will therefore approach the text you have chosen not as a random collection of words (to be looked up in the dictionary) but as an arrangement of words which form a continuous, organised piece of writing and a coherently developed argument. You might then usefully follow these steps:

1 Begin by reading through the passage which follows carefully until you have grasped the *central idea or argument*. Try to express this idea, in French, as if you were explaining the gist of the passage to someone who had not read it.

> Etre le témoin d'un accident de la route, c'est brutalement prendre conscience que 'cela n'arrive pas qu'aux autres', d'autant qu'une conduite prudente ne garantit même pas d'échapper aux facteurs impondérables. Qu'un fou du volant croise son parcours ou que son moteur vienne à défaillir et tout automobiliste peut basculer, d'un moment à l'autre, dans le camp des victimes impuissantes.
>
> Il ressort, si l'on s'en tient aux prévisions statistiques, que ce risque est de l'ordre d'un sur deux cent cinquante. La réalité, quant à elle, apparaît autrement effrayante. Dans soixante quinze pour cent des cas, les accidentés ne doivent s'en prendre qu'à leur propre façon de se comporter au volant: mauvaise appréciation des distances, réflexe tardif, coup de volant trop brusque, vitesse excessive, nervosité. Telles sont les conclusions des enquêtes réalisées, entre autres, par la Prévention Routière pour qui la faute de conduite constitue bel et bien la cause principale des accidents.
>
> Il reste pourtant que la totalité de ces défaillances humaines se voit est subordonnée un fléau plus meurtrier encore: l'alcool. Responsable d'un accident sur trois sur le réseau routier français, l'alcool tue. Plus de trois mille des accidents mortels provoqués chaque année sur les routes de France ont pour cause un excès de boisson. Il ne faut plus se résigner à recevoir le salaire de l'horreur!

2 You might briefly *summarise* the passage as follows: Certains conducteurs sont plus susceptibles que d'autres d'avoir un accident de voiture parce que la cause principale des accidents est le conducteur lui-même, et surtout le conducteur qui a bu de l'alcool.
3 Make use of your *dictionary*. Once you have grasped what the writer is saying and doing then study of the vocabulary can begin. There will be words which you have not understood or words which you have only half understood and words which you *think* you have understood (possibly because they resemble the English term). You will need to consult a dictionary. Because it is important to exploit the text for vocabulary-learning purposes it is best to use a French–English dictionary (such as *Larousse Dictionnaire du Français Contemporain*) and if you can, an illustrated monolingual dictionary (such as *Littré*). Use these tools to help you to define, in French, the *meaning* of a new word; note those *synonyms* which could replace it in the text and above all note the *example sentences* containing the new word which the dictionary provides.
4 Concentrate on *thematic vocabulary* in the passage: it is such vocabulary which is the more effectively reinforced by context. It may be of two types.
   a) vocabulary which comprises terms which relate to the *content* of the passage (and to what the writer is saying);
   b) vocabulary which comprises terms which relate to the *structure* of the passage (and to what the writer is doing).
   In the text we are studying here a) would include those terms which relate closely to driving, vehicles and accidents, e.g.:

Un accident de la route/un accidenté/le témoin d'un accident/la conduite prudente/un automobiliste/un fou du volant/leur façon de se comporter au volant/un fou du volant croise son parcours/son moteur vient à défaillir/la mauvaise appréciation des distances/le réflexe tardif/la vitesse excessive/un excès de boisson/la nervosité, etc.

b) would include those words and phrases which express cause:

> La faute de conduite constitue la cause principale des accidents/l'alcool est responsable d'un accident sur trois/les accidentés ne doivent s'en prendre qu'à leur

propre façon de se comporter/provoquer un accident/les accidents ont pour cause un excès de boisson etc.

All of these terms have been taken from the text but it is useful to find further illustrative examples in the monolingual dictionary (having first decided that the term is useful and should become part of your active vocabulary):

un témoin: personne qui a vu ou entendu quelque chose et qui peut le certifier.
Elle a été témoin d'une scène touchante, de leur dispute.
L'entrevue des chefs d'Etat a eu lieu sans témoins.

The examples will show you how to use the word with grammatical accuracy: *Elle a été* (tense) *témoin* (no article) *d'un accident* (*témoin* followed by *de*). They will also help you to understand which words 'témoin', when used in this way, may collocate with:

Elle a été témoin d'un accident.
d'une entrevue.
d'une dispute.
d'une scène.

but not
* Elle a été témoin d'un film à la télé
* Elle a été témoin du Président qui arriva à Orly.

* These sentences are ungrammatical.
All of this information is essential if you wish to reuse the word correctly.

5   *Rearrange new words* in sentences of your own creation. Experiments have shown that if the learner rearranges new words in sentences of his own creation (rather than try to learn them from a list) then memorisation of them is more efficient. In a test based on the above passage students who simply concocted 'fantasy' sentences (un accident sur trois se produit par un excès de bonbons; un accident sur trois se produit par la faute de mon grand-père) learned more efficiently than those who tried to learn the words from a random list.

6   Pay particular attention to, and try to understand, *structure* words, i.e. words which indicate that the writer is *doing* things. These may include introducing an example, or indicating that the meaning of something is to be explained, or pointing out that something is obvious, or showing that he is introducing an opposing point of view, or reaching a conclusion, and so on. From the present text you would select: Il ressort que, telles sont les conclusions, il reste pourtant que. These are words which help to present an argument and you will need a stock of such terms for your own essay-writing.

7   Study *synonyms* in the text. A way of using the text as a point of departure from which you widen your lexical knowledge is the study of synonyms. If you look up the word *s'empêcher* in the *Dictionnaire du Français Contemporain* you will find *se retenir* given as a synonym; *sage, averti, prévoyant* are given as synonyms of *prudent*. If it is possible to use these alternatives in the original sentence then clearly you will be adding to your vocabulary. However, synonyms should be treated with some caution and it is advisable to learn only those which you can be sure of as possible substitutes for the word in the original passage (and you will be sure because the dictionary examples make it clear or because you have checked with a native speaker or tutor). As there is much truth in the claim that there is no such thing as a true synonym, it is probably more valuable to try to establish the *differences* between *near-synonyms* so that you can use both terms with precision. Concentrate for example, on the *difference* between le spectacle/la vue; un conducteur/un automobiliste; une défaillance/une faute; réfléchir/se concentrer, etc.

8   Study the *thematic vocabulary* in the text. Doing this helps to form clusters of words which are then easier to memorise; memory appears to have a 'snowball effect', with like adhering to like. It is helpful to use this principle to build on the 'family' of the word and to extend vocabulary in this way. If the new word is a verb then check the dictionary to see if there is a corresponding adjective or noun which belongs to the word-family. Follow a similar procedure if the new word is an adjective or a noun. Words taken from the text above will give:

La route: routier, accident routier, un bon réseau routier, la circulation routière, etc.
Un conducteur: conduire, il conduit sa voiture avec beaucoup de maîtrise; il conduit
très prudemment.

défaillir: une défaillance; une défaillance d'attention peut provoquer un accident; tout conducteur demeure à la merci d'une défaillance mécanique.

9 Use the dictionary examples carefully to build *further sentences and phrases* which will expand the thematic vocabulary contained in the text. It is worth noting that by being able to make these *transformations* (e.g. from verb to noun, from adjective to noun, etc.) you not only increase your vocabulary but also find further ways of constructing sentences. For example, the nominalisation of *se comporter* in:

- Il risque d'avoir un accident parce qu'il se comporte d'une façon très dangereuse au volant.

This will produce:

- Il risque d'avoir un accident en raison de son comportement très dangereux au volant.

10 Produce a *plan* of the structure of the text. When you have thoroughly studied the vocabulary of the text and have recorded definitions, examples, synonyms and useful 'transformations' (e.g. verb transformed to noun, etc.) in your vocabulary notebook, it is time to turn your attention to the *way the argument or the ideas in the passage are presented*. Read the text again carefully analysing the main developments of the argument or the main stages in the author's chain of thought. The passage about road accidents earlier in the chapter has three main divisions: which correspond to the three paragraphs.

Think of a *subtitle* for *each section* and of a *title* for the *whole passage*, then note down the ideas which are developed in each section. This analysis will produce a plan such as the following:

- La plupart des accidents de la route se produisent par la faute du conducteur:
  a) Tout conducteur risque d'être victime d'un accident:
     i) la conduite prudente ne garantit pas contre le fou du volant, une défaillance mécanique;
     ii) le risque est de l'ordre d'un sur 250.
  b) Mais c'est presque toujours la faute du conducteur lui-même:
     i) dans 75% des cas il s'agit d'une erreur humaine;
     ii) conclusions des enquêtes de la Prévention Routière.
  c) L'alcool est responsable de la plupart des accidents:
     i) un accident sur 3, plus de 3 mille accidents provoqués par l'alcool
     ii) conclusion: il ne faut pas se résigner.

" A self-correcting exercise "

Working on the passage in order to produce a plan will help you to remember new vocabulary and the plan itself can be used as a means of practice and revision. When you have completed the intensive study put the original passage aside and attempt to reconstruct it orally or in writing using the plan and your vocabulary notes for guidance. By doing this you will begin the process of making passive vocabulary (that which you merely recognise) part of the stock of terms which you are able to use actively. As you can compare your own version with the original it means that you have available a self-correcting exercise which can be used as a means of revision on subsequent occasions.

REVISION AND SELF-TESTING

When you have completed the work on a text you will need to arrange your study material so that you are able to revise and test what you have learnt. You can of course list the new expressions on one side of your vocabulary notebook with the English equivalent entered against them on the other side of the page. However, it will help you to revise the lexical item more efficiently and fully if you test your knowledge of it in other ways as well and, if possible, in context.

a) You will have noted the dictionary definition of most of the new items of vocabulary. You can record the new word on one side of the page against its definition in French entered on the other side of the page and test yourself by finding the word to fit the definition.
b) The dictionary examples and sentences from the original text can be arranged as a self-testing device. Write the example sentence on one side of your book leaving the target word blank:

J'aime voyager avec lui, c'est un conducteur très —— (prudent)
La Prévention Routière a effectué —— sur les causes des accidents de la route.
(une enquête)

Il a été ——— de leur dispute, il a tout entendu.   (témoin)

On voyait des —— de toutes sortes: camions, taxis, voitures, autobus.   (véhicules)

c) You can extract a short passage from the original text, leaving certain words blank:

Etre le —— d'un accident de la route, c'est brutalement prendre —— que cela n'arrive pas qu'aux autres d'autant qu'une ——— prudente ne _____ même pas d'échapper aux facteurs ———.

"Towards a better understanding"

You will find that testing yourself in this way will make the task of learning and revising vocabulary more interesting. Also the very process of arranging and thinking about the tests themselves will help you towards a better understanding and recall of the words that you are aiming to learn.

If you follow the advice given in this chapter and make use of the suggestions on how to study a text intensively and work productively on the language in it, you will make progress in building a wide vocabulary of terms that you can understand and use with precision. In particular, the type of study proposed here will help you to prepare for the text-based use of language exercises which are set by some of the Examination Boards. A selection of exercises is provided below. Use the texts for vocabulary study and then try your hand at the examination questions. The answers have been provided so that you can correct your work.

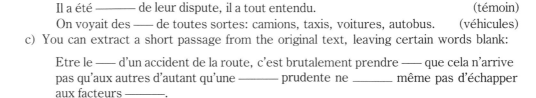

EXAMINATION QUESTIONS

Q1
Lisez attentivement le texte suivant, puis répondez aux questions.

Vers l'Europe des universités

Les discussions, au sein de l'Europe, ont longtemps porté sur le problème particulièrement embrouillé de l'équivalence des diplômes. Elles ont fait sur ce point de notables progrès, mais on est passé maintenant à une phase nouvelle et plus ambitieuse, consistant à encourager les échanges d'étudiants et de professeurs dans les universités et de professionnels dans les entreprises.

Le conseil des ministres européens a approuvé un plan dont l'objectif est de créer un réseau européen de façon à encourager, grâce à des bourses, les échanges d'étudiants, d'universitaires et de professionnels entre les universités et les entreprises d'autres pays membres.

Un autre projet plus ambitieux encore vient d'être proposé par la commission. Son objectif: faire en sorte que, à partir de 1992, 10% au moins des six millions d'étudiants européens effectuent une partie de leurs études dans un autre Etat membre. Cette mobilité donnerait aux cadres une 'conscience européenne', grâce à une expérience directe de la vie, de la culture et des mécanismes économiques d'autres pays. Les échanges s'étendraient aussi aux enseignants.

Des bourses seront attribuées aux étudiants et aux universités qui les accueilleront. Un système européen d'unités de valeur sera mis au point pour assurer la reconnaissance automatique de la partie des études faites à l'étranger.

Signalons aussi le projet de 'l'Université de l'Europe', qui est ardemment soutenu et qui constituerait un réseau de centres de recherche européens.

Mais la plus originale des initiatives en gestation est sûrement celle que prépare un groupe d'industriels. Ceux-ci réfléchissent aux initiatives susceptibles de renforcer l'Europe sur le plan économique, scientifique et technologique. Ils se sont intéressés aux problèmes de transport, de télécommunication, de technologie, d'environnement, de financement, mais aussi de formation.

Toutes ces initiatives témoignent d'un changement évident d'état d'esprit. L'idée commence à faire son chemin, la chance de l'Europe est d'abord dans son capital humain et son potentiel intellectuel. En mettant en commun ses ressources en matière grise, elle peut constituer un pôle de création et d'innovation permettant de lutter à armes égales avec les géants américains et japonais.

Questions

a) Refaites les phrases suivantes en remplaçant les mots et les expressions soulignés par des mots ou des expressions que vous aurez trouvés dans le texte. Vous ne changerez pas le sens général de la phrase, mais il faudra quelquefois changer la forme grammaticale des mots trouvés.

   i) La situation reste <u>compliquée</u>.

   ii) La manoeuvre a été <u>exécutée</u> sans la moindre difficulté.

   iii) Permettez-moi de vous <u>faire savoir</u> que je ne vais pas tolérer une telle attitude.

   iv) Le passage d'un bateau <u>était</u> la seule chance de salut des naufragés.

   v) <u>Son apprentissage</u> d'ingénieur l'aida à obtenir une situation bien payée.

b) Expliquez brièvement en français, soit par un seul mot, soit par un groupe de mots, les expressions ou les mots en italique dans les expressions suivantes, prises dans le texte.

par exemple: Il souhaite *ardemment* votre retour.
Il souhaite passionnément votre retour.

   i) Un autre projet plus ambitieux encore vient d'être *proposé* (ligne 10).

   ii) La plus originale des initiatives *en gestation* (ligne 21).

   iii) Ceux-ci refléchissent aux initiatives *susceptibles* de renforcer l'Europe (ligne 22).

   iv) L'idée commence à *faire son chemin* (ligne 27).

   v) Elle peut constituer *un pôle* de création et d'innovation (ligne 29).

c) Le passage qui suit est pris dans une autre partie de l'article d'où est tiré le texte. Reconstituez-le en remplissant les blancs. Utilisez les mot et les expressions ci-dessous – mais attention, vous ne les utilisez pas tous.

Il faut . . . (a) . . . peu à peu les . . . (b) . . . universitaires et faire travailler ensemble les établissements et les équipes de recherche.
Le conseil des ministres européens a . . . (c) . . . un programme . . . (d) . . . Commett destiné . . . (e) . . . développer la coopération entre l'Université et l'industrie. Il . . . (f) . . . , pour que ce programme . . . (g) . . . entrer en . . . (h) . . . , à se . . . (i) . . . d'accord . . . (j) . . . le budget qui lui sera . . . (k) . . . Le . . . (l) . . . de 60 millions d'ECU qui avait été . . . (m) . . . est en effet . . . (n) . . . par l'Allemagne Fédérale, qui voudrait . . . (o) . . . la somme à 45 millions.
S'il . . . (p) . . . adopté et appliqué, ce programme . . . (q) . . . les pratiques universitaires, . . . (r) . . . les méthodes n'ont guère changé . . . (s) . . . beaucoup d' . . . (t) . . . .

a été	consacré	fixé	puisse
ans	contesté	intitulé	ramener
années	cours	intituler	rapprocher
approuvé	courses	mettre	rejeté
augmenter	de	nombre	reste
avec	depuis	numéro	soutenu
bouleverserait	desquelles	passé	sur
chiffre	dont	peut	tomber
	était	pour	vigueur

(JMB 1988)

Q2

Lisez attentivement le texte suivant, puis répondez aux questions.

Hélène était venue passer les vacances d'été à Saint-Clar comme chaque année. Elle prétexta des travaux universitaires, une série de conférences du plus haut intérêt sur la physique einsteinienne, pour abréger d'un mois son séjour. M. de Balansun l'approuva tout en déplorant la tyrannie des études supérieures. Mme de Balansun posa sur sa fille un regard attristé, un peu inquiet aussi. Elle n'était pas dupe: il n'y a pas de conférences en août et septembre, les facultés sont fermées. Elle ne fit aucune remarque cependant. C'était une femme effacée, humble et discrète. Francis aussi regarda sa soeur. Il vit son expression de détresse tandis qu'elle s'empêtrait dans ses explications. Il baissa les yeux en rougissant.

Dès le premier jour, dès la première minute, Francis avait senti que sa grande soeur était changée. Il aimait beaucoup Hélène, il était fier d'elle. Cette année-là aux vacances d'été, il ne la 'retrouvait' plus. Quelque chose d'étrange était survenu. Plus de contact entre eux. Autrefois Hélène et Francis étaient comme deux enfants du même âge. Ils partageaient un certain nombre de plaisanteries vénérables, rituelles, qui n'avaient de sens et de saveur que pour eux, un stock d'allusions à tel ou tel épisode familial, à telle figure comique. Francis parlait de ses études, du collège, se faisait expliquer par sa soeur un point obscur de mathématiques. Aujourd'hui rien de tout cela ne subsistait. Dès le début des vacances Francis avait décelé chez sa soeur une gêne, un malaise qu'elle essayait de dissiper par des efforts gauches et vains. Les plaisanteries consacrées ne l'amusaient plus: son rire sonnait faux. Elle était comme absente. Francis était timide et d'une grande pudeur morale. La conscience obscure qu'il y avait quelque chose de changé chez Hélène le paralysait à son tour. Il se surprit rougir devant elle quand ils se trouvaient seuls et qu'elle tentait si péniblement d'amorcer une conversation animée. La vieille camaraderie était morte. 'C'est peut-être parce que je suis grand,' se disait Francis. 'Je ne suis plus un petit garçon. Alors forcément il ne peut plus y avoir la même intimité entre nous.' Il avait entendu dire que les affections familiales, avec les années, se diluent dans l'indifférence.

(*Les Forêts de la nuit* – J-L Curtis)

Questions

i) Refaites les phrases suivantes en remplaçant les mots et expressions soulignés par des mots ou des expressions que vous aurez trouvés dans le texte ci-dessus. Vous ne changerez pas la signification de la phrase, mail il faudra quelquefois changer la forme grammaticale des mots trouvés.
  a) Je vais vous montrer la maison de notre famille.
  b) Après le commencement du mois il ne l'a pas revue.
  c) Il voulait raccourcir sa visite.
  d) Sa mère voulait faire disparaître les ennuis de sa fille.
  e) En la regardant il percevait sa détresse.
  f) Il étudiait des problèmes de mathématiques qui l'intéressaient énormément.
  g) Elle s'efforça avec difficulté de paraître à l'aise.
  h) Jadis ils passaient tout le temps ensemble.
  i) Elle demanda à son frère de lui éclairer cette théorie de la physique einsteinienne.
  j) Ses paroles semblent dissimuler sa pensée.

ii) Etudiez ces définitions tirées d'un dictionnaire français. Chaque définition correspond à un mot dans le texte. Trouvez ces mots et écrivez-les.
  a) établissement d'enseignement secondaire
  b) qui n'est pas bien intelligible, qui se fait difficilement comprendre
  c) signification
  d) leçon donnée dans les facultés
  e) série complète des cours suivis dans un établissement d'instruction
  f) rendre un son
  g) science du mouvement
  h) (ce mot) atténue ce qu'une expression a de trop absolu
  i) exister encore, continuer d'être
  j) qualité de certaines choses qui les rend propres à captiver l'attention

TUTOR'S ANSWERS TO QUESTIONS 1 AND 2

Question 1

a) i) La situation reste compliquée. (embrouillée)
   ii) La manoeuvre a été exécutée sans la moindre difficulté. (effectuée)
   iii) Permettez-moi de vous faire savoir que je ne ne vais pas tolérer une telle attitude. (signaler)
   iv) Le passage d'un bateau était la seule chance de salut des naufragés. (constituait)
   v) Son apprentissage d'ingénieur l'aida à obtenir une situation bien payée.

(sa formation)

b) i) Un autre projet plus ambitieux encore vient d'être proposé. (soumis)
   ii) La plus originale des initiatives en gestation. (que l'on est en train d'élaborer)

iii) Ceux-ci réfléchissent aux initiatives <u>susceptibles</u> de renforcer l'Europe.

(initiatives qui pourraient renforcer)

iv) L'idée commence à <u>faire son chemin</u>. (à s'établir)

v) Elle peut constituer <u>un pôle</u> de création et d'innovation. (un centre)

a) augmenter   h) vigueur   o) ramener
b) cours   i) mettre   p) était
c) approuvé   j) sur   q) bouleverserait
d) intitulé   k) consacré   r) dont
e) à   l) chiffre   s) depuis
f) resté   m) fixé   t) années
g) puisse   n) rejeté

Question 2

i) a) Je vais vous montrer la maison <u>de notre famille</u>. (familiale)

b) Après <u>le commencement</u> du mois il ne l'a pas revue. (les premiers jours)

c) Il voulait <u>raccourcir</u> sa visite. (abréger)

d) Sa mère voulait <u>faire disparaître</u> les ennuis de sa fille. (dissiper)

e) En la regardant <u>il percevait</u> sa détresse. (voyait)

f) Il étudiait des problèmes de mathématiques <u>qui l'intéressaient énormément</u>.

(qui étaient du plus haut intérêt pour lui)

g) Elle <u>s'efforça avec difficulté</u> de paraître à l'aise (tenta péniblement)

h) <u>Jadis</u> ils passaient tout le temps ensemble (autrefois)

i) Elle <u>demanda à son frère de lui éclairer</u> cette théorie de la physique einsteinienne.

(elle se fit expliquer par son frère)

j) Ses paroles <u>semblent dissimuler sa pensée</u>. (sonnent fausses)

ii) a) faculté   f) sonner
b) obscur   g) physique
c) sens   h) un peu
d) conférence   i) subsister
e) études   j) intérêt

Further reading

Collected passages for intensive study:

S. Lee and D. Ricks. *Penguin French Reader*, Penguin
G. J. P. Courtenay. *Les Meilleures Pages du Figaro*, Longman
G. J. P. Courtenay. *Encore du 'Figaro'*, Longman
A. Deville and R. Steele. *Textes pour Aujourd'hui – Extraits de Elle*, Didier
E. Dangon, F. Weiss et al. *Lire en Français*, Hatier

Dictionaries

Dictionnaire du Français Contemporain, Larousse
Dictionnaire du Français Langue Etrangère, Bordas
Collins-Robert English-French, French-English Dictionary, Collins.

THE ESSAY IN FRENCH

VOCABULARY

IDIOM

SENTENCE STRUCTURE AND FLUENCY

GRAMMATICAL ACCURACY

COHERENCE AND SEQUENCE

CONTENT — RELEVANCE

GETTING STARTED

The essay or free composition is a major feature of all A-level examinations and accordingly is awarded a substantial proportion of the total subject mark. Writing an essay in French is a complex and demanding activity which requires competence in a variety of skills. It tests the accurate use of a knowledge of vocabulary which should be related to a wide range of non-specialist subject areas. It requires the ability to write grammatically accurate sentences and to arrange material in a coherent and logical order in French in a way which would be acceptable to a native speaker. In addition to all this, the student is expected to have a flow of ideas and to invent the content of the essay.

When getting started on preparation for the essay in French it is therefore essential to build the appropriate foundations early in your course, making sure from the beginning that your general language work and your reading in French is made to feed into your essay-writing. Ask yourself whether the grammar work in your course-book enables you to practise structures useful in narrating, describing people and places, expressing opinions, presenting an argument and counter-argument, enumerating reasons for and against and in emphasising points and reaching a conclusion. These are some of the functions which need to be performed when writing an essay and they should be practised over a period of time.

The acquisition of vocabulary should also take place progressively and should be planned to cover a wide range of everyday topics (see chapter 3). Your coursebook will probably cover a certain number of themes but you should make certain that a sufficiently wide range is provided. You might begin by checking your course-book against the topics included in the past essay questions listed in the following chapters. Treat the texts merely as a list of relevant themes to be extended by further reading. In other words, you should begin your examination preparation by organising your language work so that it always has a purpose; in this instance the improvement of your essay-writing French.

ESSENTIAL PRINCIPLES

WHAT MAKES A GOOD ESSAY?

> Interesting . . .
> entertaining . . . original?

A general reader and an A-level examiner would give rather different answers to this question but their answers ought to have a number of points in common. The general reader would doubtless say that a good essay is one which is interesting or entertaining, that it has something original to say, that the writer knows what he is talking about and that it is well written. The examiner would also be more than satisfied if he or she could write any of these comments at the end of a candidate's essay and the mark would be a good one.

However, he is interested in more than the general impression that he is left with after reading the work. He has many essays to mark. The standard will vary considerably as the writers will have reached different levels of skilfulness in essay-writing and will have made more or less progress in learning the French language. The examiner therefore needs to break down the skill of writing an essay in French to find out what the ingredients of a good essay are (or a *bad* one for that matter) in order to see how many of them are present in every essay he has to assess.

We shall discuss these ingredients later but it is important to point out here that someone who is setting out to learn the skill of writing an essay in French would do well to look as it with the same analytical eye as the examiner. When an essay has been marked 'good' or 'weak' it is not much use writing another one until you understand exactly *why* the first one deserved the mark it was given. Top tennis players analyse their game, win or lose. They do not wander along to the next tournament vaguely hoping to do better next time; they work on their weak points.

Setting goals

Trying to analyse your weak points and your strong points need not make the whole business of essay-writing an unenjoyable one. On the contrary, finding out what has to be done and then setting and achieving goals can be very rewarding. You will be able to see yourself making progress if you understand that being able to write a good language essay is a skill which can be broken down and learned gradually.

Elements of the language essay

What, then, are the elements of the language essay that the examiner considers when making an assessment? They are:

- knowledge of vocabulary and idiom
- sentence-structure and fluency
- grammatical accuracy
- coherence and sequence
- overall presentation and development of ideas
- style

We shall deal with these items in turn. It is important to understand what the examiner has in mind when he or she refers to them in the marking-grid and you should use them to identify what you can work on when you are preparing for the essay.

VOCABULARY

Is vocabulary your weak area? Do you begin to struggle with a language essay because you are stuck for words? Have a look at your recent work and ask yourself whether the errors you have made are *vocabulary errors* (including spelling, accent and gender errors) or whether the mistakes involve mainly *grammatical inaccuracies*. Then, even if you do not seem to be always choosing the wrong word or spelling it in the wrong way, ask yourself whether you are really making full use of vocabulary to make your work more readable and interesting. Do you have enough vocabulary to draw on in order to say what you want to, and so get personal satisfaction from setting ideas or opinions down in French?

Most A-level students, after submitting their essay-writing to this kind of examination would have to admit that vocabulary is a weak area. They can often 'get by' with the help of a dictionary and by falling back on a small stock of words and phrases which they have been circulating since preparing for GCSE, but this writing is not impressive, certainly not to an examiner who perhaps has read the same phrase expressing the same simple idea for the hundredth time.

The use of words

"Is it *apt*?"

As far as the vocabulary used in an essay is concerned the examiner will ask whether the writer made good use of words which relate genuinely to what is mentioned in the title of the essay. What is being tested is your ability to use words in order to express yourself on a specific topic chosen by the examiner – not on a topic chosen by yourself. It will therefore not bring you much credit if you display rich and varied vocabulary to do with an irrelevant subject which you have tried to force into an essay or if you 'pad out' your writing with collections of phrases which do not really mean anything, (such as *à tout prendre, il faut bien peser le pour et le contre, toute réflexion faite* etc.).

Range and depth

Does the vocabulary used in the essay show variety, range, depth? To understand what is indicated by range or depth, read the following paragraphs taken from recent A-level essays on the subject of television.

CANDIDATE A

Tout le monde est d'accord aujourd'hui que l'invention la plus bénéfique du 20e siècle est la télévision. En Angleterre aujourd'hui presque tout le monde possède une télévision et on dit que chaque enfant regarde la télévision pendant cinq heures chaque jour de sa vie. A l'école les enfants peuvent regarder la télévision pour apprendre l'histoire ou la géographie, par exemple. Pour les adultes il y a la 'Open University'. Mais le plus grand avantage de la télévision est le plaisir qu'elle donne. On n'a pas besoin de sortir le soir pour aller au cinéma ou au théâtre, on peut regarder la télévision chez soi sans payer. Il y a presque toujours quelque chose d'intéréssant à voir pour les enfants et pour les adultes.

CANDIDATE B

Certes, il a y a tendance à dénigrer ceux qui passent des heures devant le petit écran. On évoque souvent l'image du téléspectateur affalé dans un fauteuil qui allume son poste en se servant de la télécommande, pour regarder une émission de variétés plutôt bête ou un film de dessins animés. Mais ce n'est pas à dire que tous les programmes sont de ce niveau-là. Au contraire, un temps d'antenne important est consacré aux actualités, aux grands reportages et aux émissions théâtrales.

Assessment

It is the work of the second candidate, of course, which scored more highly because her knowledge of vocabulary showed greater depth and variety even in a shorter paragraph. *Depth*, because she could make apt use of a number of terms associated with television viewing, *variety* because she did not have to fall back repeatedly on the same expression.

Candidate A cannot avoid using the phrase *regarder la télévision* three times, which is a rather simple phrase anyway. You will notice that there are also other repetitions which suggest that the writer is restricted in the number of terms he has to choose from.

The second passage is also more interesting because the writer's greater depth of vocabulary enables her to develop ideas and to give more precise examples; television is worth watching because there are *actualités, grands reportages* and *émissions théâtrales*. Candidate A can use only the vague *quelque chose d'intéressant*; both language and ideas remain superficial and rather imprecise. Candidate B is not forced into the repetition of a phrase like *regarder la télévision*. The same idea comes across in a variety of ways: it is in *téléspectateur* or *passer des heures devant le petit écran* as well as *regarder une émission*. She can vary expression by the use of synonyms or near synonyms such as *émissions* and *programmes*.

It should be obvious from this examination of the two paragraphs that the wider knowledge of vocabulary does not simply result in there being more 'good words' for the examiner to tick: it leads to the discussion of more detailed and interesting ideas and improves readability. Candidate B went on to produce a very good essay and one of the examiner's comments was 'Interesting discussion. Candidate knows what she is talking about.'

Range and variety.

If you can use a range and variety of vocabulary you will not become mesmerised as some candidates are, into repeating endlessly key words in the title of the essay. For example, *avantages* was a key word in a recent A-level title. Numbers of candidates, because they knew little vocabulary relating to *avantages* could not avoid over-using the word, usually in very simple phrases such as *Il y a des avantages avec, un autre avantage de l'énergie nucléaire est.* Such phrases are anglicised and their repetition makes very wearisome reading.

If there had been more depth to the vocabulary which these candidates had learnt they would have been able to express the idea of being advantageous in different ways and with more variety:

– L'énergie nucléaire offre de gros avantages
– Les bénéfices de l'énergie nucléaire sont évidents
– On trouve dans l'énergie nucléaire des avantages inestimables
– L'emploi de l'énergie nucléaire constitue un avantage certain
– L'énergie nucléaire comporte de très grands avantages
– Le nucléaire présente des avantages certains
– Il y a des avantages indéniables à retirer de l'énergie nucléaire

Having established that it is the advantages which are being discussed they could have developed the idea by talking of *l'utilité, les conséquences heureuses, les effets favorables, ce qu'il apporte d'utile, les possibilités bénéfiques, les gains que permettent l'énergie nucléaire etc.*

Adjectives and adverbs

Is the vocabulary rich and interesting? One of the questions asked under this heading is: can the candidate use adjectives and adverbs to add to the meaning of the sentence? Adjectives to bring out a particular quality of a noun, to emphasise or reinforce a point; adverbs to intensify an adjective or a verb.

Rich and interesting.

The following sentences taken from A-level essays were all 'ticked' because the vocabulary was rich and interesting. The writers were able to use sometimes quite simple adjectives and adverbs to add to the meaning of a sentence. Writing in this way not only improves readability, it shows that the writer can use vocabulary to good effect.

- L'avenue parut immense, vide. Puis le ciel s'assombrit et il se mit à pleuvoir à torrents. Les gouttes de pluie étaient lourdes et larges.
- Les prairies calmes et fleuries d'aujourd'hui deviendront les chantiers sales et tumultueux de demain.
- Nos campagnes seront transformées en un vaste désert stérile.
- Quand le weekend arrive tout le monde pousse un long soupir de soulagement.
- L'énergie nucléaire coûte moins cher mais elle est incontestablement plus dangereuse que l'énergie traditionnelle.
- On a discuté à n'en plus finir des méfaits de la drogue. Maintenant il faut agir.

IDIOM

Use of idiom in the essay is also used as a criterion for judging its quality. An idiom can be defined as an expression in which the individual words cannot be translated literally:

- s'en prendre à quelqu'un = to attack or to blame someone
- ne pas y aller de main morte = to go hard at it
- se lever du pied gauche = to get out of bed the wrong side

An idiomatic usage in French is one which is characteristically French. It should be obvious why examiners take ability to use idiom as a criterion. Its presence in a piece of writing shows that the writer has a close knowledge of the language and is not thinking in English. The term idiomatic is often used by examiners to cover something wider than just choice of vocabulary. If the French in an essay is idiomatic it means that the language does not read as though it is either a translation or sounds like 'schoolboy French'. The choice of

What is meant by idiomatic language?

vocabulary, the word order and the structures are authentically French. Achieving this, of course, is not easy. That is why it can be said that a student who can write good, idiomatic French is guaranteed a very high grade in the A-level language papers.

CONCLUSIONS

What are the essential points to bear in mind as far as vocabulary and idiom are concerned? Firstly, remember that they represent a clearly defined part of essay-writing which can be worked on and revised. If you make progress here you will be achieving something very worthwhile. Secondly, do not forget that this is a part of your essay-writing to which the examiner will give particular attention and about which he will write a comment. Finally, ask yourself the following questions about your language essays:

a) Do you make good use of *idiomatic expressions*? Does the vocabulary you use really say something about the subject? Do you know enough vocabulary to vary the terms and use alternatives? Do you make good use of adjectives and adverbs to add meaning?

b) Do you rely on *common phrases* (those you have used since GCSE) and tend to over-use them? Are there few idiomatic expressions in the essay? Do you tend to use only the most obvious terms to do with the subject or aspects of it? Is there not much associated vocabulary which draws out further aspects or ideas?

c) Do you use vocabulary which is *simple* or most like the English term? Are there many repetitions? Is the vocabulary too limited for the scope of the subject? Do you invent terms? Is there no idiom?

If the answer is 'yes' to all those questions under a) then your vocabulary is likely to be very good, even excellent. If you have to answer 'yes' to most of the questions under b) your knowledge is passable but with room for improvement. If you answer 'yes' to the questions under c) vocabulary is a weak area for you and you need to work hard to improve it.

SENTENCE STRUCTURE AND FLUENCY

If you are to retain the attention of your reader and encourage him or her to read on you have to succeed in putting words together and in arranging sentences to produce a *continuity of meaning* which is interesting to follow. You have to be able to construct coherent sentences and groups of sentences. The examiner will look specifically at this kind of readability and fluency, knowing that the good A-level language essay is one in which there is a varied pattern of sentences which are correctly put together.

Read the following extracts from the work of A-level candidates and ask yourself which is more satisfying to read.

CANDIDATE A

On ne peut pas nier que la violence grandit. Pour s'en convaincre il suffit de lire les journaux ou d'assister à un grand match de football où des bagarres violents risquent toujours d'éclater. Dans les grandes villes on a l'impression que les attaques à main armée, les vols et les viols deviennent de plus en plus nombreux tous les ans, ce qui est démontré d'ailleurs par les statistiques.

La cause principale de cette violence c'est que les gens qui commettent ces crimes ne se sentent pas bien dans la société et ils l'expriment de cette façon. Pour éviter de telles choses il faudrait donner une bonne éducation à ces gens pour essayer de leur apprendre que la violence ne peut jamais résoudre leurs problèmes.

CANDIDATE B

Pendant le vingtième siècle tant de choses ont été inventées. Nous sommes beaucoup avancés par rapport aux gens du dix-neuvième siècle.

> Est-ce que les inventions sont toutes bénéfiques? Si l'on pense au magnétoscope il est très bien. On peut regarder des films chez soi, mais à mon avis le vidéo est l'invention la plus désastreuse du vingtième siècle. Avec les video-cassettes les enfants peuvent regarder des films violents et sexuels. Ils voient de mauvaises choses et ils se tournent vers la violence. Ils voient des gens qui volent, qui font la guerre et qui tuent. Comment vont-ils savoir que tout cela n'est pas bien?

CANDIDATE C

> Vers midi le vent qui s'était levé pendant la matinée a changé de direction attisant le feu et poussant les flammes vers les hauts de St. Paul. Tous les vacanciers dont les tentes et les caravanes avaient commencé à s'enflammer ont dû s'enfuir de l'autre côté de la N.98 où ils ont attendu l'arrivée des pompiers. Malheuresement, lorsque ceux-ci sont arrivés il était déjà trop tard. L'incendie avait ravagé le camping et brûlé toutes les tentes. Evidemment la mienne n'a pas été épargnée de sorte que je suis sans abri et sans argent.

Assessment

The paragraph written by candidate B is not bad work. He knows a good deal of vocabulary and the grammar is accurate. However, the passage reads as if it had been thought out and constructed *sentence by sentence* with little effort made to link the sentences up. They seem rather isolated one from another and are mainly simple (i.e. there are few subordinate clauses) and are mainly of the same pattern: On peut regarder des films chez soi; les enfants peuvent regarder des films violents; ils voient de mauvaises choses; ils se tournent vers la violence; ils voient des gens qui volent.

The other two paragraphs, on the other hand, are made up of more complex sentences (there are more subordinate clauses), the pattern of the sentences is more varied and each sentence is made to relate to the following or preceeding one more closely (N.B. in the examples below those words which link sentences or parts of sentences have been underlined).

In candidate A's work note the use of pronouns and the relative pronoun:

- Pour s'en convaincre (en stands for 'que la violence grandit', linking this sentence with the one before)

- et ils l'expriment de cette façon (l' stands for 'ne se sentent pas bien dans la société' and so links the two halves of the sentence)

- ce qui est démontré par les statistiques (ce qui stands for (le fait) que les attaques à main armée etc. deviennent plus nombreux).

In candidate C's work, note the use *qui, dont, où, lorsque, de sorte que* to introduce subordinate clauses; the use of the present participle (*attisant, poussant*) which varies the sentence structure and *ceux-ci (= les pompiers)* and *la mienne (= tente)* which link the sentence with the one before.

CONCLUSIONS

To find out whether your language essays have the qualities which the examiner looks for under the heading of sentence-structure and fluency, ask yourself the following questions:

a) Do you make *good use of subordinate clauses*? (e.g. those introduced by; afin que, de peur que, avant que, jusqu'à ce que, en attendant que, à supposer que, à condition que, à tel point que, de manière que, de façon que, de sorte que, bien, quoique etc. and by relative pronouns, qui, que, dont, lequel, ce qui, ce que etc.) Are you able to vary the pattern of the sentence (e.g. by sometimes using a present participle)? Do you use pronouns (le, la, les, leur, y, en or celui-ci, celui-là, cela, ceci, le mien, les nôtres etc.) in a natural way to link the meaning of sentences or parts of sentences?

b) Does your essay contain *some subordinate clauses only* and mainly the 'easier', more obvious ones (qui, parce que, quand, lorsque)? Do your sentences seem to follow the same pattern (e.g. subject + verb + object: les enfants [subject] regardent [verb] la télévision [object])?

c) Do you seem to write only *simple sentences* (i.e. without subordinate clauses)? Do they seem rather isolated so that the sense of the paragraph does not flow? Are they all built on the same pattern so that your writing sounds rather monotonous?

If you can answer 'yes' to most of the questions in (a) then you are likely to be producing some excellent writing. If your work fits into categories (b) or (c) then there is obviously room for improvement.

GRAMMATICAL ACCURACY

Compensating qualities.

There has been a good deal of argument in recent years about the importance of grammatical accuracy. Attitudes have changed, and it is probably true to say that inaccuracy is not penalised as severely as it was once. Examiners take the view that there may be other qualities (fluency, development of the argument) which compensate for inaccuracy and that there are different types of errors, some more serious than others. This is good news for the learner who hopes to pass an examination, but a word of warning is necessary. It certainly does not follow that grammatical accuracy is unimportant. If your essay is riddled with mistakes it is not likely to reach a pass standard. If it is inaccurate then there is likely to be poor quality in other areas: it will not have much fluency and ideas will not be clearly developed. However, you should reassure yourself that examiners take all factors into consideration and do everything they can to assess your work in a fair and balanced way.

Some errors are more serious than others. You need to realise this when you are working on your grammar. The more serious errors are:

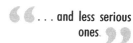

More serious errors . . .

i) those which show that you have *not learned basic forms* (e.g. of common irregular and regular verbs, plurals of certain nouns and adjectives, forms of adverbs, of the demonstrative pronouns, possessive pronoun, the gender of nouns in everyday use and common prepositions);

ii) those which show that you have *not learned basic rules* (e.g. those governing position of adjectives, question forms, rules for the definite article, rules governing the formation of the passive);

iii) those which cause a *breakdown in communication* because they obscure the meaning of the phrase or sentence.

. . . and less serious ones.

Less serious are:

i) those which are *not basic* but nevertheless would sound odd or irritating to the native speaker

ii) those which are obviously *slips* or oversights (i.e. there is evidence that the rule has been understood but that it has not been applied consistently);

iii) those which represent a '*good try*' which has not quite succeeded.

Obviously, you should aim at not making any of these errors but give priority to eliminating the serious ones.

CONCLUSIONS

It will probably be evident to you from looking at your marked language essays whether or not grammatical accuracy is a weak area for you. Nevertheless the following questions will help you to decide whether you need to take action and what you need to do.

a) Do you make very *few errors* in either simple or complex language? Are your mistakes really oversights?

b) Do you know the rules but sometimes *forget* to apply them? Do you get basic grammar right but tend to avoid/get wrong the more difficult constructions? Do you usually understand immediately why something has been underlined as wrong?

c) Do you have *serious errors* in nearly every sentence? Are there many different types of error? Do you not understand what has gone wrong?

If your work fits into category (c) you need grammar revision of a basic kind (See chapter 2) and you are not likely to pass the language papers without it. If it fits category (b) you will get by, but there is nevertheless room for improvement. If you can truthfully answer 'yes' to category (a) then you are on your way to a high grade.

COHERENCE AND SEQUENCE

When we considered sentence structure and fluency it could be seen that it is important that sentences should be carefully constructed to make for readability. That readability should be maintained throughout the paragraph and throughout the essay. It will depend on overall coherence and clear sequencing. This aspect of essay-writing depends as much on orderly thinking as it does on your knowledge of French.

Remember the reader who has to follow your line of thought. If you want to persuade him to sympathise with your point of view, which is the main reason for writing your ideas down, then do not irritate him by making him struggle to follow your argument.

Express your ideas as clearly as possible. Break down an idea into separate points and deal with them individually. When you move from one point to the next, indicate the transition. Keep in mind the points that you have made already and the forward line of your argument.

Think about what you are *doing* (e.g. I am giving an example, enumerating several points, bringing in evidence to support a point, putting an opposing point of view etc.) and make it evident to your reader.

In short, it is essential to make your reader *comfortable*. You will not do this if you:

- ramble from one point to the next
- repeat yourself
- jump unexpectedly to another point or
- run one point into the following one.

Your reader should not have the task of giving your essay a shape. That is *your* task.

CONCLUSIONS

Re-read some of your language essays, putting yourself objectively into the position of the reader, and ask yourself the following questions:

a) Does the essay have a genuine introduction which indicates direction of the discussion in a helpful fashion? Does the conclusion provide a genuine and satisfying closure? Do the paragraphs deal with complete points and are they logically linked?
b) Is the general development of the essay in terms of paragraphs clear but with perhaps some weak linking? Is the introduction or conclusion rather an artificial one, there for the form rather than as a genuine guide for the reader?
c) Is the paragraphing haphazard, with no clear indication of why a new paragraph has been started? Does the reader have to figure out for himself what it is that the writer is doing? Is the line of argument unclear or the story episodic?

Unless you can answer 'yes' to the questions in a) you should not be satisfied with the organisation and sequencing of what you are writing.

CONTENT – RELEVANCE

The importance attached to content will vary from one Board's mark-scheme to another. This is because the essay in French may be set for different purposes. For example, one of the aims of the 'topics' essay (AEB Paper 4, UCLES Paper 5, Oxford Paper 4) is to test factual content. The free composition (e.g. London Syllabus A Paper 4, O&C Paper 4) does not. However, an important criterion in all mark-schemes is *relevance*. You must keep to the subject indicated in the title of the essay. Many candidates do not, and consequently either fail the examination or get a poor grade.

What, then, are the dangers? Read the following essay on 'L'invention la plus désastreuse et l'invention la plus bénéfique du 20e siècle' by an A-level candidate and decide what went wrong and why.

> Il n'est pas possible d'ouvrir un journal sans y découvrir
> l'histoire d'un accident de la route dans lequel de nombreuses

> personnes ont été blessées ou bien de nouvelles statistiques qui montrent que le trou dans la couche d'ozone est plus grand qu'on ne croyait. Néanmoins, pour moi l'invention la plus désastreuse et la plus bénéfique du vingtième siècle n'est ni la voiture ni les aérosols. C'est la télévision.
>
> La puissance de la télévision est déjà célèbre et selon un sondage effectué par le Guardian la semaine dernière, presque quatre-vingt-dix pour cent de la population regarde la télévision chaque jour contre seulement trente pour cent qui lit un livre ou un journal. Il est clair que la télévision exerce une influence importante sur la vie de tout le monde. Mais cette influence est-elle bonne ou mauvaise?
>
> Il y a ceux qui croient que la télévision est un moyen d'éducation important. On peut apprendre beaucoup de choses en regardant certaines émissions. On ne peut pas nier que la télévision aide beaucoup d'étudiants à obtenir les diplômes de l''Open University'.
>
> En revanche, il y a d'autres qui pensent que la télévision détruit la vie de famille. Ils prétendent que la publicité à la télévision exerce une mauvaise influence sur les gens. D'autres soulignent le fait que la croissance de la violence dans notre société est liée à la télévision.
>
> A cela il faut répondre qu'il y a un choix d'émissions. Avec quatre chaines on n'est pas obligé de regarder les films violents ni les films publicitaires. Et il n'est pas prouvé que la télévision provoque la violence. Mois, je pense que la télévision est une assez bonne invention. C'est à l'individu de l'utiliser bien ou de l'abuser.

Assessment

The idea behind the introduction is quite a good one: review inventions which might qualify as 'most beneficial' or 'most disastrous' and then select one. However, the candidate seems to understand that the invention must be both beneficial and disastrous which is not very convincing. This reflects a rather unthinking reading of the title which is worded to suggest that *two* inventions should be discussed: *l'invention la plus désastreuse et l'invention la plus bénéfique*. The wording is not *l'invention la plus désastreuse et bénéfique*.

It then becomes increasingly clear that the writer does not really want to discuss the title as set. He would much rather discuss something like 'L'influence de la télévision est-elle bonne ou mauvaise?' or 'Les avantages et inconvénients de la télévision', presumably because these are titles on which he has written essays before. He therefore edges further and further away from the examiner's title. It is quite a good piece of writing but it is not an essay which addresses fully its title and it does not score full marks for relevance.

THE CHOICE OF TITLE

You should keep the need for *relevance* in mind from the moment when you choose your essay title. It is often at this point that the writer, particularly under examination conditions, goes wrong. Examine your choice very carefully and try to understand the scope and slant of the title. There is a danger in focusing on one word in it (chomâge, violence, environnement, télévision etc.) without carefully reading and analysing the whole title. You may well have written essays on these subjects already but it is unlikely that the examiner's title will be exactly the same as one on which you have already written so do not try to reproduce the previous essay. Deal with the title set.

There is a good deal of variation in the way titles are set at A-level:

i) The title could be *one word*; 'Un orage', 'La violence', 'Les villes nouvelles'.
ii) It could be *structured*; Au cours d'un voyage que vous avez fait à l'étranger, vous avez perdu tout votre argent. Comment avez-vous réagi à cette situation. Racontez comment vous avez pu rentrer chez vous.

iii) It could contain quite *detailed and precise instructions*, e.g. 'You have been staying on a campsite near the town of Plan de la Tour in southern France. A forest fire has destroyed your tent and equipment and you have had to take refuge in the village hall. Write a letter of about 150 words to a friend who was due to join you, giving details of what has happened to you and making alternative arrangements.'

It is essential when tackling questions which are like (ii) and (iii) that *you analyse the question or instructions*, list or underline the points which must be included and be sure that you respond to them in the essay.

In question ii) you would be expected to include some account of a) travelling abroad, b) losing money, c) your reactions to that loss and d) how the journey home was accomplished. In iii) you must give details of what has happened to you and make alternative arrangements. What is expected is a) some details of the fire, b) what equipment of yours is destroyed, c) how you took refuge in the village hall and d) you must remember that this is in the form of a letter. If you leave out any of the listed items your essay or letter will not be fully relevant.

> **Interpreting the title.**

It is important to interpret the title. You can do this properly only if you have understood it. Many irrelevant or partly relevant essays are written by candidates who have not understood the title which they have chosen. The following are titles in which the non-recognition of just *one word* caused the writers to produce largely irrelevant essays.

- L'importance du pétrole pour les pays occidentaux.
- Vous êtes en vacances dans une ville étrangère quand une grève éclate. Décrivez ce qui vous est arrivé.
- 'La vraie maladie de l'époque où nous vivons c'est la hâte.' Discutez.

Keywords were misunderstood. *Pétrole* as petrol, *grève* as war and *hâte* as hate. The advice must be: if you are not certain that you fully understand the title, choose a different one.

CONCLUSIONS

Always read the title and any instructions very carefully. If you are asked to discuss the influence which school has had on the formation of *your* character, then do not simply discuss *one's* character in general. If you are asked to write about the most important decisions in your life, the discussion should include more than *one* decision and if you are asked to discuss the role of sport in France, it is not sufficient to discuss sport in general. If you are asked to write a *story* entitled 'La Peur', then do not write a general discussion on the nature of fear.

Ask yourself the following questions about the content of your essays:

a) Is the material clearly related to the specific terms of the question? Would you know from reading the essay what its title was? Have you responded to all parts of the question or the instructions?
b) Is the discussion about the subject but not about the question? Do some parts of the essay have little to do with the question?
c) Are there just isolated points on the question? Would the reader have to keep looking back to the title to remind himself of what it was?

CHAPTER

5

THE DISCUSSION ESSAY

SUBJECT AREAS

PREPARATORY READING

APPROPRIATE FUNCTIONS OF LANGUAGE

GETTING STARTED

The type of essay in which you are asked to discuss, argue or explain will involve rather different language functions from those found in the narrative essay. This does not mean that you do not need to narrate when you are involved in a discussion. It may be very appropriate to recount a personal experience or to describe an incident or scene in order to reinforce an argument, but there are also other important functions which you should be able to handle. They include:

a) the expression of comparison and contrast;
b) the expression of cause and consequence;
c) the expression of hypothesis;
d) reporting and commenting on the views of another person;
e) enumerating points;
f) the expression of obligation;
g) the expression of a personal opinion;
h) indicating a conclusion.

This list is not exhaustive but it shows you what you need to do most frequently when you are putting together an argument or a discussion.

ESSENTIAL PRINCIPLES

It is best to begin thinking about how you are going to work on your essay- writing as soon as you start your A-level course. You need to know first of all what type of subjects are likely to be set for discussion. The Examination Boards do not provide detailed information as to the subject areas on which essays will be set but it is possible to establish a number of topic areas which are chosen most frequently by examiners. They are:

1   Items of *topical interest*. Those which are frequently in the news (e.g. the Bicentenary of the French Revolution, the Common Market, the Channel Tunnel, terrorism etc.).
2   *Personal issues.* Questions which require some personal, individual response (e.g. What are the qualities you would most like to possess?; What has been the biggest influence in your life? etc.).
3   *Moral questions.* (e.g. Does money bring happiness?; What do you understand by success? etc.)
4   *Sport.* (e.g. Has sport improved international relations?; Is sport a necessary part of education?; Should people be allowed to participate in dangerous sports?)
5   *School and studies.* (e.g. Is there too much liberty/discipline in school?; Is school a good preparation for life?; Why go to university?; What makes a good teacher?; What is the point of examinations?; What constitutes a good education? etc.)
6   *Youth.* (e.g. Is there a generation gap?; What is the value of youth clubs?; Are young people lazy, bored, undisciplined etc.?; What are the attitudes of young people to politics, marriage etc.?)
7   *Transport and travel.* (e.g. What are the causes of road accidents?; Is the car the plague of modern society?; The advantages/disadvantages of road/rail; Do we need supersonic aeroplanes?; The for and against of hitch-hiking; Is there any point in spending public money on space travel? etc.)
8   *Animals.* (e.g. Are we too sentimental about them?; Should we use them for scientific experiments?; Should blood sports be banned? etc.)
9   *Family life.* (e.g. How important is it to the individual?; Is it the foundation of society?; Will the family survive? etc.)
10 *Social issues.* (e.g. The rights of women; The rights of men; Equality of opportunity for men and women; What is our duty to others?; The problem of crime and punishment; The role of the police; The problem of unemployment; Should those who do dirty or dangerous jobs be paid more?; The problem of strikes; Racial problems; The influence of advertising on society; Smoking, alcohol and drugs etc.)
11 *The environment.* (e.g. Ecological problems; The problem of noise; Nuclear energy; The ozone layer; Are motorways an eyesore? etc.)
12 *Urban life/country life.* (e.g. The advantages/disadvantages of town/country life; Has life in towns become impossible? etc.)
13 *The media.* (e.g. The for and against of television; Do we have the newspapers we deserve? Is there still a role for radio? etc.)
14 *Leisure and entertainment.* (e.g. Television versus reading; Do we no longer know how to make our own entertainment? etc.)
15 *Holidays and tourism.* (e.g. The educational value of going abroad; What is the ideal holiday? The advantages and disadvantages of going on holiday with parents etc.)
16 *France and the French.* (e.g. The French character; Differences between north and south; French life and institutions etc.)

You will find that some of these topics will be dealt with in your course-book but you should supplement them with further reading. Using the above list of topic areas as a guide try to scan a French newspaper (such as *Le Figaro*) or magazine (such as *Le Point, L'Express, Le Nouvel Observateur, Ça m'intéresse)* for relevant articles. When you come across an interesting article, work on it with the specific aim of extracting ideas, vocabulary, idiom and structures which you can re-use in your own writing.

One such article entitled *L'Expérimentation animale* is printed below. It is a subject on which people have strong views; there are convincing arguments both for and against; it is a subject which is often in the news. It is therefore a possible essay subject and it is an article which will provide you with terms which are used in debate and discussion.

L'Expérimentation animale

Les raids organisés cet été par les opposants à la vivisection, ouvrent une nouvelle fois la polémique entre scientifiques et amis des animaux. Deux événements récents contribuent à alimenter ce débat. Au mois de mai des animaux dérobés dans des unités de recherche de l'Inserm près de Lyon, ont été retrouvés dans une villa du Var. La Cour d'appel de Lyon a ordonné leur restitution à l'Inserm. Autre affaire: de nombreux animaux destinés à tester des médicaments avant leur mise sur le marché ont été volés par un groupe qui s'appelle l'Arche de Noé.

Le groupe s'empare d'une centaine d'animaux – singes, chats, chiens, lapins – et dérobe aussi des registres sur lesquels sont consignés les données des expériences en cours. La police a réussi à retrouver 28 singes et un chat. Selon les chercheurs de l'Inserm, venus identifier les animaux récupérés, les singes ont inutilement souffert aux mains de leurs sauveteurs. Le groupe dément ces accusations.

Les différents acteurs de cette affaire se renvoient donc la balle. D'un côté les auteurs du raid veulent dénoncer 'les abus, commis au nom de la science, qui provoquent chaque année le sacrifice inutile de plus de 8 millions d'animaux. De l'autre les chercheurs de l'Inserm qui affirment que ces vols occasionnent 'des mois de retard dans les travaux de recherche'. Un débat qui suscite automatiquement des réactions passionnelles.

Autre aspect du problème. Les laboratoires sont prêts à payer cher les animaux sur lesquels ils effectuent des expériences, ce qui encourage les malfaiteurs. En octobre dernier, un trafic de chiens volés et puis revendus à des laboratoires avait été démantelé dans le Sud-Ouest. Une douzaine d'éleveurs et de négociants en chiens avaient été interpellé.

Aujourd'hui les chercheurs se barricadent dans leurs laboratoires et reçoivent coups de fil et menaces anonymes. Les mouvements de protection sont déterminés à poursuivre leurs actions. Dans la légalité pour les uns, dans la clandestinité pour les autres.

What do you do with such an article?

Read it carefully to extract vocabulary and structures which you think you can assimilate and re-use. Some you will discard because they are too technical or because you think they are too complex for you to handle. Look for:

a) Terms which relate to the *topic or theme* of the article.
b) Terms which belong to the *language of debate* and argument and might therefore prove useful when you are writing any discussion essay.

Under (a) you would note:

La vivisection; les amis des animaux; les mouvements de protection; tester des médicaments avant leur mise sur le marché; les expériences sur les animaux; les données des expériences; les chercheurs; les scientifiques, les laboratoires, les unités de recherche; l'Inserm (L'Institut national de la santé et de la recherche médicale); au nom de la science; les travaux de recherche; les singes, les lapins ont inutilement souffert; le trafic de chiens volés.

and under (b)

Les opposants à (la vivisection); ouvrir la polémique entre; alimenter le débat; démentir les accusations de quelqu'un; se renvoyer la balle; d'un côté . . . de l'autre; dénoncer quelque chose; affirmer que; un débat qui suscite des réactions passionnelles.

When you have made your notes, re-work the items that you have listed and try to build them into sentences which might become part of your own essay on the subject. Take a key term such as *les scientifiques* or *les amis des animaux* and use them as a basis for constructing sentences of your own.

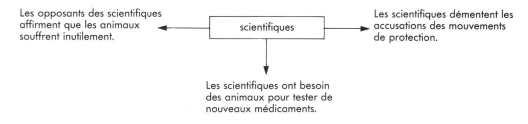

Les opposants des scientifiques affirment que les animaux souffrent inutilement. ← scientifiques → Les scientifiques démentent les accusations des mouvements de protection.

Les scientifiques ont besoin des animaux pour tester de nouveaux médicaments.

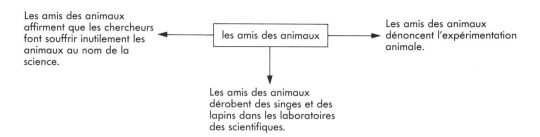

Les amis des animaux affirment que les chercheurs font souffrir inutilement les animaux au nom de la science.

les amis des animaux

Les amis des animaux dénoncent l'expérimentation animale.

Les amis des animaux dérobent des singes et des lapins dans les laboratoires des scientifiques.

Finally, on the basis of your reading try to formulate ideas which might be used in a discussion essay:

- Il faut tester des médicaments avant de les mettre sur le marché. Comment les tester sinon sur des animaux?
- L'expérimentation animale est-elle justifiée?
- Les amis des animaux devraient-ils penser à la souffrance humaine plutôt qu'à celle des animaux:
- Les mouvements de protection ont-ils le droit d'avoir recours à des actes criminels pour protéger les animaux?
- Il y a des criminels qui volent des chiens et des chats pour les vendre aux laboratoires. L'expérimentation animale mène-t-elle inévitablement à des abus?

**APPROPRIATE
FUNCTIONS OF
LANGUAGE**

COMPARISON AND CONTRAST

As you are looking at comparison and contrast with a view to essay-writing it is most useful to think in terms of the paragraph rather than the sentence. Read the following paragraph in which the writers: (1) compare Brittany and Denmark; (2) contrast the north and south of England.

1 Nombreux sont les géographes qui ont signalé les ressemblances entre la Bretagne et le Danemark. Ces deux pays, situés sur le bord occidental de l'Europe, regardant vers l'ouest, sont ouverts aux mêmes influences maritimes. Les Bretons, tout comme les Danois, sont marins et pêcheurs. Les deux pays se ressemblent également par leur climat et leur relief. Leur superficie et la densité de leur population sont pareilles, aussi bien que leur faune et leur flore. Le littoral du Finistère a sa réplique dans la côte du Jutland; un habitant d'Esbjerg ne se sentirait pas dépaysé à Lorient ou à Concarneau. Enfin, l'économie de la Bretagne autant que celle du Danemark, est fondée sur l'agriculture. L'industrie lourde (sidérurgie, chimie lourde) reste absente.

2 Le nord-est de l'Angleterre est plus dur, plus positif, plus froidement intellectuel que le reste du pays; le nord-ouest, plus 'celtique', plus proche de l'Irlande, a plus de douceur, de chaleur, de poésie. Mais dans ces deux régions, les rapports humains sont beaucoup moins froids, beaucoup plus amicaux que dans le sud (. . .) On n'est pas, dans cette Angleterre, tenu à distance par une sorte de courtoisie indifférente; au contraire, on y est chaudement, cordialement accueilli. Les enfants sont traités avec plus d'affection, les liens familiaux sont plus étroits. Les rapports humains sont moins formalistes, moins fondés sur la réserve et la peur d'autrui. Le nord, d'une façon générale, ne semble pas craindre tout ce dont le sud se protège: il ne craint pas les grands mots et les grandes idées et ne pratique pas l'*understatement*, il ne craint pas les grosses plaisanteries, le gros rire, et les comiques les plus populaires du music-hall sont des gens du nord. On travaille dur dans le nord, que ce soit à Manchester, ville du coton, et dans le grand port de Liverpool pour le Lancashire, ou à Sheffield, ville de l'acier et dans les grands centres industriels de Leeds et Bradford pour le Yorkshire, mais l'énergie va de pair avec la joie de vivre. (. . .) Que nous sommes loin du sud austère, frugal, surveillé, distingué, respectable!

(Adapted from *Grande-Bretagne* by Jean Bailhache, Editions du Seuil)

Note those terms which are used to make explicit comparisons and contrasts:

- Les deux pays se ressemblent par leur climat et leur relief.
- L'économie de la Bretagne, autant que celle du Danemark, est fondée sur l'agriculture.

- Le nord est plus dur que le sud.
- Les rapports humains sont moins formalistes.
- Au contraire, on y est chaudement accueilli.

Also note the way in which contrast or comparison is implied:

- Un habitant d'Esbjerg ne se sentirait pas dépaysé à Lorient.

CAUSE AND CONSEQUENCE

In the essays that you write you will be frequently called upon to explain, to make judgements and to give your reasons, to examine causes, and whenever you are arguing a point of view you will need to justify your arguments. You should be certain therefore that you can express cause and consequence accurately and that you can avoid over-use of a limited number of expressions. You should have no difficulty in using *parce que*, *comme* and *car* (but check the dictionary or grammar-book if you are in doubt) but you should have a more varied repertoire.

 **Improve your repertoire.**

Remember that cause may be expressed by:

1   A present participle:

- Roulant parfois six heures sans repos les conducteurs de camions sont souvent victimes de fatigue.

2   An adjective or a past participle:

- Fier de sa nouvelle voiture de sport, il la montrait à tous ses amis.
- Fatigué après une longue journée de travail, un conducteur risque de s'endormir au volant.
- Contraints de rester à la maison, les vieillards mènent parfois une vie très solitaire.

3   Using *du fait de, sous l'effet de, à force de, en raison de, à cause de, étant donné que, faute de, grâce à* followed by a noun:

- Du fait de son grand âge mon grand-père ne sort plus de la maison.
- Sous l'effet de l'alcool les réflexes d'un conducteur sont souvent tardifs.
- A force de patience on peut résoudre tous les problèmes.
- En raison des/à cause des/étant donné les circonstances la police a dû relâcher le suspect.
- Grâce à l'intervention du ministre il sera possible de monter une nouvelle campagne de prévention routière.

In your own reading find passages such as the following one which deals with the causes of road accidents:

> Il apparait, si l'on considère les résultats d'enquêtes effectuées par la Prévention Routière que *la cause principale des accidents de la route n'est ni le mauvais état des routes ou les défaillances des véhicules mais bien le conducteur lui-même. A l'origine* d'environ soixante-quinze pour cent des accidents *on trouve* une faute de conduite: mauvaise appréciation des distances, réflexe tardif, vitesse excessive, imprudence. Mais parmi les causes de ces défaillances il en est une qui les recouvre toutes par sa fréquence: l'alcool.
>
> *Un accident sur trois se produit par la faute de l'alcool.* Sur les dix mille morts *que provoquent chaque année les routes de France*, plus de trois mille *ont pour cause* un excès de boisson. C'est une proportion trop importante pour laisser indifférent.

The principal means of expressing consequence are as follows:

- pour que
- afin que
- de sorte que
- de façon que
- de manière que
- de crainte que

These conjunctions are followed by the subjunctive. For example: Il a garé la voiture de sorte que l'agent de police ne la voie pas.

- pour
- afin de
- de maînère à
- de façon à
- de crainte de
- de peur de

These terms are followed by an infinitive. For example: Il a arrêté la voiture de manière à voir l'arrivée de l'ambulance.

Make sure that these terms are part of your vocabulary. Find examples of their use in a French–French dictionary and check their grammatical use in your grammar-book.

EXPRESSING HYPOTHESIS

Many essay titles call upon you to describe 'what you would do if . . .'

- Quelles mesures prendriez-vous si vous étiez ministre de l'environnement?
- Si l'on proposait d'installer une centrale nucléaire dans votre région, seriez-vous pour ou contre une telle proposition?

Developing a hypothesis.

When you are arguing a case or discussing problems it is often necessary to develop a hypothesis over one or two paragraphs. Many candidates are uncertain of the use of tenses when doing this:

Past: Si j'avais travaillé j'aurais gagné de l'argent.
Present: Si je travaillais je gagnerais de l'argent.
Future: Si, un jour, je trouvais un emploi, je gagnerais de l'argent.
(Check in your grammar-book if you are not certain.)

Others are not able to sustain the structure throughout a whole paragraph or throughout an essay. It is therefore very important to remember what you are doing and to keep the *si j'étais . . . je ferais* pattern constantly in mind, as does the writer of the following passage.

Le développement de la civilisation industrielle a augmenté les bruits dans une telle proportion que l'on peut parler d'une véritable pollution sonore. Si j'étais ministre de l'environnement j'aurais des pouvoirs qui me permettraient de m'attaquer à ce problème. Tout d'abord, dans les villes, où le bruit des voitures est un véritable fléau, je ferais construire des écrans pour protéger les habitations en bordure des voies à grande circulation. J'imposerais des limites de vitesse plus sévères et j'interdirais le passage de poids lourds entre six heures du soir et sept heures du matin. Ensuite, j'introduirais de nouveaux règlements de construction afin d'améliorer l'insonorisation des bâtiments. Enfin, je monterais une campagne pour faire comprendre aux propriétaires de chaînes Hi-Fi, de radios et de télévision, de chiens, de tondeuses à gazon et de tronçonneuses qu'il ne faut pas importuner ses voisins et qu'il faut respecter le droit au silence.

REPORTING AND COMMENTING

If as part of your essay you are arguing a case, you are quite likely to want to refer to an opposing point of view in order to counter it:

- Le premier ministre a annoncé que le gouvernement prendrait de nouvelles mesures pour lutter contre le chômage.

It is useful to have in your vocabulary a number of those verbs which can be used to report other people's ideas and opinions:

déclarer	juger	annoncer
avertir	affirmer	protester
penser	prétendre	prévenir
être d'avis	assurer	professer
estimer	soutenir	

By choosing the right verb or phrase you can show that you are going to contradict or attack the point of view that you are reporting; e.g.

- Siméoni *prétend* que la Corse n'a jamais été qu'une terre de colonisation (and you imply that Siméoni is wrong).
- Siméoni voudrait nous faire croire
      se plaît à croire   que la majorité des Corses est d'accord
      s'obstine à croire   avec lui (but that is not the case)
      semble croire
      semble persuadé

Useful phrases include:

- à tort
- au mépris de toute évidence
- contrairement à la raison
- contre toute raison

These can be added to the reporting verb so that you can begin your counter-argument:

- Il soutient, contrairement à la raison, que la conquête de l'espace apportera des bénéfices à toutes les nations de la terre.

When you have reported the opposing point of view you can introduce your counter-argument with *mais, en fait,* or;

- Pendant les années soixante les savants voulaient nous faire croire que les centrales nucléaires ne présentaient aucun danger. Or, les accidents survenus dans les réacteurs de Windscale et de Chernobyl ont démontré que les scientifiques sont bien capables de se tromper.

ENUMERATING POINTS

By clearly enumerating the points that you make you will add force to your argument and give your paragraph and your essay a satisfactory shape. Using the following 'markers' will help you to enumerate the stages in an argument or a sequence of points:

en premier lieu	d'abord/tout d'abord
en second lieu	ensuite
en dernier lieu	de plus
	en outre
	enfin

Pourquoi tant de Français continuent-ils à voter communiste? *D'abord*, le parti leur paraît l'instrument le plus efficace dans la lutte contre le patronat. *Ensuite* parce que le parti communiste, grâce au dévouement des militants et des cadres, est beaucoup mieux organisé que les autres partis. *Enfin*, les luttes du XIXe siècle ont donné au prolétariat français un sentiment d'isolement tragique qui n'a pas entièrement disparu. Voter communiste, c'est presque une question d'honneur: abandonner le parti serait commettre une sorte de trahison.

EXPRESSING OBLIGATION

Essay titles frequently ask you what you think should/could be done concerning certain issues, what remedies should be applied to solve certain problems, e.g.

- 'On ne devrait pas punir les jeunes criminels, on devrait punir leurs parents'. Discutez.

You should ensure in the first instance that you can handle the tenses of *falloir, devoir* and *pouvoir*. Too many candidates are uncertain of these verbs, particularly in the conditional (il faudrait, on devrait etc.). You should also find other expressions which denote necessity and find paragraphs in which the writer is pointing out what should be done:

On a mille fois énuméré les remèdes à l'alcoolisme. A l'école, dans les entreprises, partout et de toutes façons, *il faudrait* expliquer les méfaits de l'alcool et favoriser la consommation de jus de fruits. *Il importe* de faire prendre conscience aux gens et surtout aux jeunes des désagréments qu'engendre l'alcoolisme. Ensuite, il faudrait améliorer l'action médicale à l'hôpital, dans des services spécialisés, avec l'aide de médecins qui auraient reçu un complément de formation en hôpital psychiatrique. Mais ces remèdes ne pourraient, tout seuls, guérir le besoin d'alcool. *Seule* une action politique et sociale de grande envergure, qui offrirait à tous des perspectives d'avenir, *distrairait les Français* de leur quête des 'paradis artificiels'.

Other phrases which express what is necessary or required include:

- il convient de
- il s'agit de
- il est question de
- il est indispensable/essentiel de
- il est de première nécessité de

These expressions are followed by the infinitive.
Note also the use of *nécessiter, s'imposer, exiger*.

- Pour s'attaquer à ce problème la plus grande prudence s'impose.
- La solution de ce problème nécessite/exige la plus grande prudence.

EXPRESSING A PERSONAL OPINION

Many essay titles invite you to express your own opinion about the subject to be discussed. You should make sure that you have the vocabulary and knowledge of grammar to be able to express:

admiration	disappointment	satisfaction
anger	displeasure	shock
approval/disapproval	doubt	surprise
astonishment	hope	sympathy
concern	indignation	
certainty	regret	

Remember that certain verbs or verbal phrases that you use to express an opinion, a feeling or a doubt require the use of the subjunctive in the clause introduced by *que*, e.g.:

- Je suis fâché/mécontent qu'elle soit revenue.
- Je m'étonne/je m'indigne/je regrette que tant de conducteurs soient imprudents.

Note: Je crois/je suis sûr/je pense que ce parti peut gagner l'élection; but when these verbs are in the negative the subjunctive is required in the clause introduced by *que*: Je ne crois pas/je ne pense pas/je ne suis pas sûr que ce parti puisse gagner l'élection.

INDICATING A CONCLUSION

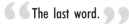
The last word.

The conclusion to the essay is important because it is your last word on the subject and your last chance to make a good impression. If it is well handled it will convince the examiner that you have good control over both language and ideas and, if the rest of the work is up to standard, it will help you to achieve a high mark.

What is a good conclusion to a discussion or an argument? It should first and foremost be seen as a coherent part of the discussion that precedes it and not as something which is simply tacked on at the end. It is not enough to produce a formula which claims that the last few lines of your essay are a conclusion (e.g. En conclusion on peut dire . . . Concluons en disant . . .). Examiners will not be impressed with these phrases if they are not used meaningfully, particularly as some candidates tend to over-use them at this stage of the essay. A conclusion will have a meaningful function:

- if it *recapitulates briefly the points that you have discussed* not for the sake of recapitulation but in order to pull together various points to form a final statement; or
- if it *recalls the main line of your argument* in order to add one final, important point; or

- if it *opens out the discussion* and invites the reader to think about future or wider implications of the points that have been discussed; or
- if it *provides an answer* to a question (even if the answer is that there is no answer) the pros and cons of which you have been considering throughout the essay.

The most effective way of learning to write satisfactory conclusions is to study the way that good French writers go about it and collect a number of models. By all means learn those words and expressions which help to form concluding statements (e.g. On voit par ce qui précède que/Il résulte de ce qui précède que/On peut conclure en disant, etc.) but learn them in a context so that their function is clear.

Study the concluding paragraph of the following passage, asking yourself what the writer is saying and doing, and how the paragraph relates to the discussion which has gone before.

Pour une majorité de Français et même d'Européens, c'est la natalité débridée des populations du tiers-monde qui est la seule cause de leur misère. Ces gens sont pauvres, affirme-t-on, parce qu'ils font trop d'enfants.

Certes, les pays du tiers-monde connaissent un taux d'accroissement démographique qu'il faudrait ralentir. Nul ne voudrait nier que le surpeuplement soulève des problèmes énormes. Il y a pourtant un fait incontestable qui ne retient pas suffisamment ceux qui veulent planifier la vie des autres: les hommes et les femmes des pays pauvres ont besoin d'enfants pour vivre et pour se garantir un soutien dans leur vieillesse; s'ils ont besoin de faire beaucoup d'enfants c'est parce qu'ils en perdent beaucoup. Ainsi, si l'on veut diminuer la fécondité il est parfaitement clair qu'il faut commencer par faire baisser la mortalité et notamment la mortalité infantile. Pour s'en convaincre, il suffit de lire le rapport présenté par la Banque mondiale à la conférence de Bucarest. Là-dessus les experts sont formels: 'Chaque fois qu'il s'est produit une baisse importante de la fécondité dans les pays en développement, cette baisse a été précédée d'un recul de la mortalité.'

Il est donc infiniment regrettable que, sur ce point, gouvernements et autorités religieuses manquent de réalisme ou de bonne volonté. Leurs efforts se portent surtout sur des programmes de stérilisation forcée ou sur la distribution gratuite de pilules avec promesses de récompenses pécuniaires. Mesures impuissantes qui tombent même dans la barbarie. Il ne s'agit point de contraindre ni d'acheter le consentement des gens mais d'assurer leur adhésion active en s'attaquant aux facteurs qui commandent la décision de faire des enfants. L'essentiel est donc de multiplier les efforts pour améliorer les conditions de vie des plus pauvres et d'augmenter en même temps le revenu monétaire des familles pour que l'enfant ne soit plus une source de revenu indispensable.

EXAMINATION QUESTIONS

Q1
'L'âge de l'ordinateur est une perspective effrayante.' Discutez.   (O & C 1985)

Q2
Les étudiants devraient-ils payer eux-mêmes leurs études?   (JMB 1982)

Q3
L'invention la plus désastreuse et l'invention la plus bénéfique du 20e siècle.
     (ULSEB 1989)

Q4
'On fait tant de beaux efforts pour sauver la baleine et le phoque que l'on oublie que dans le siècle où nous vivons l'homme lui-même est menacé d'extinction.' Discutez.
     (ULSEB 1989)

Q5
'A l'école il n'est pas bon d'être trop libre, ce qu'il faut, c'est une bonne discipline.' Discutez.   (ULSEB 1989)

Q6
Pourquoi posséder un poste de radio? La télévision ne suffit-elle pas?   (ULSEB 1990)

Q7

Savoir parler une langue étrangère est beaucoup plus important que savoir la lire ou l'écrire. (ULSEB 1990)

Q8

'Le sport international n'a pas encouragé l'amitié et la compréhension mutuelle et n'a fait qu'aggraver les tensions qui existent entre les pays.' Considérez cette observation.

(JMB 1988)

Q9

Expliquez ce qu'il faut faire pour empêcher que la violence parmi les spectateurs ne nous enlève à jamais le plaisir du football. (WJEC Specimen Paper 1987)

Q10

Le rôle de la publicité dans la vie moderne. (NISEC Specimen Paper 1988)

Q11

Les dangers de la discrimination raciale. (NISEC Specimen Paper 1988)

Q12

'La presse ne s'intéresse pas à la vérité, elle ne s'intéresse qu'aux profits.' Discutez.

(ULSEB 1988)

Q13

Devrait-on utiliser les animaux pour faire des expériences scientifiques ou médicales?

(ULSEB 1988)

Q14

Les pays de la CE (de la Communauté Européenne) et du COMECON (de l'Europe de l'Est) pourraient chercher à créer une Europe unie. Un tel développement serait-il souhaitable à votre avis? (JMB 1988)

Q15

'L'égalité des sexes, si elle était possible, serait regrettable.' Discutez.

(JMB Specimen Paper 1987)

OUTLINE ANSWER TO QUESTION 4

Bear the following points in mind when you prepare to write your essay.

  i) *Choose the right title.* Read through the list of titles carefully (there are usually six to ten questions on the paper).

- Do you understand all of the words in the title you have chosen? If the meaning is not totally clear to you, choose another title.

- Are you sufficiently familiar with the vocabulary area? Do not be misled into selecting an interesting topic if your vocabulary is not going to stretch far enough to cover it.

 ii) *Interpret the title.* (We will assume that you have chosen question 4: 'on fait tant de beaux efforts pour sauver la baleine et le phoque que l'on oublie que dans le siècle où nous vivons l'homme lui-même est menacé d'extinction.' Discutez.) What is the particular angle of the question? If it is divided into parts, what is the balance of these parts? In answering the above question you should consider:

   a) The idea that great efforts are made to save animal species (the whale and the seal are intended as examples, you do not have to discuss them exclusively).

   b) The idea that man today is threatened with extinction.

   c) The proposition that concentration on saving animal species has led to neglect of the human species.

Note that you should not see in this title an invitation to rehearse a 'pollution' essay that you have written before (Man is in danger of extinction because he is neglecting the environment). You may well be able to use some of the material from a previous essay but it *must* be re-shaped to fit a different question.

iii) Next you should *note down some preliminary ideas*. Is the statement in the title true? Partly true? Think of examples, it will help generate ideas:
Whales freed from arctic ice; protests against seal culling; attempts to preserve elephants from ivory poachers; establishment of game reserves etc.
Are these efforts justified? Does the quotation imply that they are not? Have examples like these hit the headlines making people forget about the threat to human species? Is it true to claim that the human species is threatened with extinction?
Proliferation of nuclear power stations; accidents like the one at Chernobyl; danger of destroying the ozone layer; destruction of the rain forests.

It is useful to make these preliminary notes in French. this will help you to keep within the limits of your linquistic knowledge and it will begin the process of calling to mind the vocabulary and structures needed for the essay.

You should now try to formulate the basis of an argument which can be expanded and shaped into the discussion which will become your essay.

1 It is true that there are many attempts to save animals and that these make headline news.
2 But this has not diverted our attention from dangers which threaten human life.
3 We are in fact very aware of them (global warming, damage to the ozone layer etc.)
4 Conclusion: unwise to distinguish between animals/humans because it is all life on earth which is endangered.

It is not normally advisable to write out a rough draft of the essay when you are working under examination conditions as this uses up valuable time. However, it is useful to write a résumé of your discussion. It will help you to control the development of your argument and to present it clearly to the reader.
Your résumé might be:

> *It is true* that there are many praiseworthy attempts to save animals and animal species. They often make headline news. *However*, it does not follow that interest in saving animals diverts attention from those dangers which threaten human life. We are *in fact*, made very conscious of global warming, the damage to the ozone layer, the destruction of the rain forests and radio-active pollution. *But it is also* important to realise that these same dangers threaten animal life. It is *therefore* unwise to distinguish between the human species and the animals: all life on earth is threatened, all life must be protected.

You are now ready to write your essay using the plan (points 1–4 above). Keep your synopsis in mind and pay particular attention to the way the argument develops: It is true . . . However . . . In fact . . . But it is also . . . It is therefore . . .

A TUTOR'S ANSWER TO QUESTION 16

S'il ne faut pas prohiber tout à fait le tabac, il faut du moins en interdire l'usage dans tous les endroits publics.

S'il est vrai que le tabagisme suscite aujourd'hui dans le public une certaine émotion, il faut pourtant avouer que bon nombre de nos concitoyens restent indifférents devant un problème social et médical qui risque toujours de s'aggraver. Ils n'écoutent pas les médecins qui constatent que les services hospitaliers sont encombrés de malades dont la déchéance physique est provoquée ou considérablement aggravée par l'usage du tabac. Ils ne se laissent pas émouvoir par le fait que les dépenses engendrées par les effets nocifs du tabac grèvent lourdement le budget de la Sécurité Sociale. Aux cris d'alarme des médecins, aux protestations des ministres, ils répondent que dans un pays démocratique on a bien le droit de fumer ou de ne pas fumer et qu'il s'agit là d'un choix tout à fait personnel.

Il est donc évident que, malgré les tentatives pour faire prendre conscience des méfaits du tabac, malgré la certitude des chiffres qui montrent qu'un fumeur a vingt fois plus de chances de mourir d'une maladie pulmonaire ou d'une crise cardiaque, il y aura toujours un pourcentage assez élevé de gens qui continueront à fumer. Mais les fumeurs ont-ils bien le droit d'abîmer leur santé et de courir volontairement le risque d'une mort prématurée?

Devrait-on interdire totalement la vente et l'usage du tabac pour conserver la santé de ceux qui refusent d'en prendre soin eux-mêmes? C'est là une question qui n'admet pas de réponse facile: les fumeurs, tout comme ceux qui boivent de l'alcool ou qui pratiquent des sport dangereux ont bien le droit de jouir de certaines libertés personnelles, même au péril de leur santé ou de leur vie.

Pourtant, il n'est pas question de proscrire tout à fait l'usage du tabac mais seulement d'en interdire l'usage dans les endroits publics. Proposition raisonnable et juste, car les non-fumeurs autant que les fumeurs ont des droits qu'il faudrait sauvegarder. Ils ont le droit de voyager dans un train ou dans un autobus, de manger au restaurant ou de prendre un verre au café sans être gênés par la fumée de cigarettes et de cigares, d'autant plus qu'il est maintenant démontré que la fumée est nuisible pour toute personne qui la respire, qu'il s'agit du fumeur lui-même ou de la victime innocente qui se trouve près de lui.

Il est donc évident qu'il faudrait interdire l'usage du tabac dans tous les endroits publics – autobus, trains, cinémas, restaurants – où la dissipation de la fumée ne s'effectue pas rapidement. Si les fumeurs tiennent à exercer leurs libertés personnelles qu'ils le fassent en plein air de sorte qu'ils n'empêchent pas leurs concitoyens d'exercer les leurs.

A STUDENT'S ANSWER TO QUESTION 17, WITH EXAMINER'S COMMENTS

'La télévision à l'heure du petit déjeuner, quelle idée absurde.' Discutez.

Tout d'abord il faudrait analyser de plus près les différents genres de programmes qu'on peut voir à la télévision à l'heure du petit déjeuner. Les émissions de nouvelles et des actualités sont peut-être les plus fréquentes, mais il y a aussi les films, les drames, les programmes pour les enfants jeunes et les émissions universitaires. Je ne sais pas exactement qui regarde la télévision le matin car je ne l'ai jamais fait moi-même, cependant il me semble que ce sont les enfants et les adultes.

D'un côté, regarder la télévision pendant le petit déjeuner est absurde. C'est une preuve que l'on est en train de s'assujettir tout à fait à la télévision si l'on en a besoin dès qu'on se lève. Cela fait penser à celui qui a besoin de fumer une cigarette en sortant du lit. Et si la télé est allumée à 7 heures du matin on ne peut pas prendre le petit déjeuner en famille. Personne ne parle sauf les gens à la télévision. Cela ne contribue rien à la   de famille et communiquer avec les autres seulement à travers la télévision ne contribue rien à la société.

De l'autre côté la télévision est une bonne idée. Beaucoup de gens ont décroché un diplôme à cause des émissions de l'OU. Les émissions de nouvelles sont beaucoup plus intéressantes que la radio. Il est bon de se détendre devant la télé avant d'aller faire la queue à l'arrêt d'autobus ou de courir dans les couloirs du métro. Si les enfants sont occupés à regarder la télévision leurs parents ont le temps de se parler. On pourrait trouver d'autres exemples mais je ne le crois pas nécessaire.

Peut-être que tout le monde n'est pas d'accord avec moi mais je ne vois aucune raison pour regarder la télévision à l'heure du petit déjeuner. C'est-à-dire que je ne la regarde pas moi-même mais je comprends qu'il y a plusieurs avantages. Je ne voudrais pas la condamner en disant que c'est une idée absurde.

Examiner's comments

The essay is a good one. There is a high level of grammatical accuracy, quite a good range of vocabulary and fluency. With some adjustments the essay would become an excellent one.

Paragraph 1. Not a very useful introductory paragraph. No indication of the shape of the argument to come; it does not lead into the rest of the essay. The discussion which follows does not show why it is necessary to analyse the different kinds of programmes.

Paragraph 2. A good paragraph. Ideas clear, language accurate, sentence patterns varied. However, the point about having breakfast is not well handled. It *is* possible to have breakfast together if the television is on but it is difficult to talk. Better to say: Si la télé est allumée ce n'est pas la peine de prendre le petit déjeuner en famille.

Paragraph 3. A good paragraph but some unclear thinking leads to a false comparison. The candidate should have said *Il est plus intéressant de regarder les actualités à la télévision que de les écouter à la radio.* Not a good idea to think that it is not necessary to give other examples: it gives the impression that the writer cannot think of any.

Paragraph 4. The ideas in the conclusion are not made clear enough to the reader. This is partly because the direction of the argument has not been shown clearly enough throughout the discussion. The writer wants to argue that

  i) there are disadvantages to breakfast television
 ii) there are also certain advantages
iii) because there are some valid points in favour of it the writer would not condemn breakfast television as absurd although he personally does not approve of it.

A better conclusion would have been:

De ce qui précède il est évident que la télévision à l'heure du petit déjeuner présente des inconvénients aussi bien que des avantages. Pour moi, les inconvénients l'emportent: je ne regarde pas la télévision à cette heure. Cependant j'accepte qu'il y a ceux qui ont de bonnes raisons pour le faire et qui y prennent du plaisir. Ainsi je n'irais pas jusqu'à dire que la télévision à l'heure du petit déjeuner est une idée absurde.

Useful sources of information

Technique of essay-writing:

G. Vigner. *Ecrire et Convaincre,* Hachette
G. Niquet. *Ecrire avec Logique et Clarté,* Hatier
G. Niquet. *Français – Profil Formation,* Hatier
G. Niquet. *Structurer sa Pensée. Structurer sa Phrase,* Hachette

Articles dealing with social, political and cultural topics of the 'discussion' essay type appear in the following publications:

Le Point
L'Express
Le Figaro Magazine
Le Monde Dimanche
(available in many newsagents and through European Schoolbooks, Croft St. Cheltenham GL53 0HX)

The Profil actualité and Profil dossier séries (Hatier) have many titles which relate to frequently occurring essay subjects, e.g. Les Françaises Aujourd'hui, La Réduction des Inégalités, La Famille en Question etc.

CHAPTER 6

THE NARRATIVE ESSAY

GETTING STARTED

The narrative essay will involve an account of real or imaginary events. It may include description of settings, objects or people and the portrayal of the feelings and reactions of the narrator or of characters who feature in the story. It may include dialogue. If you feel that you have some talent for story-telling or for creating characters and atmosphere, the narrative title should appeal to you.

Remember too that if you are also preparing for the Literature Paper, reading your French texts will provide you with a useful source of vocabulary and structures of a more literary nature which you can use in your own writing. This does not mean, of course, that you will be expected to write like Maupassant or Camus but you should aim at something considerably more sophisticated than the narrative compositions which you practised before you began your A-level course.

ESSENTIAL PRINCIPLES

TENSES

Accurate handling of tenses is related to the planning of the narrative, to the arrangement of events and action in the story. It is very important to have a clear notion of the *order of events* before you begin to write and this order should be established as you put together your plan. If you are clear in your mind about how the story moves forward, you will be more likely, when you are using past tenses, to handle them accurately and to make the correct choice between a narrative tense (passé composé or past historic) and the imperfect.

Narrative tense

Moving the story forward.

Remember that a narrative tense is required whenever you intend that the action of the story should move another step forward and that a series of verbs in a narrative tense implies a *series of consecutive actions or events* in the story you are narrating. If you are simply enumerating a sequence of past actions which are completed in chronological order, then a narrative tense is what is needed.

In the following passage the verbs, with one exception, are in a narrative tense, the *past historic*, because they depict events which happened one after the other:

Il se tut aussitôt; et nous restâmes plongés dans un silence plus terrifiant encore. Et soudain tous ensemble, nous eûmes une sorte de sursaut: un être glissait contre le mur du dehors vers la forêt; puis il passa contre la porte, qu'il sembla tâter, d'une main hésitante; puis on n'entendit plus rien pendant deux minutes qui firent de nous des insensés; puis il revint, frôlant toujours la muraille: et il gratta légèrement; puis soudain une tête apparut contre la vitre du judas, une tête blanche avec les yeux lumineux comme ceux des fauves.

Imperfect tense

Incompleted action.

A verb in the imperfect tense does not form part of the sequence; it does not indicate that the central narrative has moved a step further. Instead it will denote *an incompleted action*; it will *describe* what was (already) happening at the time.

As far as tenses are concerned it is important to bear in mind that they relate to how the narrative is arranged. You have control of the story, therefore structure it logically and make certain that narrative tenses and imperfects convey the meaning which you intended. Begin to decide on the way you will use tenses as you plan your essay and concentrate on the arrangement of your material. If you do not have a firm grasp of 'what happened next' and of 'what was already happening', you will not convey any clear meaning to the reader.

PROBLEM AREAS

The following passage illustrates some of the main problem areas which candidates encounter when handling tenses in a narrative account:

La jeune fille attendait dans un coin de la pièce. Elle avait peur et elle commençait à avoir froid. Jamblier, un petit homme grisonnant, vêtu d'un tablier qui lui descendait aux pieds, traînait ses savates sur le sol bétonné. Parfois, il s'arrêtait court et son regard se fixait sur le loquet de la porte. Pour apaiser l'impatience de l'attente, il prit une serpillière qui se trouvait sur une chaise, et pour la troisième fois, lava la grande table de chêne. Entendant un bruit de pas, il se releva et voulut ouvrir la porte mais sa main tremblait si fort qu'il ne put saisir la poignée.

La porte s'ouvrit pour laisser passer un homme court et trapu. Il portait une valise dans chaque main et il était sanglé dans un pardessus marron si étroitement ajusté qu'il faisait saillir ses muscles puissants. Il y eut un silence. Enfin, Jamblier s'avança et indiqua la table. Le visiteur y posa les deux valises. A cet instant, un bruit de pas et des cris se firent entendre dans le couloir. La porte fut ouverte avec violence et une dizaine de soldats allemands s'élancèrent dans la pièce.

(Adapted from *Traversée de Paris* by Marcel Aymé, Gallimard)

1 As any story requires a setting and as the action is likely to begin with the interruption of something that was happening, it is often necessary to open the narrative (or a new phase in the narrative) with description of place, characters or setting, as lines 1 − 4 of the passage above. If the story is written in the past, the tense used for this description is of course the imperfect. Most candidates understand this in theory but

are too vague when deciding which elements are descriptive. Ask yourself carefully whether a detail is properly descriptive (is it a question of a state, of something which was happening as a kind of background to the main events of the narrative) or whether it can be seen more logically as a movement forward in the narrative. If you are not sure then substitute something that you are sure about.

❝From description to narration.❞

It is also important that you make clear the transition from description to narration. The transition should be justified by the sense and by the rest of the sentence. In other words make use of adverbs, adverbial phrases and clauses of time to indicate that the story is progressing and to show the reader that he should be thinking in terms of a sequence. In the passage above, words and phrases such as *et pour la troisième fois; Entendant un bruit de pas; Enfin; A cet instant* help to indicate that the narrative is now moving forward in a sequence which justifies the past historic tense.

2 Ensure that your choice of tense has not led to an illogical or improbable statement. Ask yourself why the sense and the context would not allow the verbs in these sentences taken from the passage to be in the past historic:

- vêtu d'un tablier qui lui *descendait* aux pieds;
- (Jamblier) *traînait* ses savates sur le sol bétonné;
- une serpillière qui se *trouvait* sur une chaise;
- il *portait* une valise;
- il faisait saillir ses muscles puissants.

un tablier qui lui *descendit* aux pieds would seem to imply that the apron fell down to his feet at the moment; il *fit* saillir ses muscles puissants would mean that the overcoat (suddenly) made his muscles bulge, and these meanings would fit poorly into the context. Think carefully about the meaning of the verb in a given context when you are choosing the tense.

❝Use of *être* and *avoir*.❞

3 Give particular attention when writing narrative to the tense you use of *être* in passive constructions and for *avoir* (il y a). Many candidates would automatically write *Il y avait un silence* and *la porte était ouverte avec violence* but it is clear from the context that it is a question of events which form part of a sequence. One might write: *Puis*, il y eut un silence or *Puis* la porte fut ouverte avec violence.

4 Be careful with tenses when handling the modal auxiliaries (*devoir, savoir, pouvoir, vouloir*). A change of tense can change the meaning. Be sure of your intended meaning. Compare the following sentences:

- Il se releva et voulut ouvrir la porte (he tried to open the door).
- Il se releva parce qu'il voulait ouvrir la porte (he wanted to open the door).
- Sa main tremblait si fort qu'il ne put ouvrir la porte (he could not open it, he failed to).
- Il sortit par la fenêtre parce qu'il ne pouvait pas ouvrir la porte (he was unable to open the door).
- Je sus à 6 heures qu'il était arrivé (I found out at 6 o'clock).
- Je savais à 6 heures qu'il était arrivé (I already knew at 6 o'clock).
- Lorsque la guerre éclata je dus retourner à Paris (I had to and I did).
- Je vendis mon appartement parce que je devais retourner à Paris (because I was in the position of having to return).

Accurate use of the narrative and imperfect tenses depends in the first instance on your having *structured* the events of the story clearly. Controlling in your mind the logical sequence of the action will also help to ensure that the pluperfect tense is used when required. Too frequently, candidates who simply construct the story sentence by sentence without reference to an overall conception of the sequence of actions, overlook the logical need to indicate that something *had already happened*, that something took place when something else *had finished*:

- Voulant descendre au premier étage j'essayai d'ouvrir la porte mais quelqu'un l'avait fermée à clef.
- Lorsque le mécanicien eut réparé la voiture, Jacques partit à toute vitesse en direction de Paris.

A fundamental requirement in writing a narrative account is that of arranging the action intelligibly in time. It is important therefore that your language work should equip you to handle spontaneously a variety of structures which enable you to sequence the events and stages of the narrative.

Make a note of such structures (in complete sentences) when you come across them in your course-book or in wider reading.

Aim at compiling your own glossary and collection of examples which will include those given under the headings below.

ADVERBS AND ADVERBIAL PHRASES OF TIME

- Au bout de deux heures . . .
- Trois jours plus tard . . .
- L'équipe de sauvetage travailla du matin au soir.
- Au cours du spectacle, il y eut une panne d'électricité.
- Léon ouvrit la porte et descendit dans la rue. *Puis* il mit son imperméable et en releva le col. *Ensuite* il tira de sa poche une lettre qu'il lut attentivement. *Enfin* il se dirigea vers la bouche de métro.
- Le chauffeur s'arrêta *un instant, puis* sortit de sa poche un flacon et reprit *ensuite* son chemin.
- Soudain/subitement/tout à coup/bientôt une lampe s'alluma, puis deux, puis trois.

CONJUNCTIONS

Make sure that you are able to handle the main temporal conjunctions accurately. They are:

- Quand, lorsque, comme, pendant que, à mesure que, avant que, dès que, après que, aussitôt que, à peine

Remember that *comme pendant que, à mesure que*, when used to indicate that an action was taking place will require the imperfect tense:

- Le téléphone a sonné comme je quittais la maison.
- Pendant que j'attendais à l'entrée, une grosse voiture noire s'arrêta devant l'hôtel.
- A mesure que la nuit tombait les passants devenaient plus rares.

Avant que will require the subjunctive:

- Avant qu'il eût le temps de sortir dans le couloir, les trois hommes descendirent l'escalier.

Dès qui, après que, aussitôt que, à peine used in a narrative written in the past historic, and intended to indicate that an action happened immediately before the next action happened, will require the past anterior:

- Dès que/aussitôt qu'il eut enlevé ses chaussures il plongea dans l'eau.
- A peine l'arbitre eut-il paru sur le terrain que la foule siffla.

It is also useful to remember that instead of repeating the conjunction (e.g. to introduce a second subordinate clause after *et*) it is possible to replace it by *que*:

- *Quand* il descendit le lendemain à la petite gare et *qu*'il vit son ami qui attendait à la sortie . . .

THE PRESENT PARTICIPLE

> Adding variety to the
> narrative.

Used carefully, the present participle and the gerund (i.e. 'en' with the present participle) can add variety to the way the narrative is sequenced. It can alternate with a co-ordinate clause introduced by *et* or with a temporal clause introduced by *pendant que, comme, quand* etc.:

- En arrivant à la gare il se dépêcha de trouver une cabine téléphonique (= *lorsqu*'il arriva à la gare . . .)

- Relevant le col de son imperméable, il partit sous la pluie (= il releva le col de son imperméable *et* il partit sous la pluie).

The two examples which follow give a better idea of how the present participle and gerund can provide variety of structure in a passage of narrative:

Example 1

En me rendant compte que (= quand/au moment où je me rendis compte que) mes compagnons ne me suivaient plus, je m'arrêtai. Déposant mon sac à dos (= je déposai mon sac à dos . . . et) qui était devenue très lourd, j'en retirai la carte que Jacques m'avait prêtée. Je l'étalai sur mes genoux, essayant en vain de trouver (= et essayai en vain de trouver) la route de Bordeaux.

Example 2

En montant dans le bateau (= pendant que/comme je montais . . .) je me cognai la tête qui se mit à saigner, mais heureusement je ne perdis pas connaissance. Je me dirigeai vers l'avant et m'assis à côté de mon frère. A cet instant une grosse vague déferla sur la proue, renversant (= et renversa) un des marins qui tomba à la mer. Se levant d'un bond, mon frère lui jeta (mon frère se leva d'un bond et lui jeta . . .) une corde qu'il réussit à attraper.

ABSOLUTE CLAUSES

Temporal clauses introduced by *quand, lorsque, aussitôt, dès que*, may alternate with absolute clauses:

- Les policiers disparus, il se rendit chez les voisins (= une fois que les policiers eurent disparus . . .)
- Devenu grand, il résolut de rejoindre son père (= quand il fut devenu grand . . .)
- Libérés en 1945, les deux frères regagnèrent leur pays natal (= lorsqu'ils furent libérés en 1945)
- L'orage dissipé, les invités retournèrent à la salle à manger (= lorsque l'orage se fut dissipé . . .)
- Une fois le père mort, les fils se partagèrent la propriété (= aussitôt que le père fut mort . . .)
- Sa résolution prise, elle quitta Bordeaux (= lorsqu'elle eut pris sa résolution . . .)
- La vaisselle rangée, elle passa dans la chambre d'Antoine (= lorsqu'elle eut rangé la vaisselle . . .)
- Les cigarettes achetées, il s'attabla devant moi et commença de relire la lettre (= lorsqu'il eut acheté les cigarettes . . .)

NOMINALISATION

A temporal clause may also be replaced by a noun construction:

- Jean-Paul, *lors de sa venue* à Paris, s'inscrivit à la Faculté des Lettres (= Jean-Paul, lorsqu'il vint à Paris . . .)
- A *sa sortie* de prison, Latour s'installa à la campagne (= lorsqu'il sortit de prison . . .)
- *Dès le retour/le départ* de son père . . .
- Au moment de *son arrivée*/de *sa disparition* . . .
- Lors de *sa maladie/son mariage/sa naissance* . . .

PARTICIPLE PHRASE IN APPOSITION

- Arrivé au coin de la rue, Simon héla un taxi (lorsqu'il fut arrivé . . .)
- Remonté au sixième étage, il rentra chez lui et ferma la porte à clef.
- Revenu au jardin, il affecta de les ignorer.

- A peine assise, Madame Dufour entra dans le vif du sujet.
- Grimpé dans un arbre, Carolus tira sur les policiers.
- Rentré chez moi, je téléphonai à l'aéroport.
- Descendu pour acheter des croissants à la boulangerie d'à côté, je remarquai une voiture de police stationnée dans la rue de Londres.
- Sorti pour faire un petit tour avant de se coucher, mon père rencontra un jeune Anglais qui avait perdu tout son argent.

CONVEYING ACTION AND MOVEMENT

It is highly likely that any narrative account that you will be asked to write will involve action and movement. Sound preparatory work in acquiring the appropriate vocabulary (see Chapter 3) and practice of the structures illustrated above, will enable you to produce a controlled, lively account that will impress the examiner. You will notice that in the model answer provided on pages 59 – 60 quite simple variations in the structure of sentences together with well-chosen verbs of movement can result in French which *sounds* like French and is enjoyable to read.

CONVEYING CONFLICT AND TENSION

While the essay in French is not marked according to its literary merit (though such merit would be highly rewarded) it is nevertheless an advantage if the story is readable and lively. This is clear from the examiner's comments which appear at the end of scripts. Remarks such as 'A well-told, interesting story', 'A lively account', 'Interesting details, quite a dramatic account', indicate that the candidate's work has been marked up for the quality of the story-telling.

However, what should be emphasised again at this point is that it is not realistic to regard the essay as the exercise in creative writing which it would be if you were writing in your mother tongue. The examiner will not be impressed by attempts at imaginative or original use of language if the result is inaccurate, non-French.

The first priority remains accurate handling of structures and use of vocabulary. However, the good candidate will be able to fulfil these fundamental requirements and succeed in producing an essay which is interesting and readable.

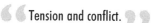 **Tension and conflict.**

It is possible to write a narrative essay with such qualities using relatively limited means. A narrative which has been planned to include three or four phases which lead progressively to a denouement and generate some dramatic interest will have the ingredients of a successful essay at A-level.

An elementary requirement of a good story is that it should be constructed to create tension or conflict. Such elements may well be prescribed in the essay title, e.g.

- Imaginez que vous vous trouvez dans une ville au moment où il s'est produit un tremblement de terre. (ULSEB 1979)
- Par une nuit de brouillard vous vous êtes égaré. Racontez vos émotions et ce qui s'est passé quand vous avez compris toute la difficulté de votre situation. (JMB 1988)
- Vous voyagiez dans un train qui s'est arrêté dans un tunnel. Soudain toutes les lumières se sont éteintes. Continuez. (ULSEB 1985)

If they are not evident in the title then it will make the story more readable if you introduce them and describe the feelings and reactions of those people involved. Such descriptions may be *specifically asked for* in the title, e.g. Un(e) réfugié(e) arrive pour la première fois dans son pays d'adoption. Imaginez ses réactions et ses émotions. (ULSEB 1983)

As part of your preparation for the essay you should concentrate on those structures which French writers commonly use when noting the feelings or reactions of characters involved in the story. You could, for example make use of:

a) *An adjective used in apposition*

- Interloqué, je regardai la liste qu'il m'avait remise.
- Gérard, muet de peur, regardait les flammes qui dévoraient la salle à manger.
- Bouleversés, ils restèrent immobiles, l'oreille tendue.
- Tenaillés par la peur, les cinq voyageurs s'étaient réfugiés dans l'autobus abandonné.
- Accablé, Jean-Pierre se retira dans un coin.

b) *Avoir + un geste, un mouvement,* to describe what is usually an involuntary action or reaction.

- Il eut un geste d'impatience et monta dans sa chambre.
- Elle eut un geste/mouvement de dépit.
- Il eut un geste/mouvement de lassitude/de surprise/de résignation etc.

c) *Appropriate vocabulary.* You should also make a conscious effort to widen your knowledge of:
  i) the vocabulary of *emotions and reactions,* e.g. expressions conveying:

surprise	respect	anxiety
satisfaction	fear	discontent
sadness	pride	gratitude
admiration	anger	bewilderment
indignation	pity	hostility, etc.

and of

  ii) the vocabulary required to express *conflict,* e.g. terms which denote:

contradiction	prohibition
disagreement	refusal
impossibility	refuting
necessity	threatening
obligation	obstacle, etc.

EXAMINATION QUESTIONS

Q1
Un voyage dans l'espace.   (O&C Specimen Paper 1987)

Q2
Imaginez que vous vous trouvez dans une ville où il s'est produit un tremblement de terre. Racontez les événements auxquels vous assistez. Décrivez la scène et les incidents.
(O&C Specimen Paper 1987)

Q3
Votre voisin ayant dû s'absenter pour un cas d'urgence, vous avez accepté de garder ses enfants pendant tout le weekend. Vous racontez comment vous vous êtes débrouillé(e).
(ULSEB 1989)

Q4
Une dispute.   (ULSEB 1989)

Q5
Imaginez que vous êtes archéologue. Vous faites partie d'une expédition qui a découvert tout à coup des traces d'une civilisation ancienne. Racontez ce que s'est passé ensuite.
(JMB 1988)

Q6
Par une nuit de brouillard vous vous êtes égaré. Racontez vos émotions et ce qui s'est passé quand vous avez compris toute la difficulté de votre situation.   (JMB 1988)

Q7
Racontez une histoire au cours de laquelle il se passe quelque chose d'inexplicable.
(WJEC Specimen Paper 1988)

Q8
Pendant que vous étiez en vacances dans une capitale étrangère une grève générale s'est déclarée. Quelles ont été pour vous les conséquences de cet événement? Décrivez comment vous avez réussi à regagner votre pays d'origine.   (ULSEB 1984)

Q9
Vous voyagiez dans un train qui s'est arrêté dans un tunnel. Soudain toutes les lumières se sont éteintes. Continuez.   (ULSEB 1985)

Q10

Pendant les grandes vacances vous avez fait un travail temporaire pour gagner de l'argent de poche. Vous racontez les incidents – amusants, désagréables, ou intéressants – qui vous sont arrivés pendant que vous exerciez cet emploi.   (ULSEB 1986)

Q11

Vous êtes gardien(ne) dans un musée important. Un jour, en entrant dans la salle dont vous êtes responsable, vous remarquez qu'un objet de valeur n'est plus à sa place. Racontez ce qui se passe ensuite.   (ULSEB 1987)

Q12

Une histoire de contrebande.   (ULSEB 1987)

EXAMINATION QUESTION AND OUTLINE ANSWER

Pendant que vous étiez en vacances dans une capitale étrangère, une grève générale s'est déclarée. Quelles ont été pour vous les conséquences de cet événement? Décrivez comment vous avez réussi à regagner votre pays d'origine.   (ULSEB 1984)

Content

The title has been worded to include a number of elements:

- holiday in a foreign capital;
- a general strike;
- the consequences for you (you should include more than one consequence);
- how you managed to return home.

Identifying the various parts of the question is the first step in tackling the essay.

An advantage of the structured question is that it provides you with an outline plan and indicates what you should write about. A disadvantage may be that it is an invitation to display knowledge of more than one vocabulary area. You should be prepared to respond to each element in the title, and within the limits of your linguistic knowledge you should put yourself imaginatively into the prescribed situations in order to make them as convincing as possible. Provide details which show that the events take place in a foreign capital and indicate that you were on holiday and not just there for some undefined purpose.

The problems encountered thereafter are caused by a general strike. Do more than announce the fact in a single sentence: give details and, if you can, make them part of the story. Do this to add interest and realism and to show that you can command the required vocabulary and structures. Similarly, you are expected to do justice to an account of the way the strike affected you and to invent convincing details of the journey home. It would not be necessary to treat each of the four elements in equal detail and at equal length but on the other hand it would be unwise to neglect one element or to give it only perfunctory attention.

Remember, when you are deciding what to put into the essay, that you could include description (e.g. of a strike-bound city) and some dialogue.

Planning

As you plan the essay concentrate on the sequence of events and the tenses that you will use. Your main narrative tense may be either the past historic or the perfect (passé composé). Be clear in your mind about the point in time at which you wish the narrative sequence to begin. You could begin with a description of how you were spending your holiday which was then interrupted by the strike and its consequences. Make the transition from the descriptive tense (imperfect) to the narrative tense clear to the reader. If you wish to refer to events which occurred before the narrative sequence starts (i.e. to why you *had decided* to spend such holiday, how you *had travelled*, where you *had already been*, etc.) then you will use the pluperfect tense. Later in the essay you may include further description (e.g. of what *was happening* when you walked through the streets, went to the airport, etc.). Think about what you are doing and arrange the tenses accordingly.

Vocabulary

The title requires knowledge of vocabulary to do with holidays, travel, strikes and personal reactions and feelings (e.g. anxiety, annoyance, frustration) experienced in a difficult situation. Other essential vocabulary will include expressions of time and place and the expression of cause and effect necessary to situate the story and make it intelligible to the reader. Use your knowledge to provide the kind of detail which will make your story interesting and convincing. If, having anaylsed the title, you feel that you have only vague knowledge of the lexical areas prescribed, then try choosing another title.

Drafting the essay

Write your essay plan and notes in French so that your mind works in French from the beginning. Write down phrases or items of vocabulary in the form you will use when you write up the essay. In this way you are more likely to generate further ideas/language by association. Do not write out the whole essay in rough first (at least, not if you are writing under examination conditions) or write out the whole essay in English and then translate it.

Outline Plan

The plan of the essay might reasonably follow the order of events presented in the title:

1   An opening paragraph which explains the situation and sets the scene (but guard against the use of an all-purpose introduction to a general 'holiday' essay).
    - Je passais quelques jours à Paris — musées, expositions, théâtres. J'étais accompagné de . . . L'hôtel se trouvait à . . . Nous étions en France depuis . . . Nous avions fait un tour en Bretagne, etc.
2   The situation is interrupted by the strike, its consequences and attempts to deal with them.
    - Rentrés à l'hôtel, nous entendîmes annoncer à la radio qu'une grève générale était prévue.
      Pas d'eau, pas d'électricité, pas de transports publics, rues presque désertes.
      Nous essayâmes de faire de l'auto-stop, sans succès.
      Manifestations, grévistes portant des pancartes.
      A la gare il y avait des piquets de grève, etc.
3   A solution to the problem is discovered.
    - Une idée lumineuse, un touriste belge à l'hôtel, on l'avait aidé. Il accepta de nous emmener à Ostende.
      Autoroute sans payer, employés du péage en grève.
4   An account is given of the journey home.
    - Très peu de voitures, aucun poids lourd.
      A Ostende, le ferry à destination de Douvres.

EXAMINATION QUESTION AND TUTOR'S ANSWER

Racontez une histoire originale — imaginée ou réelle — intitulée 'La Peur'.   (ULSEB)

Si j'avais le talent de Guy de Maupassant j'écrirais une belle histoire au sujet de la peur qui vous ferait dresser les cheveux sur la tête. N'ayant pas ce talent-là, je me contenterai de raconter une aventure qui m'arriva à une époque où, petit garçon de dix ans, j'habitais une région reculée dans le Yorkshire. Un soir, juste avant Noël, mes parents me demandèrent de promener notre chien avant de me coucher. Bien qu'il fît très froid dehors, j'acceptai pour faire plaisir à mon père. Juste avant Noël, il faut essayer de contenter un peu ses parents!

Notre maison était située dans un endroit isolé qui se trouvait à deux kilomètres d'un petit village. Comme il faisait noir comme dans un four ce soir-là, je décidai de prendre le chemin qui menait au village. C'était un petit chemin bordé de chênes et toujours désert le soir. Je partis en marchant d'un pas allègre. Le chien me suivait en tirant sur la laisse. Il était gros, le chien et n'aimait pas trotter rapidement. Je l'encourageais; il me regardait d'un oeil méfiant. Arrivé sous les arbres, je n'entendais même plus le bruit de mes pas puisque le vent hurlait et faisait tomber des feuilles mortes. C'était comme des doigts invisibles qui touchaient mon visage. Il me semblait que je n'arriverais jamais au village. Inquiet, je pressai le pas, m'enfonçant dans l'obscurité. Puis, soudain, le chien s'arrêta. Je tirai la laisse mais il regardait fixement devant lui, les oreilles dressées, refusant absolument d'avancer. Enfin, il se retourna si rapidement que je laissai tomber la laisse et le chien s'enfuit à toute vitesse. C'est à ce moment-là que je connus la peur. Il y avait quelque chose qui se tenait dans les ténèbres, quelque chose d'affreux que me guettait, qui m'attendait. Je ne le voyais pas, je le sentais. Avec une terreur croissante, je commençai à marcher rapidement en jetant des regards derrière moi. Enfin, pris de panique je me mis à courir. Je sortis du petit bois, dévalai un talus, sautai un fossé, un buisson, une clôture et arrivai, essouflé, devant la maison de mes parents.

J'entrai dans le jardin et jetai un coup d'oeil dans la niche du chien. Il dormait là, bien au chaud! Ce n'était pas la peur de l'inconnu qui lui avait fait prendre la fuite: il avait simplement eu envie de retrouver sa niche aussi rapidement que possible et de se coucher.

EXAMINATION QUESTION AND STUDENT'S ANSWER WITH EXAMINER'S COMMENTS

Vous avez été à bord d'un avion qui a dû faire un atterrissage forcé en pleine montagne. Faites le récit de cet événement en expliquant comment vous avez été sauvé(e).

(ULSEB)

> A good dramatic opening.

> Wrong tense – j'avais dû.

> d' or de l'?

> Good.

> Rather vague meaning?

> A good sentence.

> To wait until = attendre que + subjunctive.

> Improve the word order?

> Avoir chaud = to be warm.

> What does this pronoun refer to?

> Wrong term — use atteindre.

> Some apt vocabulary.

> Past participle agrees with preceeding direct object: aidés.

'Attention, attention, Mesdames et Messieurs, c'est le capitaine qui parle. Dans un instant nous allons atterrir. Le brouillard est si épais qu'il serait fou de continuer . . .'

Je me suis réveillée en sursaut, j'aurais dû m'assoupir. Je me suis vite rendu compte que nous perdions toujours d'altitude. Les montagnes menaçaient de nous enlacer et de nous écraser dans un grand manteau blanc. La neige devenait de plus en plus claire à travers le brouillard et puis, tout à coup, nous étions sur la terre sans avoir rien senti. Les autres voyageurs pleuraient et criaient, mais moi, j'ai poussé un grand soupir de soulagement. Je ne savais pas où nous étions mais, pour le moment, nous étions au moins sains et saufs.

Puis la voix du capitaine s'est fait entendre de nouveau. Il a dit que nous étions dans les Alpes et qu'il avait informé l'aéroport le plus proche de position. 'La seule chose à faire, a-t-il ajouté, est de rester calme et d'attendre jusqu'à ce qu'on vienne nous sauver.'

C'est une sensation très étrange d'être abandonné au milieu d'un désert blanc dans un avion. Nous étions si chauds dans notre petit avion pendant que le vent glacial mugissait en dehors et la neige tombait. Il était très peu confortable et moi j'étais tout en nage avec la gorge desséchée et les paumes couvertes de sueur.

Une demi-heure plus tard, cependant, j'aurais tout donné pour achever cet état de nouveau, car la température de l'avion est vite tombée dans l'atmosphère en dehors, et tout le monde commençait à grelotter. Beaucoup de voyageurs se sont mis à marcher de long en large dans le passage et on a proposé un verset de la Marseillaise pour nous réchauffer. Tous les voyageurs ont commencé de chanter de bon coeur et à ce moment-là une équipe de sauvetage est arrivée avec des fourrures, du café chaud et du cognac.

Ils nous ont aidé à aller à un grand hangar en pleine montagne pour les alpinistes qui sont obligés de trouver de l'abri pendant une tempête inattendue. Là, nous avons passé la nuit et lorsque le brouillard s'est levé, des hélicoptères ont pu nous transporter à l'aéroport. Là mon aventure s'est terminée mais je n'oublierai jamais cette nuit passée dans les Alpes.

Examiner's comment

A well planned essay. A lively, and on the whole convincing account. There is a very high level of grammatical accuracy and fluent sentence structure. There is a good range of apt vocabulary which has been used imaginatively. Overall, a very good essay.

GUIDED COMPOSITION

GETTING STARTED

The essential feature of the guided composition is that it is a writing exercise based on stimulus material which is usually given in French. This material may be one or a mixture of: notes, tables of statistics, diagrams, cartoon pictures or a short passage of instructions. On the basis of such items you may be required to write an article, a letter, the text of a short speech or talk, a dialogue, a report or a more personal account. There may be further instructions concerning the style (e.g. formal or informal) and the point of view which should be put across.

This type of exercise is quite different from the free-composition essay and you should certainly not approach it as though you were writing a free-composition.

INTERPRETATION AND ORGANISATION

PRACTICE AND PREPARATION

THE STIMULUS

ESSENTIAL PRINCIPLES

INTERPRETATION AND ORGANISATION

" What is the examiner looking for? "

When the guided composition is marked the criteria are partly the same as for the free-composition essay. The examiner looks for apt use of *vocabulary and idiom, fluency and sound sentence structure* (see chapter 4) but he or she will also appraise the way in which the candidate has put these skills together in order to *interpret and organise* the stimulus material. The basic question asked is 'Can the candidate respond to the stimulus and *do something with it?*' Responding to it means reading it, taking it in and 'making it your own', drawing ideas out of it. 'Doing something with it' means organising those ideas, building them into the structure of an argument, possibly transforming the register of the stimulus material (e.g. changing it from formal to informal or vice versa), or changing it from note-form to continuous prose.

These points are illustrated in the example question below.

Vous êtes membre d'un comité qui cherche à attirer des fonds pour faire construire un centre de loisirs pour les jeunes handicapés de votre quartier. Vous écrivez une lettre (250 mots) au chef d'une grande entreprise dans le but de le persuader de faire un don d'argent considérable pour lancer le projet.

Vous soulignerez les bienfaits d'un tel projet et ferez de votre mieux pour avoir son soutien. Vous utiliserez les notes suivantes.

1   *Quelques données*: 23 enfants et adolescents handicapés − manque total de possibilités pour les loisirs; autorités municipales favorables au projet; local déjà décerné pour la construction d'un bâtiment.
2   *Avantages*
   i) *Pour les jeunes*: possibilité de se détendre; rencontres amicales; cadre de vie plus riche; loisirs profitables; rencontres avec des jeunes sans handicaps; élargir les horizons; faire partie de la communauté.
   ii) *Pour les associés*: connaissance plus profonde de la vie d'une personne handicapée; possibilité d'intéresser le grand public à la vie de tels jeunes; aider la communauté.
   iii) *Pour l'entreprise*: association utile − réputation de l'entreprise; possibilité de jouer un rôle important dans la communauté

(ULSEB Syllabus B 1985)

Here you are told that the aim of the letter you are to write is to *persuade* the head of a firm to make a donation towards the construction of your leisure centre. You are required to construct your case on the basis of notes which give details of the situation and outline the argument that you should put forward.

For example it would be wrong to answer the question above by writing an essay on 'The need to help the handicapped' rather than use the information given in order to follow the precise instructions set out in the rubric.

" Respond, assimilate and use. "

If you have written a good guided composition you will have followed the instructions, responded to the stimulus, assimilated and used the material appropriately, developing it in a concise and logical way.

If your essay is not so good it may be because you have used only part of the material or because you have not built a very convincing structure.

If your essay is rather weak it will probably be because you have gone off at a tangent or have simply strung the points in the stimulus material together without any real development.

You should avoid following through the notes or items of information in the stimulus in an unresponsive way and simply stringing them together. Take the stimulus material in question 8 on page 70. What you should *not* do is this:

Les effets de la société de consommation sont mauvais. L'argent devient le dieu de la société et à cause des biens matériels on oublie son voisin. On croit que les possessions mènent au bonheur.

C'est une illusion parce qu'on oublie la valeur de l'effort personnel et l'importance d'attitudes sociales responsables. Souvent les possessions rendent les gens malheureux etc.

Here the notes have not been thought about and re-organised, they have simply been stitched together. Remember that this is a negative example. Compare it with the Tutor's Answer on page 71.

PRACTICE AND PREPARATION

READING PASSAGES

The guided composition does require special practice and preparation. An important part of that preparation should involve working on appropriate reading passages. These will be mainly newspaper and magazine articles dealing with contemporary issues. Recent topics which have provided the material for guided compositions include:

- the controversy of privatisation/nationalisation
- the influence of personal computers on children
- helping handicapped children
- the computerisation of personal data and the problem of civil liberties
- keep-fit and body-building clubs
- the crime rate
- the danger of nuclear power stations
- attitudes of and towards young people
- the dangers of smoking

Think about the way an examiner is likely to go about setting a guided composition question; it will help you guide your own reading and preparation. He will scan newspapers or magazines for one or more articles on a lively contemporary issue (e.g. telephone tapping, animal rights, the problem of drugs or alcohol) which incorporate visual information such as tables, sets of statistics or diagrams. He may also consider cartoons or pictures which convey interesting ideas or relate to topical questions. It makes good sense for you to base your preparation on similar material.

Take an article, reduce it to skeleton notes and at a latter date attempt to re-construct it using only the skeleton plan and the vocabulary notes that you have made. Alternatively, try to put up a counter-argument to the one contained in the original article. If you can find more than one article dealing with the same topic by looking at a selection of newspapers or magazines, try to write your own account by putting together material taken from more than one source. You will be taking yourself through a process which is very similar to the one which you need to master in order to write a guided composition.

Link-words

When you are working on a passage give particular attention to the way ideas are organised and note the *link-words* which are used to arrange ideas and make the shape of the argument clear to the reader, e.g.:

d'abord	cependant
tout d'abord	néanmoins
en premier lieu	pourtant
par ailleurs	toutefois
en outre	mais
de plus	donc
d'autre part	par conséquent
ensuite . . . ensuite	en définitive

The guided composition requires you to put forward an argument logically or to explain a situation clearly in a limited number of words. Information, ideas and vocabulary are given to you in the stimulus. You are required to shape them into an argument or an explanation. This requires practice.

The passages which follow are examples of logical arguments constructed in a clear, concise way. The link words which guide the reader through the argument have been underlined.

a) Il est incontestable que la production alimentaire totale a été augmentée à peu près partout dans le monde depuis la seconde guerre mondiale. Pourtant la quantité de nourriture dont dispose chaque individu est restée pratiquement la même, étant donné que le nombre des individus a également augmenté. Ainsi la situation des populations les plus pauvres ne s'est pas améliorée.

   En fait, en raison de la croissance démographique, la malnutrition s'est étendue. Il s'agit donc de limiter cette expansion de la population pour assurer que chaque individu mange à sa faim.

b) La prise en compte des exigences écologiques conserve beaucoup d'adversaires dans le patronat. <u>Cependant</u> elle a assez de partisans patronaux pour que son acceptation devienne une probabilité sérieuse. <u>Alors</u> mieux vaut ne pas reprocher aux puissances d'argent et aux chefs d'entreprises en leur accusant de sacrifier l'avenir de la planète pour augmenter leurs profits: cela pourrait rebuter ces patrons qui ont fait preuve de bonne volonté dans le domaine écologique. <u>Plutôt que de</u> rechercher des coupables pour les dénigrer, <u>il s'agit</u> d'attirer l'attention de tous sur les beaux efforts fournis par certains.

As an exercise, re-write the passages in semi-note form, leaving out the link-words. For (a) above:

- ■ La production alimentaire totale a été augmentée à peu près partout dans le monde.
- ■ La quantité de nourriture dont dispose chaque individu est restée pratiquement la même.
- ■ Le nombre des individus a également augmenté.
- ■ La situation des populations les plus pauvres ne s'est pas améliorée.
- ■ En raison de la croissance démographique la malnutrition s'est étendue.
- ■ Il s'agit de limiter cette expansion de la population pour assurer que chaque individu mange à sa faim.

Then, at a later date and using these notes, try to reconstruct the original passage. This exercise gives you practice in the kind of thinking and structuring involved in doing a guided composition which requires you to construct an argument on the basis of notes, quotations, facts and figures given in the stimulus.

❝ Find further passages. ❞

You can find further passages, those which seem to you to be clearly argued, in newspapers and magazines. Reading to find them, analysing them and indicating the link-words, and finally carrying out the re-construction exercise explained above, is very valuable practice for the guided composition.

THE STIMULUS

Make sure that you are familiar with the kind of material used in the stimulus. It could include a graph, a table of figures, a diagram or a cartoon. You should use such items in your preparation so that you are used to 'getting something out' of such material.

As the stimulus may include a picture, drawing or cartoon it is useful to practise analysing and explaining such items. Analyse the picture below. What ideas does it suggest to you which might be incorporated into an essay on the use and abuse of alcohol? Try to put down your findings in French.

Fig. 7.1

Comité National de défence contre l'alcoolisme. 20. rue Saint-Fiacre. 75002 Paris.

EXAMINATION QUESTIONS

Q1

Vous avez assisté à un débat très animé sur la centralisation par ordinateur de renseignements sur les individus, au cours duquel vous avez pris des notes. De retour chez vous, vous écrivez au secrétaire du comité local pour la défense des libertés du citoyen, pour l'informer de ce qui s'est passé.

Vous essayerez de faire un compte-rendu fidèle (250 mots) de la discussion, utilisant vos notes, qui sont imprimées ci-dessous. Dans votre lettre vous suivrez le schéma dressé par vos notes.

Notes

1 *Introduction*
   Mme Leblanc: question brûlante; progrès? atteinte (liberté)? deux points de vue.

2 *Avantages*
   M. Lebrun: (enthousiasme; parle bien; raisonnement fort; savant) procédé utile — médecins, police, gouvernement — économie — métiers, personnel — méthodes modernes essentielles — accès restreint — mesures de protection rigoureuses.

3 *Désavantages*
   Mme Rose: (personnalité forte; passionnée; bonne impression; bien préparée) — le point de vue de l'homme moyen — pas question pour experts — situation horrifiante — sécurité des données peu sûre; — tentations pour criminels etc. — destruction des rapports personnels (médecin/malade etc.) — fin de la société libre.

4 *Conclusion*
   Mme Leblanc: — majorité contre décisions: lettre aux députés, monter campagne, soutenir l'Association pour la défense des libertés.   (ULSEB B 1986)

Q2

On vous a invité(e) à participer à une discussion au sujet de ces jeux télélévisés où il est possible de gagner des prix de luxe. Vous décidez de vous ranger du côté de ceux qui considèrent que de tels programmes exercent une mauvaise influence sur les gens. Écrivez le petit discours (250 mots) que vous présenterez au cours de la discussion.

Vous disposerez vos arguments d'une façon claire, tout en faisant de votre mieux pour convaincre vos auditeurs que c'est vous qui avez raison.

Vous utiliserez les idées suivantes:

1 *Les programmes*: activités frivoles; encouragement de la convoitise; exploitation des mauvais aspects de la nature humaine; popularité indiscutable.

2 *Dangers psychologiques:*
   a) *participants*: désirs exagérés; perte de perspectives sur la vie; attitudes hostiles; buts douteux; objets de mépris et d'embarras.
   b) *téléspectateurs*: s'identifier avec les compétiteurs; avides de succès; encourager les excès; reflet des attitudes de notre société.

3 *La télévision menacée*: divertissement — oui, mais? la télévision — instrument de culture?   (ULSEB 1985)

Q3

Faites un commentaire (250 mots) sur le petit dessin à la page 66. Vous soulignerez l'exagération de la situation, et en expliquerez l'humour, tout en soulignant le message que Sempé veut nous transmettre.

Vous disposerez vos idées d'une façon claire et convaincante, et vous ferez de votre mieux pour persuader le lecteur que dans notre société il faut savoir mettre en perspective les deux aspects — écologie et évolution technologique.

Vous tiendrez compte des idées suivantes:

1 *le dessin*: situation exagérée, ridicule; contrastes frappants.
2 *les personnages*: situation sociale; attitudes (homme riche, femme, fermier).
3 *facteurs/mobiles*: nostalgie de la vie simple; retour à la nature; outils primitifs du paysan.
4 *humour*: plutôt cynique?
5 *implications*: évolution technique — bienfaits, mais disponibles à tout le monde? retour en arrière? profiter au mieux des développements de la science?   (ULSEB 1986)

Fig. 7.2

Ça c'est la vraie vie, ma chérie!

Q4

Vous ferez un petit commentaire (250 mots) sur le dessin (voir ci-dessous) que traite de l'influence évidente qu'a l'ordinateur sur les enfants. Vous essayerez d'en dégager les idées principales, tout en soulignant les points de vue et de l'enfant et de son père. **Vous allez vous ranger du côté du père.**

Vous ferez de votre mieux pour persuader le lecteur que vous avez raison quand vous insistez sur les dangers de cet instrument qui est devenu si populaire parmi les jeunes. En même temps vous reconnaitrez l'humour de la situation telle que l'artiste l'a conçue.

Vous utiliserez les idées suivantes pour composer votre commentaire:

Les adultes: bienfaits? Lesquels?
 disparition des activités traditionelles?
 écart entre les générations?
 jaloux?
 menace pour la culture française?
 non-développement de capacités importantes?

L'enfant: concentration assidue?
 importance — comprendre la nouvelle technologie.
 refus des activités traditionelles?
 frustré — adultes incompréhensifs.

Dessinateur: attitude plutôt cynique?
 marche du progrès?
 critique de la passivité contemporaine?

(ULSEB 1988)

Fig. 7.3

Dessin de PLANTU.

Q5   **Muscles...oui! Gonflette...non!**

Fig. 7.4

Depuis quelques années déjà, l'apparition de centres de 'body building' fleurit en France. Mais la clientèle, en général, reste méfiante: sport ou frime? Muscles ou gonflette? Telles sont les questions. Pour être fixé, il faut y aller une fois pour satisfaire sa curiosité et juger en connaissance de cause.

Déjà le club de Challans, rue Carnot, avait remis les pendules à l'heure avec ses quelque 150 adhérents assidus et réguliers depuis plus de trois ans et amplement satisfaits. Les responsables ont acquis la confiance du public grâce à leur sérieux et surtout grâce aux résultats obtenus, preuves à l'appui.

Cet été, pour la première année, une 'succursale' à Saint-Jean-de-Monts, avenue de la Forêt, propose un entraînement complet en fonction des besoins de chacun. Une dizaine d'appareils, tels que la chaise romaine ou la presse à 45°, aident pour un amincissement, un raffermissement musculaire ou tout simplement une bonne remise en forme à l'occasion des vacances annuelles.

Bruno, le moniteur agréé, déclare: **'Les gens s'intéressent d'un peu plus près à leur corps, mais ils viennent très doucement au body-building, quelquefois par manque de confiance, plus souvent par manque de courage. J'ai une clientèle à dominante féminine et le plus souvent entre 30 et 40 ans. Ma cliente la plus âgée a 60 ans, mais un corps très jeune et sain. Les femmes prennent plus vite conscience de l'esthétisme de leur personne. Avec un programme d'entraînement bien respecté et une bonne assiduité, en 15 jours, un mois au plus, on peut déjà voir les progrès, ce qui encourage les efforts'.**

C'est un véritable phénomène de société. A l'heure de l'informatisation, il était temps d'apprendre à respecter son corps et à mieux le connaître. Le club de Saint-Jean propose des forfaits de 10 séances au mois ou bien encore à l'heure. Là, le travail s'effectue en musique pour le plus grand plaisir des sportifs.

Intéressé(e) par un article de journal au sujet des 'Clubs de santé', de plus en plus populaires parmi les gens de tout âge, vous écrivez à un(e) ami(e) pour le (la) persuader de devenir membre du Club de Saint-Jean. Vous savez que votre camarade est plutôt hostile à l'idée de tels clubs.

Néanmoins, vous ferez de votre mieux pour le (la) persuader que vous avez raison, en soulignant l'importance de la bonne santé (même chez les jeunes) et les dangers de ne pas se maintenir en bonne forme.

Vous utiliserez le reportage du journal et traiterez les aspects suivants:

Avantages: résultats assez rapides
                programmes individualisés
                résultats garantis
                phénomène de société
                amincir? raffermissement musculaire?
                meilleure qualité de vie

Désavantages minuscules: coûteux?

travail dur? Oui, mais . . .

entraînement régulier? Oui, mais . . .

(ULSEB 1987)

Q6

Study carefully the following material and instructions given in French. Then write about **250 words** in **French** *in response to the material. Marks will be awarded for the logical presentation of the material and for the accuracy and quality of the French used.*
(50 marks)

Fig. 7.5

Une vie sans avenir et sans projet...

(from *Actualquarto*)

j'peux pas dire comment j'vois l'avenir, j'vois rien d'ailleurs, j'laisse venir . Par crainte : l'avenir jusqu'à présent c'était le trou total, l'angoisse totale ; si j'ai fait de la dépression, c'est à cause de cela.

Fig. 7.6

(from *Le Monde aujourd'hui*)

Fig. 7.7

Fig. 7.8

(from *Le Nouvel Observateur*)

Faites l'analyse des vues présentées ci-dessus. Dans quelle mesure, selon vous, ces opinions de la jeunesse d'aujourd'hui sont-elles vraies? Existe-t-il un point de vue plus optimiste?

(AEB 1988)

Q7
Study carefully the following material and instructions given in French. Then write about **250 words** *in* **French** *in response to the material. Marks will be awarded for the logical presentation of the material, and for the accuracy and quality of the French used.* *(50 marks)*

Et si on privatisait tout ça...

Privatiser? Pourquoi pas... Il y a effectivement des dénationalisations nécessaires comme il y a des nationalisations légitimes. Il n'est pas anormal de privatiser l'agence Havas, ni choquant à priori de désengager l'Etat de Thomson et de la CGE, pas plus qu'il n'aurait été anormal ou choquant de nationaliser la distribution de l'eau ou des pompes funèbres. Ce qui, en revanche, est débile, c'est l'idée socialiste dogmatique ou libérale sectaire selon laquelle nationalisation ou privatisation sont des solutions en soi, et dans tous les cas.
Dans un cas, on en vient à nationaliser pour l'exemple et, dans l'autre, à privatiser pour le principe. Dans les deux cas, on casse par idéologie. A cet égard, la privatisation de TF1 est aussi intelligente qu'une éventuelle nationalisation du commerce des fruits et des légumes ou des cafés-tabacs.
Dans la mesure où l'on s'engage dans cette voie, pourquoi ne pas aller plus loin ? L'armée, l'Assemblée nationale, la police, les impôts, *la Joconde*, Notre-Dame restent à privatiser. Quitte à provoquer le désordre sans raison, qu'au moins on s'amuse un peu !

(from *L'événement du jeudi*)

(from *Le Point*)

Saint-Gobain/Paribas/CGE...

En acheter ou pas

Après Saint-Gobain, Paribas entre en scène. Son succès est pratiquement assuré. Mais pourra-t-on suivre à ce rythme le train de la privatisation ? Le public, lui, a pour l'Etat la foi du charbonnier.

(from *Le Point*)

Et pourquoi ne pas continuer?

French to privatise CGE

By Robert Peston
City Staff

FRENCH Finance Minister Edouard Belladur said yesterday that the Compagnie Générale d'Electricité would be the nineth state owned company to be returned to the private sector this year.

(from *The Independent*)

Fig. 7.9

La privatisation ou la nationalisation . . . question de principe politique ou de théorie économique? Quelle position prenez-vous?
Choisissez vos exemples parmi les services publics et sociaux (par exemple, télécommunications, électricité, gaz, système éducatif etc.) . . . ou dans le monde du commerce et de l'industrie.
Vous pouvez également vous référer à la situation en Grande-Bretagne ou ailleurs.

(AEB 1987)

Q8

Votre ami(e) vous a envoyé le petit dessin (voir ci-dessous), et qu'il (elle) trouve très amusant. Se je me trouvais à la place de ce type-là . . . ! a-t-il (elle) écrit, 'ce serait le paradis! Plus d'école, plus de travail. . .' Vous lui répondez immédiatement, afin de le (la) convaincre qu'une telle attitude ne fait que refléter les mauvaises tendances de notre société de consommation.

Ecrivez la lettre (250 mots) et faites de votre mieux pour le (la) persuader qu'il (elle) a tort. Vous présenterez vos raisons d'une façon claire et convaincante, en utilisant les notes suivantes:

effets de la société de consommation: − argent − dieu de la société − biens matériels − oubli du voisin − argent = possessions = bonheur

critique: − illusion, perspectives perdues − valeur de l'effort, −importance d'attitudes sociales responsables − possessions souvent = malheur

effets psychologiques de cette société sur l'individu: − convoitise, égoïsme; refus de considérer les autres; tendance à se vanter de ses possessions; caractère peu aimable.

effets sur la société: − perte des valeurs traditionelles, − divisions profondes

le dessin: − humoristique, mais − amer commentaire sur les valeurs de notre époque.

Fig. 7.10

A TUTOR'S ANSWER TO QUESTION 8

Cher François,

Je te remercie de ta lettre et du petit dessin que tu m'as envoyés. Il m'a beaucoup amusé mais il m'a fait réfléchir aussi, d'autant plus que tu dis que tu voudrais te trouver à la place de type sur le dessin. Méfie-toi, mon vieux, tu te laisses séduire par les valeurs trompeuses de la société de consommation. Tu devrais te rendre compte que ton dessin fait un commentaire plutôt amer sur les valeurs de notre époque.

Dans une société où les gens sont exclusivement attachés à l'argent et à la possession de biens matériels, le vrai bonheur n'est pas possible. Celui qui veut gagner toujours plus est condamné à être malheureux parce qu'il n'est jamais satisfait. A un moment donné il rêve d'acheter une 2CV et une petite maison, mais à peine ce rêve réalisé, il se dégoûte de ces objets qu'il avait si vivement désirés parce qu'il est jaloux de son voisin qui, lui, possède une grosse voiture de luxe et une villa somptueuse.

Ainsi l'individu devient victime d'un égoïsme sordide. Riche, il a tendance à se vanter de ses possessions. Pauvre, il convoite les biens des autres. Il ne pense jamais à secourir ceux de ses semblables qui sont dans l'infortune. Ce qui compte pour lui ce n'est pas la valeur de l'effort personnel, c'est l'argent, l'argent et l'argent. Voilà le type de ton dessin. Tu trouves qu'il a un caractère aimable?

Réfléchis donc un peu avant d'envier le sort de cet homme. Il représente une société profondément divisée dans laquelle on serait malheureux.

Ecris-moi bientôt.

Bien à toi,
Jean-Pierre

A STUDENT'S ANSWER TO QUESTION 5 WITH EXAMINER'S COMMENTS

> **How do these two statements relate to each other?**

> **Needs further explanation.**

> **Needs further explanation.**

> **An anglicism; 'avec' is all that is needed.**

> **Say; ce qui est un désavantage.**

> **An anglicism – "deux soirs".**

> **An anglicism; say t'inscrire à .**

Cher Léon,

L'autre jour j'ai lu un article au sujet des Clubs de santé qui m'a beaucoup intéressé. Je sais que tu es plutôt hostile à l'idée de tels clubs mais je veux te persuader que ces clubs sont très populaires avec les jeunes. Ils ont beaucoup d'avantages et il est dangereux de ne pas se maintenir en bonne forme.

D'abord, examinons les avantages. Il est possible de faire des progrès très rapidement parce qu'il y a une dizaine d'appareils tels que la chaise romaine ou la presse à 45°. Aussi les résultats sont garantis parce que les programmes sont individualisés par Bruno le moniteur. Tout le monde commence à s'intéresser au body-building, c'est un phénomène de société. Si tu veux une bonne remise en forme, c'est une bonne idée pour toi.

Les désavantages sont minuscules. Il ne coûte pas très cher parce qu'il y a des prix spéciaux. Le travail est dur peut-être mais il est amusant aussi parce qu'on travaille en écoutant la musique et on peut travailler sur les appareils ensemble avec ses amis. Il faut régulièrement et c'est un désavantage mais il faut aller seulement deux nuits par semaine.

Je te conseille de joindre le club St. Jean. Il y a maintenant une 'succursale' près de chez toi. Si tu es en bonne santé tu as une meilleure qualité de vie. Même les jeunes ont besoin de faire quelque chose pour être en forme, même toi.

Amitiés,
Henri

> **Vague — be more precise "il faut s'entraine".**

Examiner's comments

The introduction is not very successful: the candidate does little more than repeat phrases from the instructions. It is a question of *being* persuasive rather than simply announcing that you are going to persuade.

The two statements in the last sentence of the first paragraph do not go together very well. It is not clear how the second one follows on logically from the first. It would be better to say *Ils ont beaucoup d'avantages, notamment celui de permettre une bonne remise en forme.*

In the second and third paragraphs, the candidate follows the stimulus without thinking his way into the situation. The explanations of why rapid progress can be made and why results are guaranteed are not very full or convincing. Throughout this paragraph the writer tends to 'lift' material from the stimulus and add it to the letter without following any clear line of development of his own.

The main problem is that the writer has not re-worked and developed the stimulus material so that it becomes part of a fluent, logical argument. He does not build his own structure because he remains focused on the stimulus material from which he picks pieces in a rather haphazard fashion. The ideas are not arranged to best persuade, challenge or interest the friend.

However, grammar, syntax and spelling are quite accurate. The guided composition would pass but it would not gain a very high mark.

EXAMINATION QUESTION AND OUTLINE ANSWER

Q9

(The following table was used as part of the stimulus in an A- level guided composition in which candidates were asked to present aspects of the crime rate in France.)

Tour de France de la criminalité en 1987

Fig. 7.11

Outline answer

At first you may wonder what you can possibly say about it or how you can say it in French. There is in fact quite a lot that can be drawn out of the table. Each sentence will contain vocabulary and structures which are useful in making a commentary of this nature.

- La lecture du tableau permet les constatations suivantes.
- La situation se caractérise par une augmentation régulière du nombre de crimes en France.
- Les années 1963 – 1986 enregistrent une forte augmentation du taux des crimes.
- Le tableau met en évidence l'augmentation de la criminalité en France.
- De 1963 à 1982 le tableau indique la montée régulière du nombre des crimes et délits.

- En 1976 le rythme d'accroissement s'est atténué mais la tendance générale est à la hausse.
- En 1986 le nombre des petits crimes est descendu à 2 675 000.
- Depuis 1963 le nombre des crimes a augmenté en moyenne de 50% par an.
- De 1967 à 1976 le nombre des crimes a doublé.
- Le nombre des crimes passe de 1,5 millions en 1972 à 2 millions en 1974 pour retomber ensuite.
- Le taux des crimes est tombé à un niveau inférieur en 1976 mais la tendance à la hausse se poursuit en 1978.
- Les chiffres indiquent une diminution de la criminalité en 1986.
- Le chiffre atteint en 1982 est maintenant largement dépassé.

Make sure that you know the meaning, spelling and gender of key words: le graphique, la courbe, le pourcentage, le chiffre, le tableau etc.

Obviously, you would not want to use all of these statements if you were writing a guided composition but it is important to give yourself practise in analysing tables and statistics in French.

Begin by examining and thinking about the material given in the stimulus; try to make notes and observations in French.

1   Les années 1963–1968 enrigistrent une forte augmentation du taux des crimes en France.

   La croissance de la criminalité se répand sur tout le territoire: de Nice au Nord, de Besançon à Brest; çà et là il y a une diminution du nombre des crimes mais la tendance générale est à la hausse; une hausse inquiétante de la toxicomanie à Nice, dans les Hautes-Alpes; persistance des grands crimes: meurtres, viols, vols à main armée.

2   Le tableau met en évidence l'augmentation de la criminalité; depuis 1963 le nombre des crimes a augmenté en moyenne de 50% tous les deux ans; le nombre des petits délits est descendu à 2 675 000 en 1986 = une diminution de 6,6%; le taux des crimes s'est réduit de 3,6% mais pour la criminalité moyenne, il y a une hausse de 11%; pour la grande criminalité une hausse de 25%

Formulate a plan:
1   Croissance de la criminalité.
        Répartition des crimes; tendance inquiétante
        Nice − Nord
        Besançon − Brest
        drogues
        grands crimes
2   Ces constatations confirmées par les chiffres:
        depuis 1963 augmentation régulière,
        petits délits, réduction
mais
        criminalité à la hausse
        grande criminalité à la hausse
3   Que faire?
     i) mieux comprendre le problème (quelles sont les heures critiques, où se trouvent les points chauds?)
     ii) mieux organiser et déployer les forces de l'ordre
     iii) monter une campagne publicitaire pour que le grand public prenne conscience du problème

LETTER-WRITING

FORMALITY/INFORMALITY

SENTENCE PATTERNS

FOLLOWING INSTRUCTIONS

GETTING STARTED

Letter-writing is a skill which is now more frequently tested at A-level. Writing a letter sometimes exists as a choice among titles set for free composition (JMB Paper 2, ULSEB Syllabus A Paper 4, NISEC Paper 3, WJEC A2) and it is a possible form of guided composition (ULSEB Syllabus B Paper 3).

As a letter is a continuous piece of prose writing the examiner will be looking for use of *vocabulary and idiom; sentence structure and fluency; grammatical accuracy; coherence and sequence* (see chapter 4).

A letter calls for some of the same uses of language as the other types of writing which are set at A-level. Practice in writing narrative essays or discussion essays would therefore help your letter-writing. Consider the following title:

■ Une tempête a sérieusement endommagé la maison de vos voisins qui sont partis en vacances. Vous leur écrivez pour expliquer ce qui est arrivé. Vous précisez les dégats et vous donner des conseils en indiquant les mesures que vous avez déjà prises.

(ULSEB 1988)

In this letter you are required to narrate (pour expliquer ce qui est arrivé); to describe (vous précisez les dégats) and to give advice (vous donnez des conseils).

However, a letter will always be different from the type of essay in which the writer has a 'general reader' in mind because the letter speaks to a specific reader. When you write a letter you are usually communicating with *one person*: an intimate friend, a relative, your bank manager. This has implications for the way you write. You would write to your friend in familiar, personal terms which you would not use in the letter to the bank manager. Getting the style and register right is important if you are going to produce a convincing letter, one that is going to sound 'real' to the examiner.

ESSENTIAL PRINCIPLES

There are two basic types of letter which you should be aware of and which you should practise: the *informal* letter and the *formal* letter. You can begin by comparing the two examples which follow.

a) Un peu inquiet/inquiète parce que vous n'avez pas vu une/un de vos amies/amis depuis quelques temps, vous lui écrivez pour faire des reproches. Vous proposez une sortie.

Chère Anne,
   Qu'est-ce que tu deviens? Ça fait déjà trois semaines que tu ne viens plus au Club d'Anglais. Je ne parviens pas à t'avoir au téléphone et tu n'as pas répondu à ma lettre. Ecoute, je suis un peu inquiète de ne pas avoir de tes nouvelles, tu t'en rends compte? Fais un petit effort! Tu as bien dix minutes à perdre pour m'écrire, non?
   En tout cas, samedi prochain Chantal et moi, allons faire une promenade en voiture pour voir ses parents à Fontainebleau. Elle veut t'inviter. Qu'en dis-tu? Si tu n'as pas le temps de m'écrire un mot tu peux toujours me téléphoner au bureau (avant onze heures). N'oublie pas, ou, alors j'aurai encore davantage de raisons de m'inquiéter.
      Avec toute mon amitié,
      Françoise

b) J.Stowe   Hôtel du Nord
   134 New Street   28 rue de Messine
   Newhaven   Lille-France
   Angleterre.

                                                     Le 4 novembre 1989

Monsieur,
   Etudiante anglaise cherchant un emploi temporaire en France, j'ai appris par une annonce insérée dans Le Courrier du Nord que vous offrez un poste de réceptioniste pour les mois de juillet et août.
   J'ai l'honneur de solliciter cet emploi. Je me permets de signaler que je parle couramment le français et l'allemand et que je possède des connaissances commerciales. J'ai déjà occupé un poste semblable à celui que vous offrez.
   Monsieur Duval et Madame Newark du collège où je fais mes études, vous donneront sur mon compte tous les renseignements qu'il vous plaira de leur demander. Vous trouverez ci-joint un curriculum vitae mentionnant les études effectuées et les postes occupés.
   Résidant à Newhaven, je pourrais facilement me déplacer jusqu'à Dieppe pour tout entretien que vous voudrez m'accorder.
   Je vous prie d'agréer, Monsieur, l'assurance de mes sentiments dévoués.
      Jane Stowe

What makes the two letters different in style?

a) In this informal letter to a friend:

- The writer uses the *vous* form.
- The vocabulary is everyday and would not be out of place in an ordinary conversation between friends.
- A conversational and personal tone is created by the direct questions (Qu'est-ce que tu deviens? Qu'en dis-tu?), the imperatives (Fais un petit effort! N'oublie pas), the reproach (Tu as bien dix minutes à perdre pour m'écrire, non?)
- The sentences are quite short and simple like those in everyday speech.
- The form of address is conventional but familiar (Chère Anne, Avec toute mon amitié)
- There are some of those terms which are used in conversation to engage and keep the attention of the person one is talking to (Ecoute; tu t'en rends compte?)

b) In this formal letter to a prospective employer:

- The letter is more formally set out.
- The writer uses the vous form.

- Some of the terms have been chosen for their polite formality (J'ai l'honneur de solliciter; Je me permets de signaler; tous les renseignements qu'il vous plaira de leur demander) or because they are the conventional phrases of a formal letter (Vous trouverez ci-joint).

- The sentences are often longer and more complex and therefore less like those used in everyday speech (Etudiante anglaise cherchant un emploi temporaire en France, j'ai appris par une annonce insérée dans Le Courrier du Nord que vous offrez un poste de réceptionniste pour les mois de juillet et août.)

If you study these points you will begin to appreciate what you need to do to make your letter formal or informal. At A-level you will not be asked to do anything more sophisticated than this in terms of style but if you can understand the distinction between formal and informal and make it clear when you write you will produce more successful and convincing letters.

FORMALITY/ INFORMALITY

What can be done to make the letter more, or less formal? You can use the appropriate form of address. There are numerous variations to choose from but it is better to keep to a few that will serve in most situations.

THE FORMAL LETTER

Open with
    Monsieur/Madame/Mademoiselle
If you are writing to anyone in their official capacity (e.g. to a manager of a shop, editor of a newspaper, in answer to a job advertisement) or to someone known to you who is clearly older than you are.
Close with
Je vous prie d'accepter, Monsieur/Madame/Mademoiselle, l'expression de mes sentiments les meilleurs.
or if you wish to show particular respect
Je vous prie d'agréer Monsieur/Madame/Mademoiselle, l'expression de mon plus profond respect/ Je vous prie d'accepter, Madame, l'hommage de tout mon respect.

THE INFORMAL LETTER

To a friend, open with
    Cher ami/Chère amie,
close with
    Amicalement/Cordialement/Amitiés.
To a close friend, open with
    Cher Daniel/Chère Anne,
close with
    Je t'embrasse/à bientôt/bien à toi/je pense à toi.
To relatives, open with
    Chers parents/Mon cher oncle/Ma chère cousine,
close with
    Je t'embrasse/Bons baisers.

Personal 'chat'

There is usually a place in the informal letter for some personal 'chat'. The following are examples which you can adapt and use:

- Ecris-moi. Dis-moi ce que tu fais et peut-être aussi quand nous pourrons nous voir, si tu as un peu de temps.

- Si tu venais dîner à la maison samedi prochain? Nous t'attendrons vers 19 heures. Qu'en dis-tu? Réponds-moi vite.

- C'est d'accord pour samedi, si cela te convient toujours. Nous arriverons vers 19 heures comme convenu.

- La soirée a été superbe, je t'en remercie. Le dessert était délicieux. Je ne me souviens pas d'avoir mangé quelque chose d'aussi bon.

- Tu ne peux savoir le plaisir que ton cadeau m'a fait. Je t'en remercie vivement. Comme toujours tu as fait preuve d'un goût exquis.
- Merci beaucoup pour les magazines. Tu es très gentil d'avoir pensé à moi.
- Je te remercie de ton invitation. Je l'accepte très volontiers. Je t'écrirai pour te dire quand je pourrai venir.
- Lundi soir j'invite quelques amis à dîner pour fêter ma promotion. Peux-tu venir aussi? Je compte sur toi.
- J'ai bien reçu ta lettre et je suis très content que tu puisses venir lundi. Si tu me préviens de l'heure de ton arrivée, je viendrai te chercher à la gare.
- Je m'aperçois que je n'ai pas encore répondu à ta dernière lettre. Pardonne-moi ce retard mais j'ai été très occupé.
- Quelques mots rapides pour te confirmer mon arrivée à Paris samedi soir.
- Excuse-moi d'avoir manqué notre rendez-vous mais j'ai été retardé au dernier moment. Je suis arrivé à 19.30 mais tu étais déjà parti.

Layout

Learn how to set out a formal letter. It may seem a small point but it helps to create the impression of a 'real' letter. Use (b) on page 75 as a model. The layout of an informal letter can be simpler. Use letter (a) as a model.

SENTENCE PATTERNS

Practise some of the sentence patterns which occur frequently in the more formal, carefully written letter. Here are three which will help you to construct a good opening sentence.

i) At the beginning of a letter it is often necessary to give your reason for writing it, or some justification for saying what you are going to say. Read the following opening sentences:

- <u>Mère de trois enfants en bas âge</u>, je vous écris pour vous dire le dégoût que m'inspire la décision de fermer la crèche municipale de Noissy.
- <u>Membre d'Amnistie Internationale</u>, j'ai lu avec intérêt l'article de Raymond Leclerc sur les prisonniers politiques en Turquie et je vous soumets mon opinion.

Note the phrase (underlined) used to give information about who the writer is and why he or she is writing. It is built on a noun (mère, membre) placed at the beginning of the sentence. No article (un, une etc.) is used with the noun. The writer could have written:

"Who and why?"

Comme je suis mère de trois enfants etc.
Je suis membre d'Amnistie Internationale et j'ai donc lu avec intérêt etc.

but the underlined version is neater and more condensed.

To practise this construction re-write the following sentences on similar lines.

- Je suis Président de l'Association des collectionneurs de boîtes de fromage. Je vous écris au sujet de votre article sur le camembert.
- Je suis professeur de lycée à Paris depuis 10 ans. J'ai été très surpris en lisant l'article de Jean Lavisse sur la violence au collège.
- Je suis une étudiante anglaise qui cherche un emploi temporaire en France. Je vous écris pour répondre à votre annonce insérée dans le Courrier du Nord.
- Je suis une Anglaise née en France. Je tiens à vous exposer mon point de vue sur la politique européenne du gouvernement britannique.
- Je suis l'épouse d'un professeur. Je comprends parfaitement pourquoi tant de jeunes enseignants quittent ce métier.
- Je suis titulaire d'un permis de conduire depuis 15 ans. Je n'ai jamais eu d'accident.
- Je suis le père de deux enfants. Je veux vous parler de mon irritation en lisant l'article de Michel Druay sur l'enseignement secondaire en France.
- Je suis une jeune enseignante mariée, mère d'un enfant de 2 ans. Je m'étonne des affirmations de Jean Paulac dans son article du 22 novembre.

ii) You can also use a present participle construction to explain why you are writing:

- <u>Connaissant bien la France</u>, je tiens à répondre aux critiques de votre correspondant Marc Lenôtre.

which is a more condensed way of saying:

- comme je connais bien la France, je tiens à répondre aux critiques de votre correspondant, Marc Lenôtre.

Practise the construction by re-writing the following sentences using the present participle of the verb (e.g. connaissant)

- Comme j'ai travaillé comme jeune fille 'au pair' c'est avec grand intérêt que j'ai lu l'article d'Anne Laroque.
- Comme je vis en Angleterre depuis 2 ans maintenant je crois utile de vous communiquer quelques faits à propos de la cuisine anglaise.
- Comme j'ai lu attentivement l'article de M. Raymond consacré à l'industrie automobile, je vous soumets mon opinion.
- Parce que je suis moi-même étudiante en lettres, je ne peux que m'élever contre les affirmations du ministre de l'éducation nationale.
- Parce que je passe souvent mes vacances dans le Midi, je m'étonne des affirmations de votre correspondant.

iii) Alternatively, you may use a construction based on a past participle.

- Attirée par la réputation de votre société, je voudrais poser ma candidature pour le poste que vous offrez.

Re-write the following sentences on this model:

- Parce que je suis alarmé par la croissance de la criminalité dans les grandes agglomérations, voici quelques réflexions qui me viennent à l'esprit.
- Parce que je suis dégoûté par le comportement de certains touristes britanniques, je vous écris pour exposer mon point de vue.
- Parce que je suis passionné par les sports nautiques, je vous écris pour exprimer mon étonnement à la lecture de votre article 'Supprimer les sports dangereux'.
- Parce que je suis surpris et peiné par l'introduction de la nouvelle loi sur l'avortement, je vous écris pour exprimer les réflexions suivantes.
- Parce que je suis étonnée par les résultats de votre sondage sur les moeurs des jeunes, je vous soumets les observations suivantes.

FOLLOWING INSTRUCTIONS

When writing a letter set as an A-level test it is particularly important to look very carefully at the question. The instructions telling you what should go into the letter are often quite detailed (look at the example on page 80). If you overlook part of the instructions you will not complete the task which has been set.

Secondly, remember that these instructions establish a life-related situation which calls for a letter to be written. Always try to treat the situation as a real one and try to think your way into it. It is rather like playing a role. Ask yourself how you would really react in a given situation. What would the recipient of the letter need to be told? What would he know already? Try to get the logic of the situation right and make your letter a convincing piece of communication. Some candidates failed to do this in a recent examination, where they were required to write a letter cancelling a meeting with a friend and suggesting new arrangements. Because some candidates had not thought about the situation there were instructions to the friend which would not have enabled him to meet the writer; there was information which he did not need to know, there were gaps in the information which would have puzzled him and insufficient time was allowed for the letter to get to him. Candidates who played the part of the letter-writer with some insight and imagination wrote letters which were much more 'realistic' and convincing.

EXAMINATION QUESTIONS

Q1
You have been staying in a campsite near the town of Plan de la Tour in southern France. A forest fire has destroyed your tent and equipment and you have had to take refuge in the village hall. You write a letter of about 150 words to a French friend who was due to join you, giving details of what has happened to you and making alternative arrangements.

(ULSEB 1989)

Q2
As a holiday arrangement you have exchanged houses with a French family. Leave a note of about 150 words in French for the family coming to stay in your house, telling them what they need to know about the area, the neighbours etc., and how best to enjoy their holiday.

(ULSEB Specimen Paper 1987)

Q3
Les parents de votre correspondant(e) français(e) vous invite à passer 15 jours chez eux. Ecrivez la réponse en expliquant pourquoi il vous est impossible d'accepter. (150 mots)

(WJEC Specimen Paper)

Q4
Voici ce que vous écrivez à un(e) ami(e) français(e) le 31 mai:

Mon cher Jacques/ma chère Jacqueline,
    Juste un petit mot pour te dire que je commence mes examens demain. J'ai beaucoup travaillé, mais comme tu le sais bien, il faut avoir aussi un peu de chance!
    Je t'écrirai dans 15 jours pour te dire comment tout cela s'est passé.
    Amitiés

Ecrivez la lettre suivante comme vous l'avez promis.   (WJEC Specimen Paper 1988)

Q5
Voici une petite annonce qui a paru dans un journal français.

Cherche pour l'été jeune personne parlant français et anglais pour travailler à la réception d'un grand hôtel. Ecrire Hôtel Majestic, Bordeaux 33000.

Ecrivez une demande d'emploi/en expliquant pourquoi vous êtes la personne qu'il leur faut et en demandant des renseignements supplémentaires.   (WJEC Specimen Paper 1988)

Q6
Un(e) ami(e) très doué(e) a l'intention de ne pas poursuivre ses études dans une université ou dans un institut universitaire de technologie. Ecrivez-lui pour l'encourager à changer d'avis.

(JMB 1988)

Q7
Un ouvrier agricole écrit une lettre au journal local, expliquant pourquoi il devait être mieux payé.

Q8
Deux de vos amis(es) se sont brouillé(e)s. Ecrivez une lettre dans laquelle vous essayez de les réconcilier.

(JMB 1983)

Q9
Une tempête a sérieusement endommagé la maison de vos voisins qui sont partis en vacances. Vous leur écrivez pour expliquer ce qui est arrivé. Vous précisez les dégâts et vous donnez des conseils en indiquant les mesures que vous avez déjà prises.

(ULSEB 1988)

Q10
Trouvant que les prévisions météorologiques sont souvent erronées et que ces erreurs font subir au public des conséquences agaçantes et parfois graves, vous écrivez à un journal pour faire connaître votre point de vue.

(ULSEB 1988)

Q11
Vous écrivez au directeur d'un journal local pour protester contre la manière dont a été relaté un accident de la circulation dont vous avez été la victime.

Q12

Vous appartenez à un groupe de jeunes désireux de fonder un foyer des jeunes. Le conseil municipal fait savoir qu'il met à votre disposition l'ancienne salle des fêtes. De la part de vos camarades vous écrivez une lettre dans laquelle vous adressez des remerciements à M. le Maire en expliquant comment vous allez utiliser les locaux.

AN OUTLINE ANSWER TO QUESTION 3

What points should you think about as you prepare to write the letter?

i) What is the appropriate *tone* to adopt? If you were writing to the pen-friend herself you could be relaxed and familiar but you are writing to her parents: the letter should be friendly but polite (you do not know them very well). Begin the letter: Chère Madame et Cher Monsieur and end it Bien cordialement à vous (NB If you had been writing to *one* of them you would have used the *vous* form).

ii) You are asked to write *150 words*. This does not give much scope to be expansive and show a wide vocabulary but try to

- choose the apt term
- aim at fluent sentence-structure
- ensure that points are coherent
- arrange paragraphs to make your points clear
- check on grammatical accuracy

iii) What would be a logical plan for such a letter? What can you say which will make the refusal a polite and friendly one? It would be normal to

- thank the parents for the invitation
- explain why you cannot accept
- express regret
- perhaps make polite alternative proposal
- show interest by referring to some aspect of their lives/your relationship with them etc.

Write the letter and compare your version with the tutor's answer below.

A TUTOR'S ANSWER TO QUESTION 3

Chère Madame et Cher Monsieur,

C'est avec très grand plaisir que j'ai reçu votre lettre m'invitant à passer une quinzaine de jours chez vous au mois de juillet, d'autant plus que vous proposez aussi un petit séjour en Ardèche, région que j'ai toujours eu envie de visiter. Malheureusement il ne m'est pas possible de répondre favorablement à votre aimable invitation.

En effet je suis prise jusqu'à la mi-août. Mes examens ne se terminent que le 12 juillet, date à laquelle je dois partir en Italie avec mes parents pour un mois.

Je sais que Marie-Hélène va être déçue mais si cela peut la consoler je le suis tout autant. Cependant j'ai une autre idée en tête pour que nous puissions nous revoir avant la fin de l'année. Aimerait-elle passer une semaine chez nous pendant les vacances de Noël? Je vais lui écrire pour lui en parler.

Je vous remercie vivement pour le très joli livre. Comme toujours vous avez fait preuve d'un goût exquis. Vous êtes très gentils d'avoir pensé à moi.

    Bien cordialement à vous,

      Jane.

A STUDENT'S ANSWER TO QUESTION 1 WITH EXAMINER COMMENTS

❝Too formal.❞   ❝Wrong tense.❞   ❝Incorrectly used.❞

❝Wrong term.❞
❝Good vocabulary and structure❞
❝Wrong word.❞

❝Wrong tenses.❞

❝A good sentence.❞
❝Negative mis-placed; "je ne veux pas".❞

❝"Tu" form required.❞

> Cher Henri,
> Je t'informe qu'il y avait un désastre ici. Avant hier un incendie a éclaté dans la forêt de pinèdes située près de notre camping. Les arbres étaient asséchés et les rafales de vent ont attisé les flammes jusqu'à ce que le camping soit tout embrasé. Heureusement les pompiers et les sauveteurs étaient en état d'alerte donc ils sont arrivés sur la scène presque immédiatement. Tous les campeurs ont déjà pris la fuite, alors personne n'était blessé. Cependant notre tente et nos affaires étaient réduites en cendres.
> En ce moment nous sommes hébergés dans la Mairie mais je ne crois pas que nous puissions rester ici après demain. Bien entendu, je veux que tu ne viennes pas ici. Je suis sûre que j'ai assez d'argent pour voyager à Paris avec Marc et j'espère arriver chez toi jeudi. Essayez de ne pas t'impatienter.
> Amitiés
> Jacqueline

Examiner's comments

- Overall it is quite a good piece of work. There is a range of structure, fluency and some variety of sentence pattern. The instructions have been followed reasonably well.

- The writer has seen the need to announce the bad news but this is not the way to do it. *Infomer quelqu'un* is too formal in this context. It would also be better to announce the news so that the friend can see immediately how it affects him. e.g:
    Je suis désolée mais je dois te dire une mauvaise nouvelle qui nous contraint à abandonner nos projets de vacances: le camping où nous allions séjourner a été ravagé par un feu de forêt. Tout notre matériel a été brûlé!

- Tenses are not always well handled when indicating a sequence of events. These are events which happened; a narrative tense (passé composé) is required:
    Notre tente et nos affaires ont été réduites en cendres (they were *reduced* to ashes, not they were in ashes).
    Personne n'a été blessé (nobody was injured, no injury occurred).

- Il y avait eu un désastre (there had been a disaster) where the pluperfect is not required but fails to use it where it *is* required:
    Tous les campeurs avaient déjà pris la fuite. They *had* fled before the fire reached the campsite.

- The candidate has attempted to use a range of vocabulary but it is sometimes a question of a 'good try' which has not entirely succeeded. The candidate did well to know *une pinède* but *une pinède* is a forest of pines; *une forêt de pinèdes* is therefore incorrect. *Sauveteur* does mean rescuer but not a member of the rescue services. The term required here is *secouriste*. *Asséchés* is close but the term needed is *desséchés; assécher* means to dry up or drain something such as a lake or pond. However, other terms used to describe the fire are apt.

THE DIALOGUE ESSAY

CHARACTERISATION AND CONFLICT

NATURAL FRENCH

TYPICAL EXPRESSIONS

FORMS OF QUESTIONING

GETTING STARTED

Including dialogue in a narrative essay is one way of making it more lively and interesting but there are other reasons for practising the writing of a dialogue. There is often a title on the essay paper which requires explicitly that you write a conversation or an interview, while other titles can sometimes be written in dialogue form if you choose to do so. The following titles, for example,

'Une dispute' (ULSEB 1989)
'Une entrevue pénible' (JMB 1983)

could be treated descriptively and what happened and what was said could simply be reported. To capture the reader's interest however, it would be better to adopt the dialogue form which is more immediate and dramatic.

A discussion essay which involves the consideration of two sides of an argument could also be tackled in this way. Indeed, well-known writers have often chosen the dialogue form to examine the pros and cons of an important problem and you will notice that when a conversation is set as an essay it usually involves people with clearly opposing points of view.

ESSENTIAL PRINCIPLES

If you read a well-written scene from a play or listen to a lively radio discussion or interview you should ask yourself what it is that makes the dialogue interesting. There are usually two main ingredients: characterisation and conflict. Try to produce a dialogue which is dramatic and realistic by giving your speakers contrasting characteristics: enthusiastic/cynical; experienced/naive; indignant/diplomatic; serious/teasing etc.

If you are able to 'get inside' the character of the person who is talking, imaginatively or by taking someone you know as a model, you will be better able to invent the material of the dialogue and make it sound convincing. It will also add interest to the 'for and against' of any discussion. The following essay title is one which shows very clearly the need to introduce and develop characterisation and conflict.

> Un jeune villageois rentre à la maison paternelle après avoir passé plusieurs mois en ville. Son père n'a jamais quitté le village et n'a aucune envie de le faire. Ecrivez le dialogue qui s'ensuit quand le fils essaie de convaincre son père qu'il devrait s'installer en ville.
>
> (JMB 1988)

There is the contrast of young and old, of experience and inexperience, of novelty and traditionalism, of enthusiasm and stubborness. Both parties should be made to put forward their own point of view. Contradicting and persuading each other and showing appropriate emotions.

If you are asked to write an interview try to make the situation as life-related as possible. Take the following essay title:

> Vous êtes journaliste et vous interviewez un vieil agriculteur qui va prendre sa retraite. Conservateur, très attaché aux valeurs traditionnelles il n'approuve pas les développements modernes qui transforment le monde rural.

As a journalist wishing to uncover the human interest of the old man's story you would plan the interview carefully. It would be necessary to prepare the ground before asking personal or searching questions. A 'real' interviewer would try to establish a rapport with the interviewee by making a certain amount of social conversation and would draw the interviewee out by making interested observations. If you were writing the dialogue you should try to create genuine interaction between the journalist and the 'agriculteur' and endeavour to make the latter speak and behave in character.

When you write dialogue you should aim to produce the patterns of natural, spoken French. It will help if you have a 'good ear' and if you have the opportunity to listen to French people talking normally in a variety of everyday situations. Many candidates have had that experience and are able to reproduce a conversational style. Unfortunately, they sometimes do it when it is not called for and in the kind of essay where only a more formal, written style is appropriate.

You should therefore distinguish between written and spoken French, limiting the use of the latter to the writing of dialogue and interviews. Even here it would be very unwise to go to extremes and overload your dialogue with slang expressions and ungrammatical French. You should aim at writing correct French but allow yourself those *expressions and constructions of everyday speech* which are appropriate to the situation you are given in the title. Keep the sentences *simple* (not simplistic but un-complex); allow some of the *hesitations and 'accidents'* of speech which occur in any conversation; make use of those *exclamations and questions* which suggest that the speakers are genuinely talking and responding to each other.

When you listen to French people talking try to note for your own use some of those expressions or formulae which come spontaneously at various points of a conversation. For example, expressions used:

i) to bring the discussion to *another subject*:
> Dites, Monsieur, que pensez-vous de ces gens qui . . . ?
> A propos, je voudrais vous poser une question sur . . .

  ii) to *interrupt* the other person:
    Ecoutez, moi je pense que . . .
    Oui, mais . . .
    D'accord, mais il faut . . .
    Exactement, c'est mon avis, je pense que . . .
  iii) to express your *point of view*:
    Pour moi, je trouve que . . .
    D'après moi . . .
    Je crois que . . .
  iv) to indicate *disagreement*:
    Non!
    Pas du tout
    Absolument pas
    Moi, je ne suis pas du tout d'accord
    Ce n'est pas vrai
    C'est faux/inexact
    C'est une blague
    Ce n'est pas sérieux
    Pas question
    Mais/quand même/tout de même
    Pas forcément
  v) to indicate *agreement*:
    Exactement
    Effectivement
    Bien entendu
    Sans aucun doute
    Je suis tout à fait de votre avis
  vi) to express your own *feelings*:
    C'est parfait
    C'est formidable
    C'est inadmissible
    C'est inacceptable
    C'est dégoûtant
    C'est incroyable

There are also many 'conversation tags' which do not mean anything in themselves but indicate that the speaker is *going to say something*:
  Eh bien, je pense que . . .
  Eh bien, voilà, passons maintenant à . . .
  Alors
  Enfin

or that he is *pausing to think*:
  Euh
  Alors
  et puis/ensuite/et en tout cas . . .

or that he has said something and is *expecting a response*:
  n'est-ce pas?
  tu ne crois pas?
  vous comprenez?
  hein?

Listen for such phrases, note when and where they are used and make use of them when you are writing your own dialogue.

FORMS OF QUESTIONING

How to formulate questions.

To write interviews or conversations successfully it is important to be as accurate in the use of vocabulary and grammatical structures as in any other type of essay. There is, however, one aspect of grammar which occurs more frequently in dialogue and particularly in interviews and that is the formulation of questions. Candidates are often uncertain about how to handle question forms, probably because in the language class they are called upon to answer questions far more often than to ask them.

However, if the language is to be used as a means of interactive communication (as in role-plays, interviews, conversations) it is obvious that it is important to know how to ask questions in correct French.

The questions which follow will help you to revise the main interrogative forms. The questions relate to the interview described in the second essay title shown on page 83. We shall concentrate on those question forms which students most frequently mis-handle.

1   Travaillez-vous tous les jours de la semaine? Cultivez-vous des céréales?
    The subject is a personal pronoun (vous, il, nous etc.). The question is formed by putting the personal pronoun after the verb (travaillez-vous). However, note that in speech two alternative question forms are frequently used:
    a) The order of words is as in a statement (as opposed to a question); *interrogation is indicated by intonation*. When you are writing down a question put in this way it is *essential* not to forget the question mark which is the only visual indication that you have written a question:
        Vous travaillez tous les jours de la semaine?
        Vous cultivez des céréales?
    b) The marker *Est-ce que* is used and again the order of words is as in a statement.
        Est-ce que vous travaillez tous les jours de la semaine?
        Est-ce que vous cultivez des céréales?

2   Vos enfants travaillent-ils à la ferme?
    The subject is a noun (vos enfants). It is not possible to invert subject and verb (Travaillent vos enfants à la ferme? is the type of error sometimes made by A-level candidates). In the correct version the noun is put in first position and it is 'repeated' by the personal pronoun which is placed after the verb.
    Note that the alternative forms (a) and (b) above, may also be used:
    Vos enfants travaillent à la ferme?
    Est-ce que vos enfants travaillent à la ferme?

3   Quand/pourquoi/comment allez-vous au marché?
    The sentence begins with an interrogative word (e.g. ou, quand, comment, pourquoi, quel = noun). The subject is a personal pronoun.
    Note that the alternative forms (a) and (b) may be used in speech. The question word in (a) is placed at the end of the sentence:
    a) Vous allez au marché quand?
        Vous êtes parti pourquoi?
    b) Quand est-ce que vous allez au marché?
        Pourquoi est-ce que vous êtes parti?

4   Où travaillent vos enfants?
    A quelle heure rentrent les vaches?
    The sentence begins with an interrogative word as in 3. The subject is a noun. The noun is placed after the verb or
    Où vos enfants travaillent-ils?
    A quelle heure les vaches rentrent-elles?
    The noun can be placed at the beginning of the sentence. It is then 'repeated' by the personal pronoun which comes after the verb.
    Again, the alternative forms (a) and (b) may be used:
    a) Vos enfants travaillent où?
        Les vaches rentrent à quelle heure?
    b) Où est-ce que vos enfants travaillent?
        A quelle heure est-ce que les vaches rentrent?

5   Pourquoi vos enfants travaillent-ils?
    Be careful when using *pourquoi*: it is a special case. When the subject is a noun, *pourquoi* is placed at the beginning of the sentence. It is *not* possible to invert subject and verb (e.g. ** Pourquoi travaillent vos enfants?). Instead, the subject (les enfants) is placed before the verb and is 'repeated' by the personal pronoun which comes after the verb.
    The alternatives (a) and (b) may be used:
    a) Vos enfants travaillent pourquoi?
    b) Pourquoi est-ce que vos enfants travaillent?

6 Où votre femme fabrique-t-elle le fromage? (fromage = the object of the verb)

Quand vos enfants partent-ils en vacances? (en vacances = closely linked complement of the verb).

The subject is a noun. The verb has an object or closely linked complement. The subject cannot be inverted (*Où fabrique votre femme le fromage?* is an error sometimes made by candidates). Instead, it is placed before the verb and is 'repeated' by the personal pronoun which comes after the verb.

The alternatives (a) and (b) may be used:

a) Votre femme fabrique le fromage où?

Vos enfants partent en vacances quand?

b) Où est-ce que votre femme fabrique le fromage?

Quand est-ce que vos enfants partent en vacances?

 The need for variety.

When you are forming questions it is always possible to use est-ce que if you are in doubt but when you are writing an interview or a conversation try to *vary* the way in which you frame the questions and make good use of those forms which are frequently used in speech.

ADVERBIAL PHRASES

When you build direct speech into a narrative you will often want to indicate the way in which the reply or the question is spoken in order to add interest to the situation. You may use an adverb:

— Non, reprit-elle *doucement*: quand on invite quelqu'un on lui offre à boire. (she said *softly*)

— Pas question! répondit-il *sèchement*, et il referma la porte. (he replied curtly)

but unwieldly forms in − *ment* are best avoided and it is often possible to use an adverbial phrase consisting of *d'une voix, d'un ton, sur un ton, d'un air* with an appropriate adjective:

dit-elle d'une voix calme (calmly)

répondit-elle d'un ton sévère (severely)

cria-t-il d'une voix un peu rauque (a little hoarsely)

reprit-il d'un ton moqueur (mockingly)

Sometimes the present participle may be used:

dit-il en la consolant (soothingly)

répondit-elle en pleurant (tearfully)

The formation of an adverbial phrase with 'avec' and a noun is another possibility:

répondit le capitaine avec courage (bravely)

cria-t-il avec indignation (indignantly)

Finally, an adjective can stand in for an adverb:

répondit Maigret, incrédule (disbelievingly)

cria le jeune homme, enchanté (delightedly)

dit Alain Robert, éperdu (bewilderedly)

EXAMINATION QUESTIONS

Q1

'Une entrevue pénible.'

(JMB 1983)

Q2

Deux jeunes gens se parlent au sujet de leur avenir. L'un d'eux a l'intention de continuer ses études, l'autre croit qu'il vaudrait mieux prendre n'importe quel emploi immédiatement. Imaginez la conversation.

(JMB 1981)

Q3

Vous êtes sur le point de partir au cinéma quand vous recevez une visite inattendue. Racontez la scène et vos réactions. (Cambridge 1981)

Q4

'Une dispute.' (ULSEB 1989)

Q5

Un jeune villageois rentre à la maison paternelle après avoir passé plusieurs mois en ville. Son père n'a jamais quitté le village et n'a aucune envie de la faire. Ecrivez le dialogue qui s'ensuit quand le fils essaie de convaincre son père qu'il devrait s'installer en ville.

(JMB 1988)

Q6

Le maire d'une commune bretonne est interviewé par un reporter. Vous êtes le reporter. Rédigez l'interview.

Q7

Vous avez garé votre voiture dans un emplacement réservé. Lorsque vous voulez repartir, vous constatez qu'une autre voiture gêne votre passage. Vous avez un rendez-vous important. En essayant de manoeuvrer vous accrochez l'aile de l'autre véhicule. A ce moment-là son propriétaire arrive. Ecrivez la conversation qui s'ensuit.

Q8

Conversation entre un hôtelier parisien et un touriste qui vient de passer une journée désagréable dans la capitale. (AEB 1987)

Q9

Vous avez invité plusieurs fois un(e) ami(e) à vous accompagner à un spectacle qu'on présente pour tracer l'histoire d'un vieux château de votre région — un spectacle *son et lumière*. Il (elle) a refusé, sous prétexte qu'une telle visite fort ennuyeuse. Agacé(e), vous lui téléphonez.

Vous ferez votre mieux pour le(la) persuader que vous avez raison, et pour (le)la convaincre que la visite ne serait pas une perte de temps. Ecrivez la conversation au téléphone (250 mots). Vous utiliserez les notes suivantes:

Votre ami(e): trop occupé(e)
aucun intérêt
autres préférences : discothèque, bars, cinéma
ennui

Vous-même: nouveauté — originalité
côté visuel — effets surprenants
historique — importance
aller seul(e)? De préférence — non
promesse — l'accompagner au cinéma — semaine prochaine

LA CASSINE
Son et lumière
DERNIÈRE REPRÉSENTATION
VENDREDI 31
Réservation
au 24.36.44.84

EXAMINATION QUESTION AND OUTLINE ANSWER

Eric Tabarly participe à la course transatlantique en solitaire à bord de son bateau Pen-Duick VI. Avant son départ de Plymouth à destination de Newport aux Etats-Unis, il est interviewé par un reporter du journal *Le Monde*. Vous écrivez l'interview. (300 mots)

A more formal interview of this nature would be structured by the questions put by the reporter. It is therefore necessary to work these out first in order to establish a plan to work to. The questions would have a logical order and progression and would be based on the areas that the newspapers' readers would be interested to know about: Is it difficult to sail single-handed across the Atlantic? What will conditions be like on board? Is Eric Tabarly going to win?

The main questions to be asked have been worked out for you and are given below. Try to complete the interview by writing up the answers using the notes which follow each question.

Reporter: Eric Tabarly, votre bateau a été conçu pour naviguer avec 6 hommes à bord. La course en solitaire ne vous pose-t-elle pas quelques problèmes?

Tabarly : Non — bonne forme physique
entraînement
beaucoup d'expérience

Reporter: Et le sommeil? Personne n'est là pour vous remplacer.

Tabarly : problème important
dormir par tranches de 3 heures
un réveil
si le vent forcit, cela me tire du sommeil

Reporter: De quoi vous nourrissez-vous à bord?

Tabarly : pâtes
riz
vin rouge

Reporter: Quelles seront les conditions météorologiques à ce moment de l'année?

Tabarly : favorables
tempêtes imprévisibles

Reporter: En combien de temps comptez-vous atteindre Newport?

Tabarly : 17/18 jours?

Reporter: Vous allez donc remporter la course?

Tabarly : confiance
bateau superbe, rapide

Reporter: Quel concurrent redoutez-vous le plus?

Tabarly : Jean-Yves Terlain,
ami, grand rival
catamaran très rapide
gagnant du Tour des Iles Britanniques

Reporter: Je vous remercie. Il ne me reste qu'à vous souhaiter bonne chance et bon voyage.

A TUTOR'S ANSWER TO QUESTION 5

— Tu sais, Papa, la vie en ville me plaît énormément. Je ne regrette pas du tout d'avoir quitté le village. Pourquoi ne viendrais-tu pas t'installer toi aussi en ville?

— Alors là, pas question. Imagine-toi que cela fait des années que je vis ici. C'est peut-être facile pour un jeune de s'adapter à un autre style de vie mais â mon âge je ne m'y vois pas.

— Mais pas du tout justement, tu te trompes. L'un des atouts de la ville c'est qu'elle offre diverses possibilités, peu importe ta profession ou ton âge. Il y a même toute une catégorie d'emplois qui ne se trouvent que dans une ville.

— Ecoute, je ne dis pas qu'il y ait pas plus d'emplois en ville mais comment veux-tu que je me fasse à la vie citadine? Moi, j'ai mes racines ici et je suis habitué à vivre tranquillement. Je ne pourrais jamais supporter le bruit, la foule, les embouteillages et la course contre la montre. Et ici, je connais la plupart des gens et presque tout le village me connaît.

— Mais justement, toi, tu t'entends bien avec tout le monde; tu pourras donc facilement te faire d'autres amis.

— Ah pardon, mais en ville ce n'est pas si facile de créer de nouveaux liens. Les gens sont moins cordiaux et ils sont parfois condescendants envers les villageois.

— Bon, d'accord j'admets qu'au début c'est un peu difficile mais qui te parle de sévrer tes liens? Avec un peu de persévérance tu verras que cela vaut le coup. En ville, les salaires sont plus élevés et tu trouveras tout ce que tu voudras pour te divertir: euh, cinéma, théâtre, sport, restaurants

— Admettons que tu aies raison sur certains points, n'oublies-tu pas une question essentielle: celle du logement? Pour toi, c'est simple, tu partages un studio avec un copain mais figure-toi qu'une maison en ville coûte beaucoup plus que dans un village. J'y perdrai au change, j'en suis sûr. Et tu sais, avec la voiture, je peux jouir des avantages qu'offre la ville sans souffrir des inconvénients.

— Papa, tu es formidable! Nous en reparlerons.

A STUDENT'S ANSWER TO QUESTION 9 WITH EXAMINER'S COMMENTS

François:	Paris vingt-deux, quatre-vingts, soixante-quatorze. Allo!
Moi:	Allo, François?
François:	Oui, c'est qui?
Moi:	Joanne, comment ça va?
François:	Bien merci, et toi?
Moi:	Assez bien, mais je ne suit pas contente aujourd'hui. J'ai besoin d'un ami pour m'accompagner au spectacle son et lumière.
François:	Ecoute, je suis désolé, Joanne, mais je n'en ai pas le temps et vendredi, tu sais, j'ai quelque chose d'importance à faire.
Moi:	C'est plus important que moi?
François:	Ah, non chérie, pas du tout. Mais, euh, l'histoire ne m'intéresse pas.
Moi:	Pourquoi pas? L'histoire du château est très intéressante.
François:	Mais non, Joanne. Tout ça ne m'intéresse pas. J'aime les discothèques et aussi le cinéma. Les spectacles son et lumière, c'est pour les touristes et les vieux.
Moi:	Mais les effets sonores seront très originaux. C'est plus intéressant qu'une discothèque. Peut-être il y aura un bar. Je suis certain que tu aimeras tout cela.
François:	Absolument pas. C'est ennuyeux.
Moi:	Pas avec moi!
François:	Mais j'ai déjà autre chose à faire.
Moi:	Pour moi, François. Je ne veux pas y aller toute seule et c'est la dernière représentation. Je suis certaine que si tu y ailles avec moi, tu ne seras pas ennuyé.
François:	Peut-être que tu as raison.
Moi:	Si je te promettes de t'accompagner au cinéma la semaine prochaine pour regarder le nouveau film, tu m'accompagnes le vendredi?
François:	Je ne sais pas, Joanne.
Moi:	Je suis amoureuse de toi, François.
François:	Tu m'as convaincu. Mais . . .
Moi:	Je te promets qu'il ne sera pas une perte de temps. N'aie pas peur! Merci beaucoup, le spectacle sera plus amusant avec toi.
François:	Mais . . .
Moi:	Maintenant tu pourras passer deux soirs avec moi.
François:	Oui.

Good.

Quelque chose d'important.

Good.

Good.

Peut-être qu'il y aura.

Not subjunctive after "si"; "si tu y allais tu ne serais pas ennuyé".

Si je promets.

Voir.

Ce.

Soirées.

Moi: Tu as de la chance, n'est-ce pas?
François: Oui.
Moi: Chéri, je dois partir maintenant, tu m'as mis en
            retard. A vendredi, n'est-ce pas?
François: A vendredi. Au revoir.

> "Mise; past participle agrees with preceeding direct object (ni)."

Examiner's comment

A convincing reproduction of spoken French with a high standard of accuracy in the use of grammar and vocabulary. The conversation is a genuine exchange in which the two speakers disagree, argue and reach a conclusion with a good deal of realism. A very good answer.

CHAPTER 10

TRANSLATION INTO FRENCH

GETTING STARTED

A-level French syllabuses have recently been revised and as a result translation into French has been substantially changed in nature or even excluded by certain of the Boards. If your Examination Board has kept translation into French as a test it will be either

a) What can be called the more traditional prose, a translation into French of a passage of English of about 240 words (O&C, NISEC, ULSEB Syllabus B, O&C Special Paper, ULSEB Special Paper)

or

b) What is sometimes called a 'mini-prose'. This is translation into French of a shorter passage (between 80 and 100 words) which may be related to a stimulus passage in French

(JMB, ULSEB Syllabus A)

You should read the syllabus to know exactly what you should be preparing for and find out whether there is a prose or mini-prose, how long the English passage is, whether there is a choice of passage and whether the translation into English is compulsory or optional.

PROSE TRANSLATION

LITERARY AND NON-LITERARY LANGUAGE

AVOIDANCE OF ELEMENTARY ERRORS

CRITERIA FOR ASSESSMENT

READING THE PASSAGE

TRANSLATING THE PASSAGE

PROSE AND OTHER LANGUAGE WORK

CHECKING YOUR WORK

THE MINI-PROSE

ESSENTIAL PRINCIPLES

PROSE TRANSLATION

How well you translate prose will depend largely on how much work you have put into your vocabulary-building, language exercises and reading in French. It is a skill which you may not be asked to practise extensively at the beginning of your language course as many teachers feel quite rightly that translation into French is an advanced skill which is best delayed until the student has an adequate command of structure and vocabulary.

Most teachers would agree that while prose is a good test of your *knowledge* of French, it is not necessarily the best means of learning *more* French. You should be prepared therefore to concentrate on other language work first as a preparation for the prose, particularly as you will not have practised this type of exercise at GCSE. You will need to start as soon as possible on building up a good working vocabulary and on improving the quality of your written French through other language exercises.

However, it is important to understand from the beginning what to expect when it comes to the examination so that you can organise your work efficiently. If you read through the selection of past questions later in the chapter you will soon realise that the passages are of different types. In question 3 there is an example of a passage which the syllabus regulations would term as 'non-literary'. In such a passage the subject matter is likely to relate to current affairs and to social, economic, political and cultural aspects of modern life — the kind of writing that you would find in newspaper articles, periodicals and non-fictional books which comment on, report and analyse topics of contemporary interest.

The passages in questions 4 and 5 could be called '*literary*' and contain the kind of writing to be found in a modern novel, short story or similar work of fiction.

LITERARY AND NON-LITERARY LANGUAGE

It would be wrong to exaggerate the differences between literary and non-literary French or English and misguided not to include material of both types in your reading programme. However, if you can be sure that the passage that you will be set will be of one type rather than another then it is clearly in your interest to direct your reading and vocabulary-building towards the area which is most relevant.

Your course-book will probably contain appropriate passages but you will need to supplement them from your own reading. When you are working out your reading programme for the course, it is therefore important to know what your needs are going to be as far as the prose is concerned and to make sure that you are laying down the right foundations.

The difficulties involved in doing prose translation should not be minimised: at an advanced level it is certainly a sophisticated exercise which demands a good knowledge of many elements of both languages. It is a test of grammatical accuracy and of precise knowledge of vocabulary. It is likely to force you to use a range of structures and terms which on other occasions (e.g. in conversation, writing free composition, etc.) you could choose to avoid if you were uncertain about how to use them correctly. There is a great deal to be kept in mind when you are tackling this exercise, particularly in the examination. It is true to say that many candidates do not always discipline themselves to be sufficiently alert to avoid errors which they do not usually make when there is less pressure, when the difficulties are less concentrated and when there is more time for thought.

> ❝ Self-discipline avoids errors. ❞

AVOIDANCE OF ELEMENTARY ERRORS

It is because they are aware of the difficulty of this test and perhaps because their first attempts at translation have been returned liberally covered in red ink that candidates are apprehensive about this part of the examination. The fact that they are facing a test which seems to be designed to find out what they do not know, that they are likely to make mistakes and that these mistakes are all going to lose them marks, understandably undermines their confidence. If you find yourself in this position it is important to understand the problem of errors and get the facts into perspective. Above all, always remind yourself that the errors which lead to a poor result are mainly elementary errors. Candidates do not fail the prose because they have not grasped the finer points of the language or cannot understand 'difficult' grammatical rules. They do badly because they make too many basic errors and because they are inaccurate in using structures and forms which they understand perfectly well, which they probably once knew but have since half-forgotten through lack of practice and revision.

The first step therefore in preparing for the prose translation is to ensure that your working knowledge of basic structures and forms is sound. You cannot afford to neglect what is elementary simply because 'we did that in the second year'.

If, when you begin to practise prose translation, your preparatory language work has been sound, you will make few errors and you will be able to handle most structures instinctively. However, it would be unrealistic to assume that you will not make mistakes and it will not be advisable to rely purely on instinct. Think carefully about your work *before* you hand it in for marking and make a point of doing something constructive about errors when you go over work that has been returned. *Classify* the errors that you seem prone to make so that you know exactly what kind of remedial action you need to take. *Check* subsequent proses to see whether this action has had any effect. If you have made no progress then get the advice of your teacher. If you organise yourself in this way it will give you more incentive to look through a translation carefully before handing it in.

Priority points

You will need to train yourself in this critical approach to your prose work. It is useful to finish the work well before the time when you are required to hand it in so that you have the opportunity to put it aside and then review it a day or two later as objectively and critically as the teacher or examiner who is going to mark it.

Find out what needs your attention.

Establish a list of priority points (e.g. forms of irregular verbs, genders, prepositions following a verb etc.) which need attention before the day of the examination. Even if you do not have enough time to work through all the items on your revision list, what you do manage to get through could very easily make the difference between a pass or a fail, a good performance and one which is merely satisfactory.

CRITERIA FOR ASSESSMENT

The translation may be marked according to a *deductive* system (e.g. a pool of marks is allotted to the passage; deductions are made for each error; the total number of penalty points is then converted to a positive mark) or a *positive* system (the passage is divided into a number of 'boxes' containing two or three words; a mark is awarded for every box which is completely right) but either system underlines the need for accuracy on the part of the candidate.

a) You must train yourself to *use vocabulary accurately*. This means that the word should be spelt correctly; it should be the right word for the sentence or group of words of which it is part and it should convey the meaning of the English as precisely as possible.
b) You must learn to *be accurate grammatically*. The words of the sentence should be fitted together correctly and in the right form and order.

The lesson is to be precise and to give attention to detail because your work will be marked in exactly the same way.

When marking the prose the examiner will distinguish between serious and less serious types of error.

Serious errors

The more serious errors include:

1   Incorrect grammatical forms. For example, the wrong form or ending of a verb, the wrong form of an adjective or of a demonstrative pronoun, the wrong plural form of a noun. In other words you would be making a serious error if you did not know that the verb *vouloir* had the forms *il voudrait, ils veulent,* that the plural of the noun *le travail* is *les travaux,* that the feminine form of the adjective *nouveau* was *nouvelle* and that the demonstrative pronoun *celui-ci* had the forms *ceux-ci* and *celle-ci* etc.
2   Failure to observe basic grammatical rules, relating for example, to the agreement of adjective and noun or of noun and pronoun, the use of the definite and indefinite article and of the partitive (du, de la, des etc.), and the choice of prepositions or conjunctions, the basic use of tenses.
3   Vocabulary errors where the term chosen conveys a completely wrong meaning; wrong genders; words which contain more than one spelling mistake.
4   Words which are omitted because of an oversight or are left out deliberately.

Less serious errors

The less serious errors would include:

1   A choice of vocabulary which is approximately correct in meaning.
2   Use of language which is not grammatically incorrect but which is clumsy and not genuinely French.
3   A word which contains no more than a single spelling mistake.

It is important to bear these principles in mind when you are going through corrected proses and analysing your own mistakes. It will help you to get your priorities right when you draw up a list of revision or remedial points.

It may seem rather alarming to you that in the prose translation every word you write seems to be under scrutiny. You can reassure yourself for two reasons. Firstly, the passage will not be littered with pitfalls designed to catch you out and secondly, examiners will accept more than one version (in some cases quite a number of versions) of any phrase or sentence, provided that it is grammatically correct. There is never just one right 'answer' which the examinee is expected to find and it is likely that some credit will be given for a near-miss. When the following section, taken from a recent examination prose, was marked, a number of different 'correct' versions would have been allowed and credit would have been given for reasonable approximations.

> When Helen realised that she was walking over the Colonel's land she felt uneasy. Perhaps she should go back, she said to herself.

In addition to any other acceptable translation which the candidates may have thought of, the examiners would have allowed:

> Lorsque/quand Hélène/Helen s'aperçut/se rendit compte qu'elle marchait sur les terres/le domaine/la propriété du Colonel elle se sentit inquiète/mal à l'aise/gênée/elle éprouva/sentit/ressentit de l'inquiétude/de l'appréhension. Peut-être devrait-elle rebrousser chemin/retourner sur ses pas, se dit-elle.

Some credit would also have been given for:

> Lorsque Hélène comprit qu'elle traversait les champs du Colonel elle se sentit anxieuse.

Note that the terms underlined are not accurate enough to be entirely acceptable.

A SYSTEMATIC APPROACH

You will practise prose translation as part of your course-work, probably as regularly as once a week. It is best to tackle this exercise only when a good deal of preparatory work has been successfully covered as it is perhaps most useful as a means of practising, testing and refining what you have already learnt. It is not the most efficient way of learning new vocabulary or new structures.

If you find that you are continually looking up words in the dictionary and that putting sentences together is a struggle which leaves you searching through the grammar-book, then you will clearly not have done enough preparatory work to enable you to cope realistically with prose translation. If this is the case then you would do well to follow the advice given in the final section of this chapter. You will also be using what many teachers call the 'look-up-bang-down-and-forget' method of language learning. Ideally you should be able to feel that the exercise enables you to reactivate and manipulate language which you have already practised and absorbed.

> "Look up — bang down — forget."

READING THE PASSAGE

Before you begin to translate into French it is essential to read the whole of the passage. If you are sure about the information in the original and the order in which it is presented you are less likely to make mistakes in the French. The line-by-line approach adopted by many candidates can easily lead them into error as the grammar of any sentence may well be partly determined by what has gone before and by what comes after. For example, in any passage in which there is a sequence of events it is important to have that sequence clear in your mind if you hope to use tenses correctly.

Understanding the sense of the whole passage will also determine the correct use of the article and partitive. If there are people involved then it is obviously necessary to know and to keep in mind the fact they they are male, female, or plural as, throughout the passage,

> "He/she/it/they?"

this will govern grammatical points such as agreement of adjective and noun, of subject and verb and of noun and pronoun (all frequent sources of error).

Having the facts of the passage clear in your mind will ensure that you do not translate *it* (it could be *il, elle,* or *ce*), *they* (it could be *ils* or *elles*), *that of* (*celui de, celle de*), etc. without realising which nouns these pronouns relate to.

Reading the passage will make situations and context clear, which is important if you are to make the appropriate choice of vocabulary. For example, the situation may require *apercevoir* rather than *voir, se retourner* and not *tourner, amener* rather than *emmener, la rue* and not *la route, la chaussée* and not *la route*. It pays dividends therefore to read original carefully. This means not just reading the words but 'reading into' the passage so that you can picture what events take place and so that, in a discursive passage, you can grasp the points and developments of an argument or discussion.

TRANSLATING THE PASSAGE

RECASTING

The prose tests the candidate's ability to render precisely and correctly a passage of English into French. The important word is 'precisely'; it is not sufficient to convey the gist of the English passage. It is here that you should be particularly careful in the way you heed the often repeated warning that the translation should not be too literal. The advice is, of course, sound and elementary but some candidates, presumably because they are anxious to demonstrate that they are following it, will recast or even add to the original in order to produce what they sometimes mistakenly consider to be a version which is 'more French'. It is true that recasting a sentence is sometimes permissible or even necessary to produce better, more natural French and meaning may be rendered by transposing structures (e.g. by rendering a verbal construction by a noun construction in French).

The following translations show that a degree of recasting can result in good French which conveys the meaning of the original with sufficient precision:

- ■ As she walked out of the room she took a key from her pocket.
- — Comme elle sortait de la pièce elle prit une clef dans sa poche. *Or:* En sortant de la pièce elle prit une clef dans sa poche.
- ■ As soon as he returned to the village he telephoned his mother.
- — Dès qu'il fut retourné au village il téléphona à sa mère. *Or:* Dès son retour au village il téléphona à sa mère.

You should, however, be careful about radical recasting, changing word order or the order of phrases and subordinate clauses, unless you are certain that there is a need for it and that it is the most effective way of rendering the meaning of the English. For example:

- ■ Helen walked rapidly down the steps carrying a large jug of water in front of her.

This sentence can be adequately translated without any recasting.

- — Helen descendit rapidement les marches, portant devant elle une grande cruche d'eau.

Unnecessay changes might distort the meaning of the original:

- — Rapidement, portant devant elle une grande cruche d'eau, Helen descendit les marches.

Rapidement is given an emphasis which 'quickly' does not have in the English sentence and therefore the sense is slightly changed. The candidate who goes in for wholesale recasting not only runs the risk of distorting the meaning of the English, but often overlooks some element in the sentence and leaves it untranslated.

You are asked for a precise translation, not a loose one, and a loose translation can also result when candidates attempt to make what they have written 'sound more French' by adding words unnecessarily. In a recent examination candidates added 'très', 'bien' and 'petit' where they were not needed, presumably because they thought that the French used these words a lot and that they were adding a touch of authenticity:

- ■ Elle avait (bien) peur d'habiter toute seule.
- ■ Il commanda une (petite) tasse de café au comptoir.
- ■ Votre fille est (très) jolie.

In fact they lost marks because they had *added* to the meaning of the English.

Paraphrase

Another cause of loose translation is paraphrase. Candidates often resort to it when they do not know the French for a word in English. It must be said that a neat paraphrase which conveys the meaning of the original and fits correctly into the sentence is very often acceptable and some (if not all) credit will be given for it.

Past candidates who did not know a closer translation of 'rocky', 'overcast' and 'middle-aged', successfully offered *un chemin couvert de cailloux* for *un chemin rocailleux*, *un ciel couvert de nuages* for *un ciel bouché* and *un homme ni jeune ni vieux* for *un homme d'un certain âge*.

However, it is advisable to avoid a lengthy paraphrase or definition to replace a single word for which you do not know the French. When this happens the candidate writes an extra number of words which often leads to further errors and frequently misconstructs the whole sentence in the attempt to fit in the paraphrase. If you are forced to fall back on a paraphrase it is as well to be brief. You should also be particularly careful with the grammar of the sentence in which it occurs.

> 66 Keep it brief. 99

PROSE AND OTHER LANGUAGE WORK

When you practise prose as part of your course-work it is important to relate what you are doing to the rest of your language work. Use your own vocabulary notebook as far as you can. If, for the purpose of vocabulary-building, you have studied texts in which the subject-matter is similar to that in the text you are going to translate, then reread those texts and try to reactivate language which you have already learnt. Cultivate the habit of retrieving words from your memory and of thinking of words in context.

Dictionaries

You will, of course, use a dictionary to look up words that you have not met before. It is essential to use a dictionary which is adequate for your needs. It is advisable to use a French − French dictionary (such as *Larousse Dictionnaire du Francais contemporain* or *Le Petit Robert*) in addition to an English-French dictionary (such as *The Collins Robert* or *Harrap's New Standard French and English dictionary*).

In this way you will have access to a greater number of example sentences containing the French word that you are seeking and you will give yourself further guidance as to whether the word is appropriate in the context in which you wish to use it, and useful illustrations of the way in which it fits grammatically into a sentence. When you look up a word, read the entire section in the dictionary if you can until, by comparing examples and taking note of the indications given, you have an understanding of the register of the word (is it familiar or formal, etc.?), its meaning and the contexts in which it can be used.

The small pocket dictionary is not suitable for this work. It is probably the use of such a dictionary combined with an attempt to translate the English word for word which leads to such errors as Le *bal* commença à *évier* (for 'the football began to sink') and Dans le vestibule il y avait une odeur de *polonais* (for 'in the hall there was a smell of polish').

CHECKING YOUR WORK

Nowhere is the advice 'check your work before handing it in' more applicable than to the prose. Ideally you should be able to produce French with spontaneous accuracy but experience shows that candidates must subject their work to thorough, reflective checking.

Careful checking, which implies much more than simply reading the work through, requires practice which should begin as soon as you start to do prose translations for your course-work. Most students are able to correct an error once it has been pointed out to them. The difficulty is spotting the error in the first place. When the translation is neatly written out it is easy to persuade yourself that there is nothing wrong with it. Clearly it will help if you use a method of reviewing your work which makes you read critically.

Look for specific types of error (those which experience tells you that you are prone to make): agreement of adjectives, verb endings, genders, prepositions following a verb.

Make sure that concentrating on an obvious difficulty in a given sentence has not led you to overlook less obvious problems. Analysis of candidates' scripts shows that this frequently happens. The candidate spots the difficult point (e.g. the need to use the subjunctive or a past anterior), deals with it successfully and then goes on to make elementary errors in the rest of the sentence. You should check very carefully the whole of the sentence in which you have identified a 'trouble-spot'.

Your final reading should be made in order to check that you have considered every word in the original passage. Careless omissions occur too frequently, particularly under examination conditions, and marks are lost needlessly. Check first to ensure that no sentence has been omitted (it can easily happen when the French version makes perfectly good sense without the missing sentence), and secondly to make sure that no single word has been overlooked. There are certain English sentences which seem to lead very frequently to omissions: they are those which contain many apparently insignificant words. In a recent examination, this sentence gave rise to frequent omissions;

- They both suddenly remembered that the new manager often stayed very late in the office on a Friday.

Candidates lost marks because they simply overlooked words (such as 'both', 'new', 'often', 'very') which they would have had no difficulty in translating.

THE MINI-PROSE

Everything that has been said about prose translation applies to the mini-prose. If you practised prose translation and became quite good at it you would find little difficulty in coping with the mini-prose which is shorter and less demanding. It is really an intermediate step between the kind of work that you did for GCSE and the more traditional type of translation into French. However, there are points to be understood which relate specifically to the mini-prose and not to prose translation in general.

The Stimulus Passage

The mini-prose set by two major Boards (JMB and ULSEB Syllabus A) is always connected with a stimulus passage. Look at the example on page 100. The French text provides help with the translation in the following ways:

- It helps you get your mind working in French before you start translating into French. It is therefore important to read the stimulus passage slowly and thoroughly before you begin on the mini-prose.
- It will provide you with some of the vocabulary that you will need for the translation either directly or by presenting you with other terms which will jog your memory and help you to recall vocabulary which is not in the passage itself. As it makes it less likely that you will have to struggle with vocabulary it frees you to spend more time on getting the structures right in your translation.

It is important to use this help properly. Therefore:

- Spend time on reading and understanding the French text so that you do not borrow the wrong term.
- Usually the equivalent of the more difficult words in the English text will be found in the French passage but do not assume that it contains *all* the words that you do not know and do not spend unnecessary time searching for words and guessing their meaning.
- When the French text contains a word or phrase that you can re-use it will often need some grammatical adaptation before you use it in your mini-prose. For example, you have to change a noun from singular to plural and change the form; an adjective may need a different agreement; a verb may need to be used in a different tense or be given a different ending. Be careful to make these changes: students, when given vocabulary to use, have a tendency simply to re-use it in the form in which it is given.
- There is usually more than one answer when you are translating. If you have used a term of your own which is satisfactory it will get full credit. You are not penalised for 'missing' a term given in the French passage.
- When you have finished the translation always read it, *and* the stimulus passage through once more.

EXAMINATION QUESTIONS

Read through these passages in order to give yourself practice in grasping fully the ideas or situation and in anticipating the problems discussed in the previous section of the chapter.

Q1

As a housewife walks past the shop windows in the High Street, a hundred and one different goods compete for the limited amount of money in her purse. Should she buy beef or chicken for the Sunday dinner? She compares the prices and asks herself whether the pleasure her family will obtain from them will be worth their cost.

But it is not only the housewife who has to economise. The businessman faces the same problems in running his factory. Should he produce this article or that, or some of both? How many of each? Should he employ extra labourers or would it be better to install a machine to do the work? Would it be more profitable to hire transport or buy his own lorry? And so on.

Open the newspaper any morning, and it soon becomes obvious how the government is also forced to choose as it plans the broad lines upon which the economy shall develop. More houses, new roads and better hospitals − all are competing for the materials and capital used by the building industry. Extra playing fields, new factory sites, and farmland − all are claiming a share of the limited land available. In these and many other instances, the government has the task of making the most of the nation's resources.

(O&C Specimen Paper 1988)

Q2

A day or two later, Treece took his test again on his motor-bike. It was the same examiner and Treece felt that a sort of friendship was growing between them; it was as if both of them realised that they would be busy doing this little task for a long time. It was an icy day and Treece's ears were cold. 'I feel nervous again,' he stammered. 'Don't worry,' the examiner reassured him, 'I'm not going to kill you, you know.' They went out into the road. 'Go up this little hill and come back down; then I'll cross the street in front of you and you will have to stop as quickly as you can, as if I was an ordinary pedestrian.'

Treece went to the top of the hill and turned around. Suddenly, from behind a car, a figure appeared. Treece braked, nothing happened, and he ran into him. Papers and a hat flew into the air. Treece suddenly saw with horror that the examiner was lying on the ground. The poor victim's suit was dirty, but otherwise he was alright. He told Treece to continue his test. Afterwards, when it was all over, Treece asked with some embarrassment: 'Did I pass?'

The examiner burst out laughing: 'He knocks me over, and then he wants to know if he's passed!' Treece was becoming almost a friend. 'Let me know how much it costs to have your suit cleaned. See you again soon,' Treece shouted to him. 'Unless I see you first!' replied the courageous official. (NISEC Specimen Paper)

Q3

In the spring of 1981, when the Left won control of the government of France for the first time in twenty-three years, it was thought that the hopes of May 1968 would finally be realised, through what was called Mitterrand's 'gentle revolution'. The student revolt that had eventually spread throughout the entire French nation during that spring filled with hope had failed to produce authentic social change. When the French people asked to choose a new government, it had elected a solid Gaullist majority that would, at best, produce only modest reforms with the aim of satisfying the demands of both students and workers.

But May 1981 was to be different. The parties of the Left would seek to carry out the reforms which it had already established in its Common Programme in 1972. The Mitterrand government began its programme with the nationalisation of important sectors of the economy. In this way it sought to increase government control in those domains. However, this action forced the government to introduce new austerity measures in 1983 and 1984, in the hope of slowing down inflation in France.

It was clear in 1984 that the President's austerity plans were worrying some of the more radical members of his own party, such as Edmond Maire, who declared himself to be particularly concerned about the high level of unemployment. However, it seemed obvious at that time that Mitterrand would continue as President until the election in 1988.

(ULSEB Syllabus B, 1986, from Contemporary French Civilisation, Vol viii, Nos. 1 and 2)

Q4

After leaving the narrow lane we found ourselves in an orchard not far from the cottage. I could make out its white walls beyond the trees. Despite his air of authority, I was glad that Jacques had offered to come with me as it was getting dark and without him I could easily have lost my way. We stopped for three or four minutes. Nothing was to be heard but the distant cry of an owl in the wood below the farm. If Durand had left, he ought to be somewhere in that wood, for the road passed through it.

We went on waiting. The darkness and the silence weighed heavily on me and I began to feel that we were being watched. Suddenly I heard a noise and turned round in terror. 'It's nothing,' whispered Jacques, drawing closer to me. 'An apple must have fallen. Shall we go on?'

'Wait a bit,' I said coldly.

I looked towards the wood. Almost immediately I saw someone emerging from the trees. It was Durand marching quickly along the road. He had taken a long time to get through the wood, but it must be him. I waited until he had disappeared.

'All right. Let's go.'

'Don't be afraid of the dogs, they won't hurt you. They know me.'

I nodded but said nothing, and we began to make our way towards the cottage.

Q5

Charles got out of the car and opened the door for Nicole. A policeman was standing at the entrance to the block of flats, talking to the caretaker, and as they approached he turned towards them.

'You can't go in there, sir,' he said.

At once Nicole explained who she was and introduced Charles. The policeman stared at her for a moment, obviously surprised.

'Lefranc? the daughter of General Lefranc?'

The girl nodded and he asked to see her identity card. She got it out of her bag and handed it to him. After examining it carefully he looked once again at Nicole. Then, although he did not seem entirely convinced, he let them pass.

'I'll come with you,' the caretaker said suddenly. 'I'll bring the key of the flat.'

'Just give it to me. There's no need for you to come up.' Nicole replied.

'It's my job, Miss Lefranc. I'm responsible for everything in there.'

'I'm his daughter,' Nicole insisted angrily.

When, finally, they had succeeded in obtaining the key, Charles and Nicole went up the stairs to the first floor. Once inside the flat they began to go through all the cupboards and drawers, but found nothing interesting. In one corner of the sitting-room was a large desk.

'It's locked, unfortunately,' said Charles in a disappointed tone.

Nicole smiled.

'It doesn't matter. I know how to open it.'

Q6

The Gare d'Orsay, the abandoned railway station on the Left Bank of the Seine opposite the Louvre, has been reborn as a museum devoted to all the arts of the nineteenth century. The new Musée d'Orsay, inaugurated today by President Mitterrand will be open to the public from 9th December.

Last week a huge bronze elephant and rhinoceros were carefully placed outside the entrance amid an indifferent crowd of demonstrating students. Facing them are six statues representing the six continents. They once belonged to the Trocadéro Palace, which disappeared a long time ago, and were found by accident far away in Nantes.

The station itself with its elegant stone facade is a symbol of the Belle Epoque whose finest artistic products are now settled in it. Built in only two years by Victor Laloux for the Paris-Orléans railway, the station is a work of the Paris 'Iron Age' like the Eiffel Tower and the Grand Palais.

The station was due for demolition in 1953 and saved by the late Jacques Duhamel, then Culture Minister. It was used for despatching prisoner-of-war parcels and was also a centre for people returning after liberation. Orson Welles, attracted by its vast space, used it to make a film of Kafka's Trial, and Jean Louis Barrault presented plays there.

The decision to convert the station into a museum was made by Valéry Giscard d'Estaing in 1977. He was invited to the ceremony by President Mitterrand who confirmed the project and threw out Socialist suggestions to drop it. It is, therefore, a symbol of France's coherent museum policy which has continued through three presidencies of different political colour.

Q7 (Mini-prose)

Les paysages des Basses-Alpes sont toujours beaux, mais souvent austères. La route étroite suivait le fond d'un vallon, entre deux chaînes de montagnes, et, comme un autre vallon traversait le nôtre, Bébert freina brusquement, et nous montra sur notre gauche, au fond de ce vallon, une haute colline en tronc de pyramide dont le sommet semblait couronné de ruines et d'arbres.

   — C'est sûrement ça que nous cherchons, dit-il.

Il s'engagea dans une sorte de chemin de bûcherons.

Nous arrivâmes au pied de la colline. Il fallut abandonner les voitures: le chemin muletier n'était plus assez large, et il montait en lacets dont les virages étaient dangereusement serrés.

Nous commençâmes l'ascension de ce tortueux raidillon: en levant la tête, on voyait un spectacle tragique. Le sommet vers lequel nous montions était couronné des derniers pans de murs de maisons effondrées.

Nous débouchâmes sur la place du village. Elle était entourée de maisons aux facades crevassées: le porche de l'église s'était abattu dans l'herbe, derrière un gros figuier dont une branche avait traversé un vitrail. Il restait cependant une rue étroite jonchée de tuiles brisées et bordée de maisons, dont certaines étaient inexplicablement assez bien conservées, si ce n'est que leurs fenêtres n'avaient plus de volets ni de vitres. On avait aussi emporté presque toutes les portes. Dans une cuisine, sur une table vermoulue, il y avait un soulier de paysan, dur comme du bronze, et sur l'évier, les débris verdâtres d'une cruche cassée. Des hommes et des femmes avaient vécu là; ils avaient dansé sur la place du village, ils s'étaient aimés, ils avaient eu des enfants, puis, un jour, ils étaient partis, les uns après les autres, vers les villes que les jeunes avaient découvertes en faisant leur service militaire, ou vers le cimetière du village, et tout ce qui restait de leur dur labeur c'était ces ruines pathétiques, ce cruel témoignage de l'émouvante faiblesse de l'homme qui passe comme une ombre rapide sur cette terre minérale, nourrisseuse obstinée de l'herbe éternelle.

Traduisez en français le texte qui suit, en utilisant le text ci-dessus pour vous aider. Vous pouvez vous servir ou bien du passé composé ou bien du passé simple.

After leaving the car at the bottom of the hill, we had to turn along a narrow path which led up to the ruins. On reaching the top, we found that the former inhabitants must have removed everything useful. In one of the woodcutters' houses, for example, there were only the remnants of an old sink scattered everywhere. There was hardly any trace of those country folk who, one by one, had left to find work elsewhere.

(JMB 1988)

OUTLINE ANSWERS TO QUESTIONS 1, 2 AND 5

The following translations have been prepared as an examiner would prepare them with, whenever possible, alternative versions for each section. This will help you to self-correct your work when you attempt the translation yourself. Use the alternatives that you did not think of to extend your knowledge of structures and vocabulary.

Question 1

	une/la ménagère		les vitrines
Quand	la maîtresse de maison	passe devant	les devantures
	la mère de famille		les étalages

	mille et un		
de la Grande Rue	mille	d'articles	
	je ne sais combien	d'objets	différents
		de produits	

se disputent	la somme	d'argent limité	
se font concurrence pour		le contenu limité	qui se trouve dans
		le peu d'argent	que contient

son porte-monnaie sa bourse	Doit-elle acheter Achetera-t-elle Choisira-t-elle Prendra-t-elle	du boeuf ou du poulet

pour le déjeuner repas	de dimanche? dominical?	Elle compare les prix et se demande

si le plaisir que sa famille	en retirera ressentira	justifiera mérite une telle dépense	la dépense le coût

Mais	la ménagère n'est pas la seule il n'y a pas que la ménagère ce n'est pas seulement la ménagère	qui	se trouve dans l'obligation de soit obligée de soit contrainte de doive

faire des économies. économiser être économe.	l'homme d'affaires

se trouve devant les mêmes problèmes
fait fâce à des problèmes identiques

quand il	dirige gère	son usine. son entreprise.	Doit-il Faut-il	fabriquer sortir

cet article-ci ou les deux? Combien de chaque sorte?

Doit-il	faire appel à employer recruter	des	travailleurs ouvriers employés	supplémentaires de plus

ou vaudrait-il mieux serait-il préférable	d'installer une machine pour faire le travail?

Serait-il plus	profitable avantageux rentable

de louer le transport ou d'acheter son

propre camion? Et ainsi de suite.

Ouvrez le journal Il suffit d'ouvrir le journal	un matin n'importe quel matin et

il est bientôt	évident clair manifeste	que le gouvernement aussi	est obligé est forcé se voit dans l'obligation

de choisir de faire des choix	quand	il établit les décide des élabore les	grandes lignes sur lesquelles

l'économie	se développera. va se développer. sera fondée.	Plus de	maisons logements

de nouvelles routes

et de meilleurs hôpitaux — tous sont	en compétition rivalisent	pour les matériaux

et	le capital utilisé les capitaux utilisés	par l'industrie du bâtiment. Terrains de sport

supplémentaires,   emplacements

terrains à bâtir pour de nouvelles usines, terres agricoles

	demandent	leur part	du peu de
tous	réclament	leur partie	de la quantité limitée de
	revendiquent		

terres disponibles.
superficie disponible.   Dans ces cas-là et dans bien d'autres,

le gouvernement   a pour tâche   de tirer le meilleur parti possible des
                a le devoir   d'utiliser au mieux les

ressources   nationales
             de la nation

Question 2

Un ou deux jours
Quelques jours   plus tard, Treece

se représenta aux épreuves du permis de conduire une moto.
passa de nouveau son permis sur sa motocyclette.
repassa son permis-moto.
repassa son examen pour le permis-moto.

                                   sentit
C'était le même examinateur et Treece   eut l'impression
                                   avait l'impression

	certaine amitié		s'établir	
qu'une	sorte d'amitié	était en train de	grandir	entre eux.
	espèce d'amitié			

C'était comme s'ils comprenaient tous (les) deux qu'ils   allaient
                                              devaient

se livrer à ce petit exercice pendant   un bon bout de temps.
                                    un certain temps.

C'était une journée glaciale   avait froid aux oreilles
Il faisait un temps glacial   et Treece   avait les oreilles gelées

'J'ai de nouveau le trac'   bredouilla-t-il
'Le trac me reprend'   balbutia-t-il
                            bégaya-t-il

'Ne vous inquiétez pas'
'Ne vous en faites pas'   le rassura l'examinateur
'Ne vous tourmentez pas'

'Je ne vais pas vous   tuer   vous savez.'
                     manger

Ils   sortirent   sur la route.
     allèrent

'Allez jusqu'en haut de cette petite colline et redescendez; à ce moment-là
Montez en haut

je traverserai devant vous   et vous devrez vous arrêter
                          et il faudra que vous vous arrêtiez

net
pile
le plus rapidement possible, comme   si j'étais un piéton ordinaire
                                             pour

Treece   alla   en haut   de la colline et fit demi-tour.
            se rendit   jusqu'au sommet

Soudain
tout à coup   de derrière une voiture   une silhouette   apparut.
                                              une forme   surgit.

                     sans résultat   lui rentra dedans
Treece freina,   rien ne se produisit   et il   l'accrocha.
                     sans aucun effet   la renversa.

Des papiers et un chapeau   s'élevèrent dans les airs
                               volèrent de tous côtés

Treece   s'aperçut   soudain   à sa grande horreur
            vit   alors   à son grand effroi   que l'examinateur
                                       avec horreur

était étendu   sur le sol.   de la pauvre victime
gisait   par terre.   Le costume   du malheureux
                  à même le sol.   du pauvre homme

était   sale   Mais   à part cela   (elle) n'était pas blessé(e)
           sali   autrement   il allait bien.

Il dit à Treece de   continuer à passer les épreuves.   Plus tard, quand
                        passer aux épreuves suivantes.

tout fut fini, Treece   demanda   avec   un certain embarras
                           s'enquit   une certaine gêne

             j'ai réussi?'
'Est-ce que je l'ai eu?'   L'examinateur éclata de rire
             je l'ai'

'Il me   renverse   et il   vient me demander   s'il a réussi.'
            rentre dedans   veut savoir

Treece   devenait   presque un ami
            était maintenant

'Envoyez-moi la note du pressing
'Faites-moi savoir combien coûte   le nettoyage de votre costume.
'Faites-moi savoir combien vous aura coûté

J'espère   vous revoir bientôt'   lui cria Treece.
              que je vous reverrai bientôt'

                                                              fonctionnaire.
'Pas si je vous vois   en premier'   répondit le courageux   employé.
                          d'abord'   officiel.

'Pas si c'est moi qui vous aperçoit le premier'

Question 5

Charles	descendit sortit	de la voiture et ouvrit la portière pour Nicole.

Un agent un policier un gendarme	se trouvait se tenait	à l'entrée de l'immeuble	et s'entretenait avec s'entretenant avec en train de converser avec

le concierge la concierge	et	comme ils s'approchaient à leur approche	il se tourna il leur fit face	vers eux de leur côté

'Monsieur, vous ne pouvez pas (y) entrer' vous n'avez pas le droit d'y entrer' dit-il

Nicole (lui) expliqua	aussitôt tout de suite immédiatement	qui elle était et présenta Charles

Le policier	la regarda fixement la dévisagea	quelques instants un instant un moment	avec une surprise évidente. avec un étonnement évident. évidemment étonné.

'Lefranc? La fille du Général Lefranc?'

La jeune fille	acquiesca de la tête fit oui de la tête	et il demanda à voir sa carte

d'identité.	Elle	la sortit de la retira de la prit dans	son sac à main et la lui	tendit. présenta.

Après l'avoir L'ayant	examinée étudiée inspectée	avec soin avec attention attentivement	il regarda	à nouveau de nouveau

Nicole.	Puis Alors	bien qu' quoiqu'	il	ne semblât pas ne parût pas n'eût pas l'air	entièrement absolument	convaincu,

il les laissa il leur permit d' il les autorisa à	entrer passer.

'Je viens' 'Je vous accompagne' 'Je vais venir avec vous'	dit fit	soudain tout à coup	le concierge.

'J'apporte 'Je vais apporter	la	clé clef	de l'appartement.'

'Mais donnez-la-moi tout simplement.   Vous n'avez pas besoin de monter'
'Vous n'avez qu'à me la donner.   Il est inutile de monter'
'Il vous suffit de me la donner.   Ce n'est pas la peine que vous montiez'

répondit Nicole.	'C'est mon métier, 'Ça fait partie de mes fonctions,	Mademoiselle Lefranc.

Je suis responsable J'ai la responsablité	de	tout ce que s'y trouve. tout ce qu'il y a là-dedans.

Mais, je suis sa fille	quand même tout de même	insista Nicole	avec colère. furieuse. furieusement.

Quand ils eurent finalement réussi	à obtenir à se procurer	la clef, Charles et Nicole

montèrent (l'escalier)
gravirent les marches   jusqu'au premier étage.

Une fois à l'intérieur de l'appartement	ils commencèrent ils se mirent	à fouiller

tous les placards et les tiroirs, mais	ne trouvèrent ne découvrirent	rien d'intéressant.

Dans un coin du salon	il y avait se trouvait	un grand bureau.

'Malheureusement, il est fermé à clef,' dit Charles	déçu. désappointé. d'un ton déçu.

Nicole sourit.

'Ça n'a pas d'importance   je sais (comment) l'ouvrir.'
'Ça ne fait rien   je sais comment il s'ouvre.'
'Peu importe   je sais comment on l'ouvre.'

A TUTOR'S ANSWERS TO QUESTIONS 3, 4, 6 AND 7

Question 3

Au printemps de 1981, lorsque la gauche obtint le contrôle du gouvernement de la France pour la première fois en vingt-trois ans, on crut que les rêves de Mai 1968 allaient enfin se réaliser, au travers de ce que l'on appela 'la révolution tranquille' de Mitterrand. La révolte des étudiants qui avait fini par se répandre dans toute la nation française lors de ce printemps débordant d'espoirs n'avait pas réussi à produire un changement social authentique. Lorsqu'on avait demandé aux Français de se prononcer sur le choix d'un nouveau gouvernement, ils avaient élu une forte majorité gaulliste qui devait, au mieux, mettre en oeuvre quelques modestes réformes visant à satisfaire les doubles revendications des étudiants et des travailleurs de l'industrie.

Cependant, Mai 1968 devait s'avérer différent. Les partis de gauche allaient tenter de mettre en place des réformes qu'ils avaient déjà élaborées dans leur Programme Commun de 1972. Le gouvernement Mitterrand commença la réalisation de son programme par la nationalisation d'importants secteurs de l'économie. Il visait ainsi à accroître le contrôle du gouvernement dans ces domaines. Cette action obligea pourtant le gouvernement à adopter de nouvelles mesures d'austérité en 1983 et 1984, afin de ralentir l'inflation en France.

Il ne faisait aucun doute en 1984 que les plans d'austérité du Président suscitaient l'inquiétude, au sein de son propre parti, de quelques éléments les plus radicaux tel Edmond Maire, qui se déclara particulièrement troublé par les taux élevés du chômage. Mais, à ce moment-là, il paraissait évident que Mitterrand exercerait ses fonctions présidentielles jusqu'aux élections de 1988.

Question 4

Après avoir quitté le chemin étroit nous nous trouvâmes dans un verger à peu de distance de la chaumière. J'en distinguais les murs blancs au-delà des arbres. Malgré son air d'autorité, j'étais content que Jacques eût offert de m'accompagner puisqu'il commençait à faire sombre et sans lui j'aurais pu facilement me perdre. Nous nous arrêtâmes pendant trois ou quatre minutes. Rien ne se faisait entendre que le cri lointain d'un hibou dans le bois en bas de la ferme. Si Durand était bien parti, il devait se trouver quelque part dans ce bois, car la route le traversait.

Nous continuâmes d'attendre. L'obscurité et le silence pesaient lourdement sur moi et je commençai à sentir que l'on nous guettait. Soudain j'entendis un bruit derrière moi et me retournai, saisi de terreur.

'Ce n'est rien,' chuchota Jacques, en s'approchant de moi. 'C'est une pomme qui a dû tomber. On continue?'

'Attendez un peu,' dis-je d'un ton glacial.

Je regardai vers le bois. Presque immédiatement je vis quelqu'un qui sortait de parmi les arbres. C'était Durand qui marchait à pas rapides le long de la route. Il avait mis longtemps à traverser le bois. J'attendis qu'il eût disparu.

'Bon d'accord. Allons-y.'

'N'ayez pas peur des chiens, ils ne vous feront pas de mal. Ils me connaissent.'

Je fis oui de la tête mais ne dis rien et nous commençâmes à diriger nos pas vers la chaumière.

Question 6

La Gare d'Orsay, gare de chemin de fer désaffectée sur la Rive Gauche de la Seine en face du Louvre, vient de renaître en tant que musée consacré à tous les arts du dix-neuvième siècle. Le nouveau Musée d'Orsay, inauguré aujourd'hui par le Président Mitterrand ouvrira ses portes au public à partir du 9 décembre.

La semaine dernière un énorme éléphant et un rhinocéros de bronze ont été soigneusement mis en place devant l'entrée parmi un rassemblement indifférent d'étudiants protestataires. En face se trouvent six statues représentant les six continents. Elles appartenaient autrefois au Palais du Trocadéro, depuis longtemps disparu, et ont été retrouvées par hasard loin de là à Nantes.

La gare elle-même avec son élégante façade de pierre est un symbole de la Belle Epoque dont les plus beaux chefs-d'oeuvre y sont maintenant exposés. Construite en deux ans seulement par Victor Laloux pour le chemin de fer Paris-Orléans, la gare est typique de 'l'Age de Fer' de Paris au même titre que la Tour Eiffel et le Grand Palais.

La gare qui devait être démolie en 1953 fut sauvée par le regretté Jacques Duhamel, qui était alors Ministre de la Culture. Elle avait servi de centre d'expédition pour les colis aux prisonniers de guerre et de centre d'accueil pour ceux qui revenaient après avoir été libérés. Orson Welles, attiré par cet immense espace s'en était servi pour filmer le Procès de Kafka et Jean-Louis Barrault y avait monté des pièces de théâtre.

La décision de reconvertir la gare en musée fut prise par Valéry Giscard d'Estaing en 1977. Il fut invité à la cérémonie par le Président Mitterrand qui confirma le projet et rejeta certaines suggestions socialistes de l'abandonner. Nous trouvons donc là un symbole de la politique cohérente de la France concernant les musées qui s'est prolongée sous trois présidences d'opinion politique différente.

Question 7

Après avoir laissé la voiture au pied de la colline nous nous engageâmes dans un chemin étroit qui montait vers les ruines. En arrivant au sommet nous trouvâmes que les anciens habitants avaient dû emporter tout ce que pouvait servir. Dans l'une des maisons de bûcheron, par exemple, il n'y avait que les débris éparpillés d'un vieil évier. Il n'y avait presque pas de traces de ces paysans qui, l'un après l'autre, étaient partis pour trouver du travail ailleurs.

A STUDENT'S ANSWER TO QUESTION 4 WITH EXAMINER'S COMMENTS

"Un pommier" is an apple tree.

Vocabulary half-known; the word is "chaumière".

Good.

Spelling.

An anglicism.

Don't add words unnecessarily.

Imprecise.

Good.

Tense of "pouvoir" used well.

Imprecise.

Wrong tense.

A careless error?

Verb has two subjects so plural.

Good vocab, but candidate has changed sex of narrator.

Tense of "devoir" used well.

It is not a *street*.

Has confused two expressions: Il avait mis longtemps/Cela lui avait pris longtemps.

Use s'approcher de .

Après avoir quitté le chemin étroit nous nous trouvâmes dans un pommier pas très loin de la fermière. Je distinguais ses murs blancs derrière les arbres. Malgré son air d'authorité j'étais contente que Jacques eût offert de m'accompagner comme il devenait noir et sans lui j'aurais pu facilement perdre mon chemin. Nous nous arrêtions pendant trois ou quatre minutes. Rien ne se faisait entendre que le cri lointain d'un oiseau dans le bois sous la ferme. Si Durand était parti il devrait être quelque part dans ce bois.

Not "underneath".

Nous continuâmes de attendre. L'obscurité et le silence pesait lourdement sur moi et je commençai à sentir que nous étions regardés Tout à coup j'entendis un bruit derrière moi et je me tournai, saisi de terreur.

Turned *round*.

'Ce n'est rien,' chuchota Jacques, en venant plus près de moi. 'Une pomme a dû tomber. On continue?'

Anglicism.

'Attendez un peu' dis-je, d'un ton froid.

Je regardai vers le bois. Presque tout de suite je vis quelqu'un sortait du bois. C'était Durand marchant rapidement le long de la rue. Il avait pris longtemps pour traverser le bois, mais ce devrait être lui. J'attendai jusqu'à ce qu'il ait disparu.

Attendre + que +! subjunctive.

'Bon d'accord. Allons-y.'

Wrong form.

'N'ayez pas peur des chiens, ils ne vous feront pas de mal. Ils me connaissent.'

Je fis oui de la tête mais ne dis rien, et nous commençâmes à marcher vers la fermière.

Wrong tense, this is what happened. ①

Good knowledge of idiom. ②

Phrase omitted — care needed! ③

Re-phrase – passive awkward. ④

Either "*qui* sortait" or "*sortir*". ⑤

Further practice

If you need extra practice in prose translation you will find it easiest and most profitable to work on the retranslation of passages which you have translated from the French yourself. Retranslation is most effective if you link it to the intensive study of texts. When you have completed the intensive study of a passage as part of your vocabulary-building programme, translate the passage, or better still a simplified or slightly rearranged version of it, into English. After an interval of two or three days, translate it back into French using the original passage and your own study notes to self-correct your work. You will find that the differences between your retranslation and the text you started with will help you to understand the technique of translation and the nature of language.

Make your translation practice emerge naturally from your own reading and language-learning programme. You can ensure that you are working on texts which are totally relevant to your examination needs and you will be using translation as a productive revision exercise, retrieving words and phrases from your memory rather than from the dictionary. With a little experience you will be able to build into the target passage, and therefore into the English passage intended for retranslation, those points on which you need to test yourself.

It is also useful to work on parallel English – French texts. A range of French or English translations is available in paperback (Gallimard folio, Penguin etc.). Work initially on an original French passage using it for intensive study and then use the English translation for retranslation practice. You will be carrying out a productive language exercise rather than just setting yourself a test. You will also be in a better position to look critically at the translator's version and will learn that even a professional translation can often be improved upon.

CHAPTER

11

READING COMPREHENSION

USING THE SYLLABUS

CRITERIA FOR ASSESSMENT

REASONS FOR POOR PERFORMANCE

ACTIVITIES FOR IMPROVING YOUR READING COMPREHENSION

TYPES OF MEANING

TYPES OF QUESTION

EXAMINATION TECHNIQUE

GETTING STARTED

You will already be familiar with reading comprehension in one form or another because it is a very frequently used language exercise at all levels; a text in French is studied closely and its vocabulary and structures are practised through a series of questions and answers. However at an advanced level, although the format may be similar (a passage of French followed by a number of questions), reading comprehension is likely to demand more sophisticated skills and a wider reading vocabulary and understanding of structures than the 'questions on the text' that you are probably used to. The reading comprehension test may well be less familiar and more challenging than you have ssumed and you would therefore be advised to prepare carefully for it.

ESSENTIAL PRINCIPLES

USING THE SYLLABUS

The first step is to find out as much as you can from the syllabus and from past papers about the type of passage and questions which will be set. The syllabus regulations will probably give only brief indications such as 'The intention of this Paper is to test the candidate's ability to understand a passage (or passages) of quite complex contemporary French in a non-literary register' (ULSEB, syllabus B) or 'The passage will be in the form of a narrative with elements of analysis and dialogue' (AEB), but what it says can guide you to the main type of reading material which you should use when preparing specifically for this paper. This is important because the most useful way in which you can prepare for the test is to read as extensively as you can and to develop your comprehension skill through practice.

> **Extensive reading; the foundation of all your language work.**

Extensive reading, of course, should become an activity which is the foundation of all your language work and it will therefore be valuable to read a wide variety of texts. However, if the reading comprehension test in the examination is clearly going to be of a specific type (e.g. a non-literary passage or a passage of narrative) it is essential to work on plenty of passages of the appropriate type. A passage of argument or discussion in a non-literary register will present different analytical problems and require a somewhat different approach from a passage of narrative and dialogue.

The syllabus regulations will give you information about the time allowed for the test and the length of the passage (or passages). If you consult past papers (or specimen papers if the Board has recently changed its syllabus) you will have an idea of the type of questions which you will be required to answer.

There is a variety of possible question types: *multiple* choice questions, sentences for completion, gapped passages to be filled in, 'true or false' questions and of course, Why? What? How? questions.

There is also quite a wide variety in the passages which are set. You will find short items, longer magazine and newspaper articles, advertisements, extracts from brochures published by the SNCF (Société Nationale des Chemins de Fer Français) or the PTT (Postes Télégraphes, Téléphones), passages based on photographs and drawings as well as material in tabulated form.

At A-level the questions are usually set and answered in English on the grounds that it is the candidate's comprehension of French which is being tested rather than the ability to write it, but there are one or two exceptions. It is therefore a point to check.

> **Confidence and a sense of purpose.**

Sometimes the syllabus will give quite detailed information as to the number and type of questions; 'There will be not less than 6 and not more than 10 questions on the passage. Some of these will test comprehension of specific elements, others gist comprehension, and they may require the candidate to draw inferences from surface content of the passage' (AEB). Find out all that you can. It will give you confidence and a more defined sense of purpose.

If only a little information is given there is no cause for alarm. If you follow the advice in this chapter it will help you to improve your comprehension skills generally and to prepare yourself for tackling different question types. Indeed, it is a wise approach to be ready for a number of possibilities.

These preliminary investigations will enable you to begin to set up a reading programme designed to support not only your practice in reading comprehension but the rest of your language work. Extensive and intensive reading are essential for training in reading comprehension but they are also vital for vocabulary acquisition and for familiarisation and revision of grammatical structures. The reading in French that you do to develop your comprehension skills will also help you to improve your essay-writing in French together with your prose and translation work.

CRITERIA OF ASSESSMENT

Before considering in detail what is involved in applying and developing the skill of reading comprehension, it is as well to discuss briefly the way in which the test is usually marked and to mention some of the common pitfalls which candidates should learn to avoid.

The purpose of the reading comprehension is to assess the ability of candidates to express their understanding of a passage of written French. As it is a test of comprehension, not translation, candidates are not expected to translate directly from the original but to express themselves clearly in their own words in order to answer the questions on the text. The main requirement is that *all* relevant information should be given and that precise information or explanation should be provided. You will therefore not gain full marks for an answer when necessary details are omitted or when the answer is not expressed precisely enough. If you include too many details you are not likely to be penalised unless the extra information which you provide distorts the meaning of the correct answer.

Mark distribution

When there are several questions on a passage (on the longer passages there are usually between six to ten questions) you will find that the marks are not distributed evenly to each question. The number of marks given to an individual question will depend on the amount of information which must be retrieved from the text in order to provide a satisfactory answer. The number of marks carried by each question is almost always printed on the question paper.

REASONS FOR POOR PERFORMANCE

When candidates do not do well in the reading comprehension test examiners find that it is mainly for one or more of the following reasons:

1   Candidates try to translate sentences from the text instead of reading it and thinking about it in order to identify relevant points and ideas. This superficial approach often leads the candidate to miss the point or to produce half-meaningful English which may falsify the answer.
    So read into the passage and do not try to translate it!
2   Many candidates appear not to have had sufficient training in reading texts of the right length and of sufficient complexity. They have therefore not developed the skill of identifying and following the main theme of the passage and of picking out and remembering its points and counter-points. Instead they adopt a piecemeal, line-by-line approach and as a result misinterpret points or miss them altogether.
    Aim at an overall understanding of the passage.
3   Candidates do not always give sufficient attention to the rubric. They may therefore fail to read the text with precise comprehension.
    Read and follow all instructions carefully.
4   The passive or reading vocabulary of too many candidates is not sufficiently wide. Some candidates have not developed the strategy of using context and global understanding of the passage to help them discover the meaning of lexical items which they do not recognise.
    Work at building up a wide reading vocabulary.
5   Candidates do not read the questions on the text carefully enough, particularly those questions which ask for precise information. The result is a general answer which will not score full marks. All terms of the question should be taken into consideration.
    Read all parts of each question carefully.
6   Some candidates have not understood the nature of the test and spend time commenting on the text in vague terms or on agreeing or disagreeing with opinions and ideas expressed in it.
    Answer the question set.

These, of course, are faults which you should make sure of avoiding. Some of them would never arise if candidates had a better understanding of what reading comprehension really involves. Making clear what it involves is the purpose of the section which follows.

ACTIVITIES FOR IMPROVING YOUR READING COMPREHENSION

EXTENSIVE READING

There are a number of reading skills which you can learn which will help you to tackle the reading comprehension efficiently. These will be discussed below, but the best way to improve your performance in this test is to ensure that you *read regularly and as widely as possible in French*. If you read frequently in your own language you will probably find that it is not difficult to motivate yourself to read in French. You will be able to transfer some of your reading interests from one language to another.

If you are not an enthusiastic reader you should ask yourself why, and see whether you can cultivate an interest in reading in French. Remember that there is a range of reading material which is appropriate now that you are studying French at an advanced level. It is to be found in newspapers, advertisements, illustrated magazines, instructions, short stories, poems, novels, plays, biographies, reference books, encyclopaedias, books on geography, history, science and so on. Select topics which interest you and try to read with a purpose. If you are studying other subjects make an effort to read books on that subject in French. Set yourself tasks which will motivate your reading.

 **Read French!**

If you can buy regularly, or have access to, a French newspaper such as *Le Figaro* or *Le Matin*, or to a French magazine such as *Elle*, *Le Point* or *L'Express*, use it to follow up a topical theme or to document a place or person of interest. Read French to find out information and you may find you want to read more French.

What is proposed here is *extensive* reading, rather than *intensive* reading (which also has an important place in your language work but is a different activity) which would involve you in analysis of grammar and vocabulary. Your primary objective when you embark on a programme of extensive reading is to read with interest and with fluency. Foreign language learners tend not to read in this way. They have often developed the habit of concentrating on every word instead of taking in groups of words and blocks of meaning. It may be of course that they are forced into this approach simply because the text contains too much unknown vocabulary and too many unfamiliar structures.

More often the apparent inability to read with fluency is the result of old habits. These persist because the reader does not realise that it is not necessary to understand every word in order to maintain the thought process involved in continuous reading and to prevent interest from flagging. At first you will find it taxing to get through a short story, a novel or a long newspaper article but sometimes it is important to keep going even if you have only a rather hazy idea of what the novel or article is about. Remember that when you are reading to improve fluency it is better to avoid over-use of the dictionary. Meaning can often be inferred from the context and by reading on you will often come across clues which will elucidate troublesome vocabulary.

When you meet words that you do not understand it is valuable to go through a process of inferring or intelligent guessing instead of, or at least before, checking the word in the dictionary. It is an important way of developing your comprehension skill. It will mean, of course, that you do not read each section of the text at the same speed but this does not necessarily mean loss of fluency. It is quite normal for a fluent reader to read certain sentences and to read some parts of the text more slowly than others.

Choice of texts

In the initial stages you will need to be discriminating in your choice of texts. A certain amount of difficulty is tolerable and, if your attitude is relaxed, will not prevent you from making reasonable progress; but clearly some reading matter will be too inaccessible and is best discarded or left until later.

To begin with, in order to have reading material which does allow fluent reading, you could make use of simplified versions of authentic texts such as the series *Textes en Français Facile* published by Hachette. You could also try textbooks and junior encyclopaedias intended for younger native French readers. If you have access to a French newspaper or periodical concentrate on the easier sections such as reports of events in the news about which you already have a background knowledge or on the *Courrier des lecteurs* which provide shorter, less complex passages of French until you have the confidence to read more generally. If you have difficulty in locating or selecting authentic material of an appropriate standard then consult your tutor and the suggested reading at the end of this chapter.

Fluent or even semi-fluent reading of a range of material will help you to develop those comprehension skills which are essential for dealing successfully with the reading comprehension test. Such reading will also become a very important part of your general language-learning programme. It is the most effective way of building up an extensive receptive vocabulary, of rehearsing known but half-forgotten lexical items and structures and of generally keeping in use language that you have already learnt. This is a major difficulty for the learner who is not living in a French-speaking environment. Reading fluently is also a way of acquiring a feel for what is grammatically correct and of assimilating syntactic patterns.

Setting yourself clear reading goals and establishing good reading habits is something that you cannot afford to neglect.

INTENSIVE READING

When it comes to tackling the type of passage set as a reading comprehension test you will be required to read it intensively. Nevertheless your extensive reading, particularly if it has been directed towards finding out information, will stand you in very good stead. You will be used to identifying main points and to separating them from less significant detail. You will also be more able to read rapidly or to scan a text in order to retrieve a specific piece of information. When it comes to the reading comprehension test these are useful skills.

When you work on the passage set you will need to read it a number of times, closely and analytically, and then rapidly scan it as you search for the information asked for in the questions. Extensive reading will also have improved your background knowledge or your 'knowledge of the world'. When such knowledge corresponds to that of the writer you will be able to deal with assumptions which are left inexplicit and with those lexical items which do not mean very much unless you are aware of the reality to which they refer. Examples of such terms are: les collectivités locales; une caisse de sécurité sociale; le social; le nucléaire; la cohabitation. The words seem easy enough but without some background knowledge the reader may well ask: 'What exactly do they mean?' It is this knowledge as much as the dictionary which will help you to understand that it is a question of communities such as the 'communes' and 'départements' in France; the offices where social security matters are dealt with; that which is to do with industry; the nuclear energy sector; the power-sharing of opposing political groups.

The format of the paper may vary from one Examination Board to another. You may find a range of short items but there is almost always a lengthier passage as well (400 – 600 words) and sometimes the whole reading comprehension test is based on just one passage of that length.

Working on a passage

When you start work on a passage, short or long, *first read it continuously*, without lingering over details which are not immediately understood, in order to arrive at an overall understanding of the passage. It is best to work from a global understanding to the understanding of smaller units: paragraphs, sentences and then to individual words. In this way you will have an outline of the text in your mind from the beginning. Knowing the context will help you to elucidate specific parts of the text which, initially, may have caused difficulty. Remember that the examiner will have approached the text in this way when setting the questions and that most questions will be designed to test not just understanding of individual sentences but of sentences in context.

If you are not working under exam conditions and you are practising reading comprehension on a passage of your own choosing, it is a good idea, before you study the text closely, to try to anticipate what the writer is going to say. First read through the text rapidly in order to get an overall view of its main points. Then write down the questions that you think the text should answer. Finally you study the text closely, looking for the answer to your questions. Predicting information contained in the text will help you to read with a purpose and working out your own questions will give you some insight into the way an examiner might approach the passage when setting questions on it.

Any text that you may be faced with, in the examination or elsewhere, will inevitably contain vocabulary that you do not recognise and constructions that you are unable to unravel. There are ways of dealing with specific difficulties of this nature and they are discussed in chapter 13. However, it is important to realise that there is more to understanding a text than understanding separate words and structures or even separate sentences.

TYPES OF MEANING

To comprehend a text fully you must practise 'reading into' it and in order to do this effectively you should be aware that any given sentence can have more than one type of meaning.

1 Firstly, there is the meaning that a sentence can have on its own, i.e. its *independent or propositional meaning*:

Nous sommes aujourd'hui deux milliards et demi d'humains.

2 Secondly, a sentence which is part of a text will also have a *contextual meaning* which is created because the sentence is related to other sentences which precede and follow it. It then takes on a function which derives from the writer's reason for using it. When it

stands alone the sentence in French above has no function, but it takes on a function when it follows another sentence:

> Il est important de reconnaître qu'il y a une limite au peuplement de la planète. Nous sommes aujourd'hui deux milliards et demi d'humaines.

Here it is a justification of the first statement and we can see how it fits into the writer's argument. The relationship between the two sentences would, of course, be more clearly indicated if they were joined by *parce que* or *car* but you will often find that the relationship is not marked explicitly. The reader *interprets* it by referring to the context and through his global understanding of the text.

3   Thirdly, there is the type of meaning which a sentence can carry and one which a reading comprehension question may require you to interpret, namely the *meaning that reflects the writer's attitude* or feelings:

> Avec 8,43 sur 20, Christine avait été jugée 'irrécupérable' par ses professeurs. A 9, apprirent peu après ses parents, elle aurait été admise à redoubler. Admirable certitude des chiffres!

The closing sentence, which is to be taken ironically, expresses the attitude of the writer who is not at all convinced that marks are as precisely reliable as Christine's teachers were apparently prepared to believe.

Every sentence can have these three kinds of meaning and if you aim to understand a text fully you should be prepared to interpret all three meanings. Ask yourself what a writer is saying in a sentence but also ask yourself what he is doing (i.e. is he giving an explanation, providing an example, establishing a reason, introducing a counter-argument, etc.?) by placing it in relationship with other sentences. Aim to discover what attitude the writer is conveying by using the sentence in the way he has used it.

The fact that a sentence can have these different meanings can be of positive help when you are interpreting a text as one meaning can lead you to infer another. For example, you would probably have understood from the rest of the passage that the writer was being ironic in the final sentence of the above quotation. Even if the meaning of the two preceding sentences had eluded you, you would have at least been able to infer that Christine had suffered rather harsh treatment because of her marks and the thread of the writer's argument would not have been lost.

POINTS TO CHECK WHEN TRYING TO INFER MEANING

If the meaning of part of a reading comprehension passage escapes you there are a number of points that you can check.

1   Use the aproach described in chapter 13 to help you *disentangle the syntax*.
2   Check those words which are used to indicate the *function* of a sentence, i.e. those which tell how a writer is using the sentence and what he is doing with it:

cependant	en fait	enfin
mais	d'ailleurs	or
toutefois	en outre	en somme
néanmoins	par ailleurs	ainsi
pourtant	en revanche	ensuite
en effet	d'autre part	

Words such as these (they are sometimes called '*markers*') indicate that the sentence is carrying out one of a number of possible functions such as expressing an opposition, making a concession, giving an example, sequencing, specifying, resuming, commenting, focusing attention, passing from one point to the next, enumerating or concluding. It is not possible to provide an exhaustive list of such words or even of the functions that they mark but the important point is that you should be aware of them. Identify them in your reading and use them in order to read a text with full comprehension. They provide useful clues. For example, in the following sentences:

- Cette histoire semble invraisemblable; elle est *pourtant* vraie.
- Si les objectifs n'ont pas totalement changé, on note *en revanche* une nette divergence sur les moyens d'y parvenir.

If you had not understood *invraisemblable* the word *pourtant* would give you a clue because it tells you *invraisemblable* is opposed in meaning to *vraie*, and if you had not grasped *une nette divergence sur les moyens d'y parvenir*, *en revanche* would tell you that it goes against the meaning of the first part of the sentence in some way and this would enable you to edge closer to the meaning of the whole sentence, or at least to reach enough understanding of it to be able to deal with a comprehension question.

3   Check what are called the *reference words* in the text. They are those words which tell the reader that he has to find their meaning in another part of the text. The pronouns *il, elle, elles, le, la, les, lui, leur, eux, y* and *en* are obvious examples:

- Lorsque le directeur m'a demandé des renseignements sur la conférence de presse du Président je lui ai dit qu'*elle* avait été remise au lendemain.
- Quand tu *le* verras, dis à Paul de me téléphoner.
- Le bâtiment se trouvait près du port et l'odeur des poissons *y* pénétrait.
- Si les gens veulent partir je ne peux pas *les en* empêcher.

Other words of this type are the relative pronouns *qui, que, quoi, dont*, a preposition with *lequel, où, ce qui, ce que, ce dont, ce à quoi* and the demonstrative pronouns *celui-ci, celui-là, cela, ceci, ce*.

When you study a text, examine the way in which these terms relate backwards or forwards to other parts of the text. If the meaning of a sentence or paragraph eludes you, make sure that it is not because you have misunderstood the function of one of these reference words. It is very good practice to ring such terms when you read a text and to link them visibly to other elements in the passage to which they refer.

4   The use of words to indicate the function of a sentence and reference words are two of the elements which make a text hang together and work as a process of communication. There is another factor which makes a text cohesive: a writer will use different words to refer to the same thing at different points in the text. These words may be *synonyms* of the word already used but often they will add to the meaning as well as providing a substitute term. It is therefore possible to talk of a *synonymic development* which runs through a text. If you are aware of it and can identify it this will help you to follow the sense of the passage.

The following words and phrases, all taken from a text on over-population, represent what we have called the synonymic development of the text:

La croissance de la population . . . l'extraordinaire développement de l'homme . . . la multiplication de l'espèce humaine . . . la prédominance de l'homme sur la terre . . . l'accroissement démographique . . . ce problème . . . le peuplement de la terre . . . ce danger . . . le nombre d'individus, etc.

It is a useful task to set yourself to trace such a development when reading a text. It will help you to grasp the way in which the ideas are organised and developed through different paragraphs and will improve your ability to relate one part of the text to another.

TYPES OF QUESTION

The questions which follow the reading comprehension passage are nearly always put and answered in English as questions on the text. However, comprehension may be tested in a number of other ways. You may be required to summarise a given section of the text in your own words, to give the gist of a selected number of lines or possibly to write a brief report on the passage. You may even have multiple choice or sentence-completion questions in French. It is as well to check the syllabus to find out exactly how comprehension will be tested.

66 Check the syllabus. 99

DIRECT REFERENCE QUESTIONS

Questions on the text may be of different types. The first and simplest type is the direct reference question. It is simple because the answer can be reached by translating (or by 'lifting', if the answer is in French) the relevant part of the text without 'organising' the material in any other way.

Pourquoi tant de Français continuent-ils à voter communiste? D'abord, probablement, parce que le parti leur paraît l'instrument le plus efficace dans la lutte contre le patronat, pour la défense des intérêts des travailleurs. De façon directe, par son action et celle de la CGT — sa filiale — dans les combats pour les salaires, la sécurité et les avantages sociaux. De façon indirecte aussi, par la peur qu'il inspire aux chefs d'entreprise et aux pouvoirs publics. Le pourcentage des voix communistes aux élections a fini par devenir une cote d'alerte: s'il s'élève, patrons et gouvernements sentent qu'il faut 'faire quelque chose' pour les ouvriers, lesquels ont fort bien compris cette situation. D'autre part, l'admirable dévouement des militants et des cadres n'a pas d'équivalent dans les autres partis, lesquels ressemblent plus à des comités de politiciens professionnels qu'à des organisations de masse: cela aussi maintient l'attachement au PC. Enfin, l'intégration morale de la classe ouvrière dans la nation est probablement en retard sur son intégration matérielle. Les terribles luttes du XIXe siècle, les massacres de Juin 48 et de la Commune ont donné au prolétariat français un sentiment d'isolement tragique, qui n'a pas encore entièrement disparu. Voter communiste, c'est presque une question d'honneur, de dignité: abandonner le parti serait commettre une sorte de trahison.

(*De la Dictature* by Maurice Duverger, Julliard)

A direct reference question and answer relating to these lines would be:

Q: Why do so many French people vote Communist?
A: Because the Communist Party seems to be the most effective way of fighting the employers.

Such a question tests only literal comprehension and is *not* the type of question that you should expect at A-level.

INFERENCE QUESTIONS

Another type is the inference question. To answer it you will have to relate different sentences or parts of the text, reorganise the information contained in them and examine the text to see what, if any, implications there are. It is a question of not only reading the lines but of 'reading between the lines'. It may be necessary to refer to information which is scattered quite widely throughout the text in order to make a deduction or to check that your deduction is correct. The following are inference questions set on the passage above:

Q: Why is the Communist Party an effective party organisation?
A: Because it is a party which has a mass membership and has loyal and hard-working party workers and officials.
Q: Why should the working class feel a sense of honour and dignity in supporting the Communist Party?
A: The working class feel a sense of honour and dignity in voting Communist because it is an act of solidarity and loyalty. Events in recent history have made them feel that they stand apart from the rest of the nation; therefore they feel that they themselves must stand together.

INTERPRETATIVE QUESTIONS

The third type may be called the interpretative question. It requires you to not only understand the text but to interpret it in the light of wider knowledge or of common sense.
    — Nous parlions de Mlle Lagarde.
Simon s'agita.
    — On se connaît elle et moi depuis un an!
    — Je sais.
    — Elle est sensationnelle! dit-il et il se mit à froisser l'extrémité de sa cravate. Pauline, c'est la jeune fille la plus . . . elle est merveilleuse! Vous verrez . . .
    — Simon, tu te rends bien compte que dans une petite ville comme Sault, un grand garçon ne peut pas fréquenter une jeune personne sans que les gens bavardent.

(*La Parade* by Jean-Louis Curtis, Julliard)

Q: What is Simon's attitude towards his mother when she questions him?
A: He is ill at ease and hesitates to assert himself.

Here it is necessary to understand the literal meaning of the French and to use common sense to understand that this behaviour (fidgeting, playing with his tie, inability to articulate what he wants to say) is a sign of nervousness and uneasiness.

EVALUATIVE QUESTIONS

Finally, there is the evaluative question. It is the one which involves you in making a judgement about the writer's attitude and about what he is trying to do in the text. You could be asked to describe the author's opinion of the facts that he is relating or explaining, even though that opinion is not explicitly stated in the text. Questions of this kind are perhaps the most advanced of all as the reader has to analyse his response to the text and discover the objective reasons for it. The way in which the ideas are presented, i.e. the author's style, will help indicate whether he is being ironic, flippant, indignant and so on.

The comprehension questions set in an examination are likely to involve a mixture of these types and any one question could require both literal comprehension and a measure of inference or interpretation. What the different types should show you above all is that reading comprehension will need considerably more than a literal, sentence by sentence, understanding. The skill being tested is the ability to read the text as connected French and to be alert to all its levels of meaning.

EXAMINATION TECHNIQUE

When you tackle reading comprehension under examination conditions you should remember the following points:

1   Do not be in too much of a hurry to get to the questions. Study the text intensively and when you feel that you have worked your way sufficiently into the passage, try to establish a rough plan of it by identifying the main developments of the argument or the main stages in a chronological account, depending on the type of passage. These divisions will not always correspond to the paragraphs in the passage, you may find that two or even three paragraphs will relate to one main idea. It is useful to indicate the natural divisions visually be bracketing them together on the paper. Then, in each division, underline the key sentence, the one which seems to contain the central idea. It is also helpful to ring those words which signpost the various stages in the argument or the account. Your plan may be somewhat 'rough and ready' but working on it will improve your understanding of the passage and help you to hold it in your mind.

> **Planning.**

2   Once you have the 'feel' of the passage, study the questions carefully and pay attention to every word. If the question asks for 'causes', 'advantages', 'factors' in the plural then expect to find more than one. Use the clues which are in the questions. Sometimes the way in which the question is framed will indicate that you may have to make an inference or a supposition in order to reach the answer. (e.g. Why does the factory *seem* to be important? What *appears* to be the French view?)

> **Study.**

It will help if you have practised interpreting questions set on past papers; you will be used to some of the terms which examiners use (factors, attitude, indications, evidence, etc.) to avoid giving too much of the answer in the question.

Read the English carefully. A question such as 'What motivates Y's attitude?' is not the same as 'What is Y's attitude?' and if you think about it the question on page 115, 'Why should the working class feel a sense of honour etc.?' is slightly different from 'Why do the working class feel a sense of honour?' If a question really does seem ambiguous then indicate in your answer that it could be reasonably interpreted in two ways.

3   Make brief notes in rough for each answer. Until you have read the passage with complete understanding it may seem that some questions overlap. As subsequent readings improve your grasp of the passage you may well find that what you have jotted down for one answer is more applicable to another. It is therefore best to work through all the questions in rough before you start to write on the answer paper.

> **Make notes.**

It is usual for the order of the questions to follow the order of the text (the examiner will not have jumbled them deliberately to confuse you) but you should not assume that having taken an answer from say the first few lines that you can forget about them. They may have further relevance. This is why it is important to have a global view of the text.

4   Remember that you are required to give all relevant information in answer to a question. When you have identified the relevant point in the text always read on to see whether there are further elements which should be included. The information which you are seeking may be scattered. Sometimes, of course, it is difficult to decide whether the extra information is necessary or not. This need not give you cause for too much concern. The inclusion of non-essential details is not likely to be penalised unless it distorts the correct answer.

> 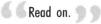 **Read on.**

5 Express your answer as clearly and as simply as you can and ensure that it says what
you mean. Concentrate on answering the question and do not be satisfied with locating
what seems to be a relevant section of the text and translating it into English. You are
likely to miss the point.

Answer the question.

Certain questions will specifically ask you *not* to translate. For example:
'In your own words, explain the ideas in paragraph X'
'Without translating, outline the points made in paragraph Y'
This does not mean that you are not allowed to use the English equivalent of some of
the words in the French. It means rather that you should make clear your
understanding of the essential points without struggling with the niceties of translation,
and that the examiner is not looking for an answer in clumsy 'translationese'.

EXAMINATION QUESTIONS

Q1

Read the following passage carefully and then answer in English, giving all relevant details,
the questions which follow it:

Quand, sur la recommandation de la directrice de son cours, Anne avait reçu une
convocation des Papeteries Réunies, une joie conquérante s'était emparée d'elle. Elle
s'était présentée à l'heure indiquée. Mais à peine frachie la grille, elle s'était trouvée, sans
bien savoir comment, dans un petit bureau triste et sombre où d'autres candidates
attendaient anxieuses, assises sur le bord de leur chaise . . . Il n'y avait plus de siège. Elle
avait dû rester debout jusqu'au moment où une porte s'était ouverte sur une grande femme
revêche qui les avait interpellées.

— Pour le poste de sténodactylo . . . Nous allons faire un essai . . . Si vous voulez bien
me suivre . . .

Dans une salle, des machines à écrire étaient préparées. On leur avait distribué un
texte. Il lui avait fallu un prodigieux effort de volonté pour dominer sa nervosité, éviter des
fautes de frappe et, un peu plus tard, retrouver en sténo sa vitesse habituelle.

L'épreuve finie, la femme les avait sèchement remerciées:

— On vous écrira . . .

Elles s'étaient retrouvées dehors toutes les six, se regardant avec un peu de méfiance et
un curieux sentiment de gêne qui ressemblait à de la honte.

Ils avaient écrit cependant, un imprimé rempli d'une main hâtive. Une visite encore
avant de signer sa lettre d'engagement. Un salaire moins important qu'elle ne l'avait
espéré, mais qu'elle avait accepté, trop heureuse, après cette attente, d'avoir la place.

Anne ouvrit la porte de l'appartement, traversa l'entrée obscure et pénétra dans sa
chambre dont elle claqua la porte. Elle chercha ses pantoufles et courut vers la cuisine où
Louise s'affairait. Elle saisit sa mère dans ses bras, l'embrassa avec fougue et s'écria:

— Ça y est, maman, ça y est! Je suis acceptée! Je commence demain!

— Quelle chance! dit Louise. J'espère que tout le monde sera gentil pour toi.

— Naturellement, ma douce! On ne va pas manger ta fille, répondit-elle, taquine. Et, tu
sais, c'est une grosse boîte . . . Plusieurs millions d'affaires par an . . . Quinze
sténodactylos et neuf cents francs par mois pour débuter. Ce n'est pas si mal. Et puis je
monterai en grade. Que crois-tu que père va en penser?

— Il sera content, bien sûr . . . Tiens, le voilà.

La porte d'entrée s'ouvrit avec fracas et Léon Moiraud entra en chantant.

— On l'a acceptée aux Papeteries Réunies, dit Louise. C'est une maison sérieuse; elle
commence demain.

Léon tapota la joue de sa fille.

— C'est bien, fillette. Le travail, vois-tu, il n'y a que ça. Mais il faut en profiter quand on
est jeune.

A quarante-cinq ans lui n'était plus assez jeune pour accomplir cet effort quotidien.
Après quelques années de dur travail comme transporteur, la guerre et quatre ans de
captivité en avaient fait un autre homme. Le beau garçon plein d'allant et de drôlerie avec
qui Louise avait connu quelques années de bonheur n'avait plus le coeur à l'ouvrage. Il
passait au café le plus clair de son temps, jouant aux cartes ou revivant les aventures
imaginaires de sa vie de prisonnier. Il n'avait gardé de sa jeunesse que sa gaieté, son
humeur tapageuse et un optimisme qui croissait avec sa paresse.

Louise s'usait à faire des travaux de couture pour colmater les brèches que la prodigalité et l'insouciance de Léon creusaient dans son budget. Il ne semblait pas, cependant, qu'elle fût malheureuse. Elle accueillait les extravagances de son mari avec une indulgence que la résignation ne suffisait pas à expliquer. Bien qu'Anne eût moins d'indulgence et souffrît de vivre dans ce logement inconfortable et de voir sa mère s'épuiser à la tâche, elle s'amusait, elle aussi, de la verve intarissable de son père.

Séduisant, son père avait dû l'être. Il avait ces yeux chauds de Méridional, ce teint basané qui plaisent aux femmes. Mais ces séductions ne suffisaient pas à compenser les privations de toute une vie et l'angoisse de la misère.

Anne aussi était gaie, avait envie de rire, de chanter, et elle se sentait prête à mordre à belles dents dans les fruits dorés de la vie. Mais elle se promettait bien de ne pas tomber dans les pièges auxquels Louise s'était laissé prendre.

Ce soir, elle avait remporté sa première victoire, fait ses premiers pas sur la route qui devait conduire au succès. (*Le Revers de la Médaille* by Pierette Sartin, Casterman)

Questions

a) What kind of test did Anne have to carry out? *(2 marks)*

b) How many candidates were called for the post, and in what state of mind were they before and after the test? *(6 marks)*

c) What are we told about the firm to which Anne applied? *(6 marks)*

d) What evidence is there in the text to show that Anne was ambitious? *(7 marks)*

e) What else are we told about Anne? *(9 marks)*

f) How did the war affect Léon Moiraud? *(6 marks)*

g) What was Louise's reaction to these changes in her husband? *(6 marks)*

h) In what ways could Léon Moiraud be described as attractive? *(6 marks)*

(AEB Specimen Paper)

Q2

Read carefully the following passage, *which is not to be translated*, then answer in English the questions. Tabulation may be used if appropriate. In the assessment of your answers accuracy, appropriateness and quality of language will be taken into account.

L'industrie en Europe

Berceau de la première révolution industrielle, l'Europe jouera-t-elle encore les premiers rôles à l'avenir? Pour provocatrice qu'elle soit, la question doit être posée aujourd'hui. Qui ne voit qu'au fil des ans son influence scientifique et économique, culturelle et militaire — en un mot, politique — s'érode?

Si l'Europe demeure un marché convoité, elle a été détrônée par le Japon comme principal partenaire-concurrent des Etats-Unis. Ce sont les entreprises nipponnes qui inquiètent outre-Atlantique, non les entreprises européennes. Sur un plan militaire, Américains et Soviétiques la considèrent plus comme un pion — certes non négligeable — que comme une entité autonome et responsable. Dans le reste du monde les jeunes Etats s'interrogent sur les capacités de l'Europe à offrir une alternative aux Super-Grands.

Attendant anxieusement de recueillir les miettes d'une reprise économique outre-Atlantique, assistant impuissante aux sauts capricieux d'un dollar plus dominateur que jamais, manipulée de sommets en sommets par un Président Reagan qui mène le bal, la vieille Europe donne bel et bien l'impression de jouer un rôle secondaire.

Ce déclin, dont on commence à prendre conscience et à s'inquiéter dans les capitales européennes et au siège de la CEE, ne date pas d'aujourd'hui. Les causes en sont multiples. En fait, tout se passe comme si les Etats européens, à commencer par la France, n'étaient pas parvenus à maîtriser le phénomène concomitant d'une crise économique durable et de l'arrivée des nouvelles technologies électroniques.

Le drame des Dix réside dans l'étroitesse de chaque marché national et la duplication des efforts entre ses membres sur des programmes qui mettent en jeu des dizaines de milliards de francs. Vu les moyens en hommes et en argent que mobilisent les Etats-Unis et le Japon, appuyés également sur de larges marchés intérieurs, seule la coopération entre les industriels européens peut permettre au Dix de rattraper globalement leur retard. Coopération qui implique une relative répartition des tâches, une concentration des efforts dans certains domaines.

Ce concept avait présidé au début des années 70 à l'aventure d'Airbus. Mais les forces centrifuges hostiles à l'idée d'une Europe forte, indépendante des Etats-Unis, allaient, la crise aidant, l'emporter. Les vieilles rivalités entre voisins, entre groupes industriels, ressurgissaient. Depuis 1975 la coopération industrielle européenne marque le pas. Comme si chaque industriel préférait jouer son propre jeu international. Comme si, derrière les déclarations de foi européenne des gouvernements, chacun cherchait à mériter le titre de *meilleur élève de Washington* ou de *meilleur ami de Tokyo*. Quitte à affaiblir longtemps l'Europe.

Après tout, dira-t-on, il est normal que des industriels tiennent d'abord compte de leurs propres intérêts. Leur logique première n'est pas forcément de privilégier les coopérations avec leurs concurrents les plus proches. Il revient donc aux Etats, à la Communauté, de créer un cadre tel que les firmes du Vieux Continent trouvent une motivation à coopérer entre elles.

La France paraît attacher aujourd'hui le plus grand prix à la relance d'une coopération industrielle européenne, seule voie − selon elle − pour donner un second souffle à l'Europe. Le président de la République en a reparlé lors du sommet de Stuttgart.

Les esprits sont-ils mûrs? L'environnement, le climat politique et psychologique sont-ils favorables à une telle relance de l'idée européenne à partir de coopérations industrielles? Rien n'est moins sûr.

(*La Coopération industrielle: un impératif pour l'Europe* by J M Quatrepoint, *Le Monde* 2.8.83)

Questions

1   What, according to the writer, is the crucial question
    facing European industry, and why does he ask it now?   (*5 marks*)
2   What factors does the writer see as supporting his point of view?   (*5 marks*)
3   What evidence does he produce suggesting the 'devalued' role played
    by the EEC in world affairs?   (*5 marks*)
4   What, for the writer, are the underlying causes of the present situation? (*5 marks*)
5   Indicate clearly the ideas in paragraph 5. Do not translate.   (*10 marks*)
6   Why, according to the writer, did the idea of unity fail, and what has
    characterised the political and industrial situation since 1975?   (*10 marks*)
7   What must EEC industries do to remedy the situation?   (*3 marks*)
8   What appears to be the French view?   (*4 marks*)
9   What is the writer's conclusion?   (*4 marks*)

(ULSEB Syllabus B, 1985)

Q3

Fig. 11.1

Questions

a) Who is this videocassette service for? *(2 marks)*

b) From what sources is the recorded material taken? *(2 marks)*

c) How often are the cassettes issued, and on what basis? *(2 marks)*

(Oxford AS-level Specimen Paper)

Q4

Carte d'abonnement privilégié

L'Express s'engage à vous faire bénéficier d'une remise exceptionnelle de 40% sur le prix normal de L'Express : vous recevrez le premier magazine d'information français à votre domicile, pendant 30 semaines, au tarif réservé aux abonnés de votre pays de résidence (voir tableau) au verso).

Vous n'avez rien à régler aujourd'hui: nous vous adresserons ultérieurement votre facture.

En outre, nous serons heureux de vous offrir gratuitement, en cadeau de bienvenue, la pendulette-réveil exclusive de L'Express (délai de livraison : 6 semaines après réception de votre paiement).

Offre valable jusqu'au 11 juin 1986.

Fig. 11.2

Questions

a) What precisely is on offer? *(2 marks)*

b) When should you pay? *(1 mark)*

c) What extra inducement is on offer? *(2 marks)*

d) When will you receive this extra inducement? *(1 mark)*

(JMB AS-level Specimen Paper)

Q5

On croit volontiers, parce que des marchands sont installés au bout d'un chemin de terre, que leurs pommes de terre sont de la ferme, leurs carottes fraîchement cueillies. Or, très souvent, ces revendeurs écoulent les fonds de stocks de Rungis. Ils achètent, à très bas prix, des marchandises dont ne voudrait pas la plus mal tenue des collectivités. Cela peut être le stock d'un camion qui, pour une raison ou une autre, a tardé à arriver à Rungis et qui aurait dû, normalement, aller à la benne. Ce sont des cageots qui comprennent un pourcentage excessif de fruits tachés. Bien souvent sur ces étals du bord des routes, à la fraude sur la qualité, s'en ajoute une autre, sur la quantité. On vous vend un plateau de fruits de six kilos alors qu'il n'en comprend que quatre . . .

Questions

a) Why are farm fresh goods not necessarily so? *(3 marks)*

b) What does one find at Rungis? *(3 marks)*

c) What are the two risks of buying 'fresh food' at a roadside stall? *(3 marks)*

(from NISEC A-level and AS-level Specimen Paper)

Q6

Le débat nucléaire en Europe

Avec cent quarante-trois réacteurs installés dans dix pays d'Europe, fournissant environ le quart de ses besoins énergétiques, et trente-sept autres en construction, l'industrie nucléaire fait quand même grise mine. L'Europe termine actuellement les programmes déjà lancés mais les carnets de commandes commencent à se vider: neuf réacteurs en tout en 1985. Pourquoi ce désenchantement après tant d'espoirs? La sensibilité écologique et la montée des Verts dans les pays anglo-saxons pèsent certes beaucoup. Mais elles ne sont pas seules en cause. La croissance de la consommation s'est beaucoup ralentie avec la disparition des vieilles industries grosses consommatrices comme la sidérurgie. De plus, dans certains pays comme la Grande-Bretagne, de nouvelles réserves d'hydrocarbure ont été découvertes depuis les années 70, rendant le nucléaire moins vital. Enfin, dans les pays comme l'Italie, où la décentralisation et la pagaille sont de règle, les compagnies électriques ne sont pas parvenues à réunir les fonds qu'il faut pour financer les programmes voulus. Si l'avenir du nucléaire en Europe était déjà peu encourageant, la catastrophe de Tchernobyl risque de le compromettre plus encore en renforçant les préventions, donc en allongeant les délais de réalisation. Jointes à l'envolée des taux d'intérêt, ces rallonges ont beaucoup alourdi les coûts. Les compagnies d'électricité européennes, largement pourvues pour encore une dizaine d'années, devront, en effet, pour faire face à leurs besoins à la fin du siècle, investir. Et le choix n'est pas aisé. Le nucléaire coûte très cher en investissements. Pour le moment le pétrole a certes le vent en poupe, mais la baisse des prix a peu de chances de durer. Le charbon est abondant et bon marché mais il pollue, lui aussi, et les équipements de désulfuration imposés pour éviter les pluies acides renchérissent son coût.

Questions

1 How significant was nuclear power as a source of energy in Europe in 1985? *(1 mark)*
2 Why was there an atmosphere of gloom in the nuclear construction industry? *(1 mark)*
3 What has been the effect of 'la montée des Verts'? *(2 marks)*
4 What general economic factor has reduced the immediate need
   for further expansion? *(2 marks)*
5 What particular circumstances have affected nuclear development in Britain? *(1 mark)*
6 What problem has the Italian electricity industry had? *(1 mark)*
7 What has been the specific effect of the Chernobyl disaster on the industry? *(2 marks)*
8 Why does the electricity supply industry need to plan
   over 10 years ahead? *(2 marks)*
9 State the disadvantages of the two non-nuclear sources of energy
   mentioned in the text. *(8 marks)*

(ULSEB AS-level Specimen Paper)

Q7

Read the following passage through carefully, and then answer in English the questions below the passage. As much **relevant** detail as possible should be given in your answers, but this need not be in the form of complete sentences.

Aussi étonnant que cela puisse paraître, aucune étude d'ensemble ne permet de dire combien de jeunes vivent entre eux, par petits groupes et qui ils sont. Les rares chiffres disponibles établissent pourtant qu'il s'agit d'une réalité quantitativement importante.

Même si elle échappe largement à l'investigation sociale, cette vie à plusieurs est une réalité très 'contrôlée', en ce sens qu'elle fait l'objet, de la part de la plus grande partie de la population, d'attitudes de rejet très fortes. Les voisins craignent le bruit, les propriétaires redoutent dégâts et loyers impayés; mais le refuse a aussi des sources plus troubles. Mixte, le groupe de jeunes suggère la licence, voire la débauche sexuelle. Non mixte, il n'est pas mieux vu. Les réactions enregistrées manifestent un soupçon presque systématique à l'égard de la sexualité des jeunes, ressentie comme une menace d'explosion anarchique.

La vie à plusieurs en 1988, est, on le voit, un véritable kaléidoscope. On peut littéralement tout voir: ici, un groupe bon enfant, mais vivant dans un désordre et dans une saleté à peine croyables; là trois jeunes qui cohabitent sans jamais se dire un mot; ailleurs, quatre garçons qui ne réussissent à rester ensemble que parce que l'un d'eux s'est résigné à servir de 'nounou' aux autres. A l'autre extrême des réussites quasi miraculeuses malgré les ombres inévitables; comme celle d'un groupe rencontré à Tassin, près de Lyon, qui a appris à faire cohabiter dans un climat d'étonnante gentillesse six jeunes, dont quatre ont entre dix-neuf et vingt ans, plus deux visiteurs quasi permanents, dans trois pièces tout juste moyennes: un couple argentin venu en France pour des études; François, étudiant en arts déco, bouddhiste, à qui a été laissé l'usage solitaire d'une pièce, pour y mener la vie austère qu'il désire et y psalmodier ses prières à haute voix; et dans la troisième pièce, Agnès et Jonathan, elle étudiante en psychologie, lui un jeune noir employé dans un restaurant; et puis, dans la même chambre Helyette, la Hollandaise. A vingt ans ils ont acquis une expérience humaine que d'autres n'atteindront jamais.

Pour tous, la vie à plusieurs signifie la découverte du poids du travail ménager, une plongée souvent suffocante dans le monde des nécessités quotidiennes. Les garçons sont évidemment les plus mal préparés à ce type d'aventure, et beaucoup de groupes masculins n'en réchappent pas; mais force est de constater que, dans la presque totalité des groupes rencontrés, le travail domestique est à peu près équitablement partagé entre les deux sexes. Autre constante dans ce domaine: le refus de toute organisation. A peu près partout, on compte sur la bonne volonté de chacun, et si celle-ci se révèle insuffisante, le groupe se disperse plutôt que de s'imposer des règles précises. D'une manière générale, ceux qui ont un minimum de projet commun surmontent beaucoup mieux que les autres ce type de difficultés.

Beaucoup de groupes connaissent une première période débordante d'animation; drainant la jeunesse alentour, il leur arrive même de mourir de leur succès. En réchappent ceux qui réussissent à s'imposer et à imposer à leurs visiteurs des moments où ceux-ci ne sont pas admis. Vient alors une période plus calme: 'on a demandé aux copains de téléphoner avant de venir.' Plus tourné vers lui-même le groupe n'en manifeste pourtant, en général, que peu d'intérêt pour les activités d'intérieur classiques. C'est que l'intérêt de la vie à plusieurs est ailleurs et d'abord dans la parole, l'échange. Les interminables soirées passées à discuter en sont des moments-clés.

Questions

1. What information is given in the first paragraph about groups of young people who live together?
2. What sort of public reaction do they arouse?
3. What explains the attitude which people adopt towards them?
4. What is surprising about the group living at Tassin?
5. Why does François have a room of his own?
6. How do the young people benefit from communal life?
7. What do all the groups of young people have to face?
8. What are we told about the way housework is done?
9. Having come together, what two stages do many groups pass through?
10. Why do they not take part in the usual indoor leisure activities?   (*50 marks*)
(ULSEB 1989)

OUTLINE ANSWER TO QUESTION 1

You should work through the passage in rough as you would in the examination.

1. *Read it several times* and try to find three main divisions. You should find that these can be sub-divided.
2. *Think through the questions* (a) – (h). Watch for those which might require you to consider more than one part of the text, e.g. (c), (d) and (e). Are there any others? Take all parts of the question into account. In (b) for example, look for: (i) number of candidates; (ii) state of mind before; (iii) state of mind after. What is implied exactly when the question says 'What are we told?' Does it mean 'What does the author say directly to the reader?' or does it mean 'What can we tell from the text?' In (h) you are asked about 'ways' in the plural, so expect to find more than one.
3. *Make brief notes* for each answer. Decide whether the information in the notes is appropriate.
4. *Check by re-reading* the text that all the relevant information has been noted.

A TUTOR'S ANSWER TO QUESTIONS 1 TO 6

Question 1

a) A test in typing and shorthand.
b) There were six candidates. Before the test they were uneasy and tense; afterwards they experienced a kind of embarrassment which was like a feeling of shame.
c) It was called *les Papeteries Réunies* and therefore presumably produced stationery. It is said to be a large establishment with an annual turnover of several millions. It employs fifteen shorthand typists.
d) Her ambition is revealed by her sense of triumph at being called for interview and at being offered a post in a good firm. She was confident of promotion and of increasing her salary and felt that she had taken the first steps on the road to success.

e) She was cheerful and fun-loving and ready to enjoy what life had to offer. She was amused by her father's lively nature but less tolerant than her mother. She did not like living in uncomfortable accommodation and seeing her mother work so hard, so vowed to avoid ending up like her.

f) The war had changed him. He no longer had any enthusiasm for work. He would spend most of his time in cafes, playing cards or reminiscing about his imaginary adventures as a prisoner of war. He had not lost his good humour, his cheerfulness or optimism.

g) She tolerated his behaviour and was not unhappy. She worked hard to try to compensate for the cost of his shortcomings.

h) He was cheerful, lively and optimistic and with his warm eyes and tanned complexion he was physically attractive.

Question 2

1 Will Europe play a leading role in the world in the future? He asks the question because Europe's scientific, economic, cultural and military influence is being eroded.

2 Japan has overtaken Europe economically and it is Japanese firms which threaten the United States; the USA and USSR do not consider that Europe is a military force in its own right; the rest of the world doubts that Europe is a credible alternative to the superpowers.

3 Economically Europe depends passively on the USA, trying to profit as best it can from American economic recovery and remaining at the mercy of the dollar's fluctuations. Europe allows itself to be manipulated at summit level by President Reagan.

4 The fact that Europe cannot control a situation in which there is the problem of dealing with new electronic technology at a time of long-term economic crisis.

5 The problem is that each member country is limited to its national market and therefore operates separately in an area of spending involving millions of francs. What is required (following the American and Japanese example) is co-operation between leading industrial organisations throughout the ten countries and this would mean some division of labour with concentration on particular areas

6 There were forces which worked against the idea of a strong, independent (and therefore unified) Europe. Old rivalries between countries and industrial groups re-emerged. Since 1975 there has been no further industrial co-operation; in spite of government claims of a belief in a united Europe there has been individual action from separate organisations.

7 The industries must co-operate with each other instead of always following the natural inclination to compete.

8 France appears to attach great importance to a renewal of European industrial co-operation as the only way of leading Europe to recovery.

9 It is uncertain that people are ready, politically and psychologically, for a renewal of the idea of Europe based on industrial co-operation.

Question 3

a) For people abroad, anywhere in the world.

b) It is taken from programmes broadcast by the 3 television channels.

c) Every month. The cassettes are for hire.

Question 4

a) 40% reduction on a 30 week subscription to the news magazine L'Express.

b) At a later date.

c) A free alarm clock.

d) 6 weeks after you have paid the subscription.

Question 5

a) Because they may not have come from the nearby farm itself.

b) Low-priced merchandise which has been left or has arrived late and which should normally have been thrown away; crates of fruit containing a high proportion of damaged fruit.

c) It may be sub-standard and less than the quantity which has been paid for.

Question 6

1 It supplied ¼ of the energy required.

2 There were fewer orders for new reactors; only 5 in 1985.

3 It has had a good deal of influence in making people disenchanted with nuclear power.
4 The demand for nuclear power has decreased with the disappearance of old industries such as the iron and steel industry.
5 New stocks of hydrocarbon fuel have been discovered making nuclear energy less vital.
6 Electricity companies have not been able to finance the necessary constructions programmes.
7 It could compromise the future of the nuclear industry by increasing the demand for safeguards which would mean that it would take longer before it was possible to go into production.
8 Because they have provision only for the next ten years and must invest to cover needs until the end of the century.
9 Oil prices are not likely to remain low. Coal causes pollution and the measures taken to prevent the acid rain which it causes add to the cost.

A STUDENT'S ANSWER TO QUESTION 7 WITH EXAMINER'S COMMENTS

" Misinterpretation; point is that no information is available. "

" This changes the meaning. "

" A literal translation which makes no sense. "

" Not a likely answer; meaning? "

" Good. "

" Does not answer the question. "

" Good. "

" Literal translation. "

" Does not mean anything. "

" Details omitted and last sentence not clear enough. "

" Note-form acceptable if meaning clear. "

1 No information is allowed to be given but there is an important quantitive reality.
2 Very negative attitudes. " Details omitted. "
3 The neighbours fear the noise and landlords are fed up with damage and unpaid rents. If the group is mixed, people think that sexual debauchery is going on. If the group is not mixed, people don't see it. They fear an anarchic explosion. " Literal translation. "
4 That there is a wide range of organisation represented.
5 The fact that one of the boys is prepared to act as a kind of nursemaid to the others.
6 There are 6 people living together. Four of them are between 19 and 20. There are also two people who are almost permanent visitors. They have three rooms which are only just big enough.
7 That people from such different backgrounds all live together in harmony.
8 Francois has a room to himself so that he can lead an austere life as a Buddhist and sing his prayers in a high voice.
9 At the age of 20 they have experience of life which others will never have.
10 They have to face housework. " Details omitted. "
11 Boys are less well prepared and many male groups do not escape.
12 In most groups housework is shared more or less equally between the sexes. They rely on goodwill to do it.
13 Lively at first but this threatens survival of groups. Then calm period when friends must telephone before calling.
14 The group is turned in on itself and is more interested in talking and exchanging ideas. " Good. "

28/50

Examiner's comment

Quite a good level of comprehension is maintained. Where the full mark for an answer has not been gained it is because the candidate has omitted irrelevant details or has not given a clear enough answer.

Further reading

Textes en Français Facile — Four star level — e.g. Simenon. *L'Affaire St Fiacre* and numerous other titles, Hachette

Periodicals (available through European Schoolbooks, Croft St. Cheltenham GL53 0HX):

Clé: Votre Journal en Français (articles on current affairs, sport, fashion, music etc. 4 issues per annum)

Revue de la Presse (4-page illustrated newspaper containing articles from the French daily press)

Elle (covers a range of topics of interest to women together with studies of wider issues)

See Gallimard Folio catalogue.

LISTENING COMPREHENSION

BASIC EQUIPMENT

AIMS

TYPES OF QUESTIONS

INTENSIVE AND EXTENSIVE READING

EXAMINATION TECHNIQUE

TRANSCRIPTS

GETTING STARTED

All A- and AS-level examinations in French and most other advanced examinations in French now include some form of listening comprehension test and, of course, the skill also plays a part in the oral. Part of your examination preparation should therefore be devoted to improving your ability to understand spoken French. If you do this successfully you will do far more than improve your chances in just one part of the examination. If you make use of the right kind of listening material (news bulletins, radio and possibly television plays, films, talks, discussions, panel games and interviews) you will provide yourself with a valuable source of French which will help you to build up your vocabulary and to keep what you have learnt in circulation. Listening comprehension may be examined and practised as a separate skill but you should see it as an integrated part of your language learning.

Many people would argue that for anyone who is intending to use his or her French in real life situations, listening comprehension is the most useful of all the language skills. As a non-native speaker you are likely to do much more listening than speaking or writing. When you are in a French-speaking environment you will find that the major difficulty is understanding the native speaker rather than making yourself understood. There is therefore great practical value in developing your listening ability, which is a consideration which should give you extra incentive to spend time and effort on it.

ESSENTIAL PRINCIPLES

Like all the other linguistic skills listening comprehension needs regular practice over a long period of time. This need not be a source of drudgery. On the contrary, if you make yourself an active listener and if you make an effort to use a wide variety of material, listening to French can become the most enjoyable part of your learning programme. Many students are encouraged by the progress they make in this area and many find that they learn more French aurally than from the printed word.

" Equipment for listening. "

In order to get started you will need some basic equipment such as a cassette player or better still a radio cassette recorder and a source of listening material. There is a very wide range of authentic material available commercially (see for example the catalogue published by Radio France; Cassettes Radio France). The cassettes are expensive to buy but if you have access to a language laboratory or centre with a tape library you should be able to borrow them. It is also worth making enquiries at your local public library. You might even make your own recordings from France Inter (details of French radio programmes are to be found in *Le Monde* or *Le Figaro*). The advantage of being able to use a tape library is that the tapes are usually classified according to difficulty, and transcripts of the recordings are sometimes available. If you have difficulty in getting hold of taped material you could always try approaching the language centre at a local polytechnic or university.

At an early stage in your course and while you are looking for material it is important to consult the syllabus regulations and past papers to see what kind of listening comprehension test is set by your Examination Board. Find out how long the listening comprehension test takes (it varies from 45 minutes to 1½ hours according to the Board), the type of questions that will be asked and the kind of material you will be required to listen to.

In fact, the Boards use very similar sources for the listening comprehension material. It is likely to be taken from radio news bulletins, news flashes, radio advertisements, weather forecasts, announcements, radio 'phone-ins', games, quizzes, discussions and interviews. This means that the material produced by any Board is going to provide relevant practice for you. It is useful to bear this in mind in view of the fact that there is not a great deal of commercial material at the right level available whereas cassettes of past listening comprehension tests can usually be obtained from any Board's Publications Department.

With regard to the level, you should note that the material used in A-level examinations, although the Boards call it authentic and say that the French is spoken at normal speed, is less difficult to understand than much of what you are likely to hear if you tune in to French radio or television. This is because the material for the examination is carefully selected, edited and sometimes re-recorded at a more manageable speed.

You should, of course, listen to genuine 'off-air' radio programmes but you should not be dismayed if at first your understanding is limited: firstly, your comprehension will improve with practice and secondly you can remind yourself that the A-level examination will not be as difficult. Naturally, it follows that if you reach the point where you are able to listen effortlessly to almost any radio or television programme in French, you will be able to cope easily with the French in an A- level listening comprehension.

" What should you listen to? "

Regular practice is important and it is essential to listen to a variety of spoken French if you can. For example, in addition to news bulletins which are really printed texts read aloud, listen to unscripted talks, discussions or interviews in which French is spoken more spontaneously. You will then get used to the repetitions, false starts, changes of direction in mid-sentence, exclamations and even the mumblings which are all features of natural speech.

The aim of the listening comprehension paper is to test the accuracy and extent of the candidate's understanding of the French. It is not just a test of hearing. The exercise inevitably involves the ability to interpret the meaning of the question, to switch from English (as the questions are usually in English) to French, to select and retain the information which has been asked for and finally to return to English in order to present the answer in a satisfactory form.

TYPES OF QUESTIONS

There are various types of question. Depending on which Board has set your Paper you will be faced with one or more of the following:

- Questions in English to be answered in English.
- Questions in French to be answered in French.
- Choosing between 'true or false' statements in French about what you have listened to.
- Completing statements or filling in tables in French relating to what you have listened to.
- Writing a summary in English of what you have listened to in French.

What you are most likely to find are questions in English to be answered in English. They may be direct reference questions, which means that the answer is directly stated in the original but inference questions are also frequent. To answer this second type it is necessary to interpret what you hear and make certain deductions. The questions may test understanding of specific items in the original or the broad outline of what has been said.

You will probably have realised by now that the kind of listening required in an A- or AS-level is not quite the same as the relaxed listening which occurs in everyday life and in one's own language. For the examination you have to train yourself to use your ears and your mind with a great deal of concentration.

It is usual for the questions on the Paper to follow the order of the material you are listening to. This helps you to select the pieces of information needed for each answer. However, it is always important to try to reach an overall understanding of the text which you will always hear at least once as an uninterrupted whole. You are given the opportunity to listen at least twice to all the material.

Marks are awarded according to the amount of information needed in the response and in all A- and AS-level examinations the number of marks awarded for each question is printed on the question paper.

Allowance is made for the fact that candidates have limited time to answer each question, therefore answers are usually acceptable in note-form but it is important to ensure that the information is clearly conveyed.

In their reports on candidates' performance in this part of the examination examiners draw attention to the following points:

1 Many candidates appear to have given insufficient time to practising listening comprehension. The test requires specific practice.
2 There is a need for clear presentation of answers, which must be relevant. The wrong approach is to write down everything you can think of in answer to a question. The inclusion of irrelevant information is penalised if it distorts the information which has been asked for.
3 Candidates need to listen to a greater variety of texts in order to build up a wider receptive vocabulary.
4 Some candidates are not able to recognise words and particularly combinations of words spoken at normal speed although they would be familiar with their written forms.
5 It is essential to treat the exercise as more than an exercise in listening. Most candidates do not have difficulty in identifying what they hear but do not always succeed in processing it and retaining it in the short-term memory in order to answer the questions satisfactorily.
6 Some candidates have clearly not practised the art of note-taking. They attempt to take down too much information which sometimes prevents them from hearing and selecting relevant points or from reaching an overall understanding of the text.

INTENSIVE AND EXTENSIVE LISTENING

There are two main types of listening practice which will improve your listening comprehension as a means of language learning. They are *intensive* listening which concentrates on detailed comprehension and on listening to particular features of the language, and *extensive* listening which should involve listening more widely for meaning and information. Both will help you to prepare for the listening comprehension paper and the oral.

INTENSIVE LISTENING

If you have difficulty in following spoken French, it will help you in the early stages of the course to work on selected phonetic exercises. A major obstacle for the learner whose experience of the language is based mainly on written texts is that the spoken sentence can sound like a single, long word or just a succession of syllables. Students therefore complain that the French is too fast or that all they can hear is a blur of sound.

Linking

If this problem arises it is advisable to study the way in which syllables and words are grouped when French is spoken. French tends to end syllables on a vowel (e.g. particulièrement: par-ti-cu-lière-ment; ridicule: ri-di-cule) and if a consonant follows, it becomes initial in the following syllable even if that syllable is part of the next word. The result is that words are often linked. The phrase *avec une amie* becomes (avekynami) rather than (avec – yne – amie). This phenomenon is called *linking*.

Liaison

It is further complicated by the problem of *liaison*. This involves the pronunciation of a linking consonant at the end of certain words when they are followed by a vowel. It means that in practice many French words have two spoken forms, one containing a liaison consonant which is heard in certain combinations and a more frequent form in which the liaising consonant is absent.

By making yourself aware of linking and liaison and, better still, by practising it yourself, you will begin to distinguish sense-groups and the meaning of sentences more readily.

Stress

Understanding where the stress falls in the sentence will also help you to follow a passage of spoken French. Stress falls on the last syllable of the word (the syllable is stronger and more prominent) but also on the last syllable of a word-group. As the word-group is a grammatical unit and a unit of meaning it is important to identify it when you are listening.

Intonation patterns

Intonation patterns (the rise and fall of pitch) can also indicate the limits of sense-groups in speech as well as signal a question, a plain statement, an instruction or changes in the speaker's attitude or intention which can become important clues to meaning.

A course in French pronunciation will provide practice in identifying and imitating features such as stress and intonation patterns, linking and liaison.

There is a further problem for the learner who is more familiar with the way that French looks on the printed page than with the way that it sounds when spoken. In everyday speech delivered at normal speed there are contractions of words and groups of words which cause certain vowels and consonants to disappear or become distorted. If you compare the following sentences with their phonetic transcription you will see that recognising them in normal speech could cause difficulty:

- Il te voit   [itvwa]
- Tu as fini   [tafini]
- Je ne sais pas   [chépa]
- Deux chevaux   [deuchvo]
- Je le vois   [jelvwa]
- Un faux jeton   [un faucheton]

Exercises which will help you to recognise such contractions are provided in *Le Pont Sonore* (see *Further Reading*). If you are preparing for a listening comprehension test which aims to use authentic speech it will help you to practise these or similar exercises. *Le Pont Sonore* contains further exercises which help with aural recognition of tenses. There are also self-correcting, gap-transcription exercises on the recognition of selected items of vocabulary. It is simple to do your own exercises. Select a short passage of recorded speech and by using the pause-button on your cassette player listen to and write down what you hear in phonetic spelling, indicating the links, liaisons and contractions. Short, intensive study like this will help you to 'tune in' to spoken French.

EXTENSIVE LISTENING

Intensive listening is important but the greater part of your practice should be devoted to extensive listening based on a wide variety of oral texts so that you will develop the skill of hearing, understanding and processing information which will be tested in the examination.

Getting the gist.

As you make the transition from intensive to extensive listening you should learn not to concentrate on distinguishing the sound and meaning of every word. Instead you should aim to follow the text continuously in order to 're-create' the gist of the passage and to maintain a global understanding of what you are hearing. It is important training for the listening comprehension test in which you will have to structure the passage and retrieve items of information from your short-term memory.

It is in fact not necessary to hear every detail. You do not hear clearly everything that is said when listening in your own language. You will not hear everything when you attempt listening comprehension under exam conditions but it does not mean that your comprehension will not be adequate. It is good practice to listen to texts in which there is some form of natural hindrance such as interruptions, two people talking at once, hesitation or even background noise. You will learn to tolerate gaps in what you hear and to infer meaning from other clues. The text which you hear in the examination may include little or no interference of this kind but learning to cope with it is an important way of developing your own listening strategies.

Plenty of varied listening practice will also help you to build up a stock of vocabulary that you are able to recognise aurally. This is important because there is good evidence that in understanding speech we rely more on registering the meaning of words, and particularly keywords, than on the grammar of the sentence. We pick out semantic elements first and only go back over the way the sentence is put together if there is any ambiguity. This means that you need a wide recognition vocabulary and that you should ensure that when you learn new items of vocabulary you learn to recognise their sound.

Transcripts

One way of learning the written form of the word with its sound is to listen to recorded material with a transcript. Commercially produced listening materials often come with a transcript. (Cassettes Radio France produce a series of tapes plus transcript) You should check the index in your tape library.

A useful variation on listening with a transcript which will help you build up recognition vocabulary is gap transcription. You follow the recording which has items of vocabulary deleted so that the learner can fill in the gaps.

Clues to meaning

Of course, it is also essential to listen to French without the support of the printed word so that you train yourself to use other clues to meaning. One very important clue is your knowledge of the context of what is being said because this knowledge helps you to make predictions and make sense out of what comes next. Quite a lot of what you comprehend comes not from the actual words we hear but from the context, and we hear more clearly what we *expect* to hear. When listening in our own language to a weather forecast, a joke or a lecture the fact that we have a vague idea of what is going to be said helps towards understanding.

Being aware of the context and creating an outline of the 'script' can help you both in your listening practice and in the examination. If you are going to listen to recordings which you have taken yourself from French radio it is a good idea to work on news bulletins or programmes about current affairs. You will always have an idea of what the broadcast will be about, particularly if you have read about the topic in a French newspaper, and you will be able to make predictions and inferences from context which are an essential part of aural comprehension.

In the examination you have no choice of what you listen to, but there is usually an introduction to the text and the context will be partially outlined by the questions which you have to answer which you are usually allowed to read through before you begin listening. It must be remembered, of course, that knowledge of context is not based solely on what you know beforehand, it is built up as you listen, which is why it is important to try to reach a global understanding, and is continually used to make further predictions.

If you have access to a tape library you will find it quite easy to select a range of listening texts. They should include news bulletins, weather forecasts, radio (and possibly television) plays, interviews, advertisements, panel games, 'phone-ins', speeches and recorded readings from novels and of short stories. This list will probably include the type of listening text that you will be given in the exam but check to see that you are giving yourself sufficient practice with appropriate material.

If you have access to televised programmes through satellite television or video cassettes, make good use of them. Many students find that understanding French is considerably easier when there are the visual aids of facial expression and gestures and when you can see what is being talked about.

You will no doubt be given practice in answering listening comprehension questions as part of your course but there are other activities which you can bring to your private listening. If you listen to an interview of a well-known personality, tabulate information to build up a biographical picture of the interviewee. You could listen to a news report on a bank robbery or a hijacking and draw a plan or diagram of what happened or you could use a map to fill in information gleaned from a weather forecast. A news item describing a state visit could lead to the drawing up of an itinerary and timetable.

These activities will not only ensure that your listening is not passive but as they involve the selection of information they will improve your ability to make succinct notes (a skill which is essential for success in the listening comprehension test). Indeed note-taking and summarising the gist of what you hear should be regularly practised. If you train yourself to listen and process you will be well prepared for the examination and will not feel, as one student put it, like 'a non-swimmer in a sea of sound'.

> > Listen and process. > >

EXAMINATION TECHNIQUE

On the day of the examination make sure that you give or have given attention to the following points:

1 It is important to be familiar with the *mechanics of the test*. You will have to listen and write only when instructed, so make sure beforehand that you know what is going to happen and when. You should also know:

- whether the questions and answers are to be in English or French and whether note-form answers are accepted;
- how many times you will hear the text and whether it will be divided into parts;
- whether the instructions for the test are given in English or French;
- at what stage you may read the questions;
- at what stage you may take notes;
- how many questions there will be and how long you will have to write the answers;
- how many marks are allotted to each answer.

2 Try to adopt a reasonably *relaxed attitude* when you listen to the text. Remember that the inexperienced candidate who is desperate to hear everything often concentrates too much on one part and sometimes misses what comes next or fails to reach a global understanding of the passage. If you miss words do not panic: you can afford not to understand everything clearly.

3 During the first listening try to *reach an overall understanding* of the text. Use the introduction or title of the text, and the questions, to form an idea of what the text is going to be about. It is often a help to memory if you make an effort to visualise as you listen. Try to picture a narrative account. If you are listening to an interview, imagining the positions and gestures of the speakers can help you to remember who says what and even what has been said.

4 *Read the questions carefully and underline keywords* to remind yourself what the main point of the question is. You will probably have to answer more than one question on any section of the text that you hear, therefore it is important to distinguish one question from another. In a text on immigration for example, you are likely to meet the word 'immigrants' in several of the questions: but if you read attentively you may discover that in the first question you are asked about illegal immigrants, in the second about unemployed immigrants, in the third about married immigrants and so on. If you look at the questions analytically it will enable you to structure the text even before you hear it and it will be less likely to come over as a blur of information. Working actively on the questions before you begin listening and answering will help you to internalise them. If you have them in your mind you will avoid the confusion of reading questions in English at the same time as listening in French.

5   You should *practise note-taking* so that it is a help to you. If you spend too much time writing when you should be listening, then taking notes could be a hindrance. Before the stage when you listen and write notes it is useful to number the lines of your answer sheet to correspond to the numbering of the questions. (Some Boards provide a booklet with spaces for the answers under each question and room in the margin for rough-work). Keep your notes as brief as possible, just one or two words to help you recall the information from your memory.

It is best to make your notes in French as they are intended to recall relevant parts of the text. At the note-taking stage you do not have time to start formulating an answer in English. However, if an English term occurs to you and it is brief, use it. You can also make use of simple symbols to save time. e.g.

- to indicate the idea of increase, growth, becoming more important, rise etc. use the symbol +
- to indicate that someone announced something, put forward a view, made a speech etc. use speech marks as a symbol e.g. The President made a long speech about the Common Market = Pr. "EEC. If you use symbols it is best to use a small number and to develop your own.

Practice in 'listening and doing' will have helped your note-taking; you will have developed the technique of selecting information and of listening with a purpose. Also, the more you have practised listening to the linguistic patterns of French the easier note-taking will be because you will be able to choose the right moment to jot things down: when the speaker pauses, when you can predict what the rest of his sentence will be, when he is adding a detail or repeating himself rather than making a main point. With practice you will find that very brief notes are adequate. A professional interpreter's notes made for a consecutive interpretation will usually contain only a few abbreviated words of French and English and a number of symbols.

6   When you answer the questions the main requirement is to *give all the relevant information*. This means that it is often not enough to supply the main point; relevant supporting details are also required for full marks to be awarded for the answer. It is sometimes difficult to know where to draw the line when it comes to secondary details, but if in doubt it is usually safer to include them. As a general rule the examiner will not penalise the addition of unnecessary details unless they vitiate the main point of the answer or are simply invented.

Do not expect the answer to be stated directly in the text, it may need to be inferred. However, it is unlikely in a listening comprehension that the information to be retrieved will be dispersed throughout the text. The questions follow the text chronologically. It is not a test of English and you will have limited time to write down your answers but it is important that you present the information clearly. If note-form is allowed then make sure that the notes are not ambiguous; the examiner should not have to try to deduce what you mean.

7   A common fear among candidates is that the French will be too fast for them to understand. Again, the remedy is *practice*. If you have had plenty of varied listening to a variety of authentic texts spoken at normal speed or near-normal speed you will be well prepared.

EXAMINATION QUESTIONS

To get the maximum benefit from these questions, the transcripts of the listening comprehension texts (see pp 137–145) should be read to you (or recorded) by a friend or tutor.

Q1

In this phone-in quiz programme, hotel guests are invited, through the owner, to participate in a game. You will hear the conversation between the presenter of the programme and the hotel owner.

Transcript 1

Questions

1	Where exactly is the hotel situated?	*(4 marks)*
2	By whom is room 27 occupied?	*(2 marks)*
3	When did they arrive and how long ago was it?	*(2 marks)*
4	Give details of the terms of their booking.	*(2 marks)*

(Total of 10 marks)

Listen carefully to this news item.

Transcript 2

Questions

5	Where and when did this incident take place?	*(4 marks)*
6	What did the union leaders of the CFDT call on their members to do?	*(1 mark)*
7	Why did the CFDT feel this was necessary?	*(2 marks)*
8	What action had the owners of the shop taken?	*(3 marks)*

(Total of 10 marks)

Now listen to this extract from an interview with the Mayor of Levallois-Perret, a suburb of Paris.

Transcript 3

Questions

9	How does the interviewer describe the role of the mayor?	*(2 marks)*
10	What areas of responsibility does the mayor identify in his answer?	*(6 marks)*
11	Describe the composition of the town council in Levallois-Perret.	*(6 marks)*
12	Outline the mayor's view of the principles underlying the work of the council.	*(4 marks)*
13	What is the extent of the cleaning problem in Levallois-Perret?	*(5 marks)*
14	Indicate additional measures now being taken to deal with this.	*(7 marks)*

(Total of 30 marks)
(AEB 1989)

NB The examination paper does not have this format. The questions are printed in a booklet and there is a space for the answer after each question.

Q2 (Approximately 45 minutes)
You will be told to turn over the question paper and you will be allowed 3 minutes to look through all the questions. Further instructions for the test will be given in French on the recording. You may take notes at any time during this paper.

Transcript 4

Answer the following questions in English. Your answers should give all relevant information but need not be in the form of complete sentences.

Première partie

1	What activity has begun at Acy-Romance?	*(1 mark)*
2	Who is eligible to take part?	*(1 mark)*
3	What may be provided for the participants?	*(1 mark)*
4	What was reported at Joigny-sur-Meuse?	*(1 mark)*
5	How did it happen?	*(1 mark)*
6	What had happened at the school?	*(1 mark)*
7	What did the caretaker discover?	*(1 mark)*
8	How was access gained?	*(1 mark)*

Deuxième partie

9	As far as local radio is concerned, what information does Didier give about (a) the audience and (b) the stations?	*(1 mark)*
10	How does he propose to deal with this subject in his talk?	*(3 marks)*
11	According to him, what has been a general feature of the development of local radio in France?	*(1 mark)*

Troisième partie

12   What information does the first lady give about her home town and its setting?

(*4 marks*)

13   What historical features are there? (*4 marks*)
14   What is the interviewer's first question to the second lady? (*2 marks*)
15   What is said about the physical features of the 'ville-dortoir'? (*1 mark*)
16   Give two features of the life-style of each community. (*4 marks*)

(*30 marks*)

(ULSEB 1989)

Q3

Part i)

In this part you will hear short passages. After the first announcement of the passage number there is a short pause in which you should read the introduction and questions. Each passage will be played twice. If you so wish you may take notes while listening. After the first hearing there is a short pause in which you may take notes or begin to answer questions. After the second hearing there is a longer pause in which you should complete your answers. These pauses vary in length according to the amount you need to write. Your answers can be brief so long as all essential points are included. You do not need to write full sentences, provided it is clear what you mean, but you must be sure that what you write is not vague or ambiguous.

Questions

Passage 1 (an extract from a news broadcast)

(Transcript 5)

1   What is the purpose of the campaign? (*3 marks*)
2   Why is this campaign necessary? (*2 marks*)
3   Why is this campaign being directed at parents as well as drivers? (*2 marks*)

Passage 2 (an advertisement)

(Transcript 6)

4   What is being advertised here? (*1 mark*)
5   Give three reasons why it is superior to other similar products.
   a) (*2 marks*)
   b) (*2 marks*)
   c) (*2 marks*)
6   When is each part on sale and at what price? (*2 marks*)

Passage 3 (an extract from a radio review of the morning papers)

(Transcript 7)

7   What does *Le Quotidien* say about the EEC decisions? (*3 marks*)
8   What will be the effect on motorists of
   a) lead-free petrol? (*2 marks*)
   b) catalytic exhausts? (*2 marks*)
9   Why have German environmentalists been pressing for this agreement? (*3 marks*)
10   What further demands are these environmentalists making? (*4 marks*)

Passage 4 (an extract from an interview with a travel agent — the travel agent speaks first)

(Transcript 8)

11   What comments does the travel agent make about holiday brochures? (*3 marks*)
12   According to the travel agent, what two things have tended to be lacking in Austrian winter sports results? (*2 marks*)
13   How do prices in France compare with those in neighbouring countries? (*2 marks*)

Passage 5 (a French woman talks about her family)

(Transcript 9)

14	What does Catherine say about herself and her family:	(*4 marks*)
15	What does she say about the benefits and the disadvantages of her work?	(*4 marks*)
16	Indicate fully in what ways her husband's attitude has changed and give instances of this.	(*7 marks*)
17	What difficulties does she have with the children?	(*2 marks*)

Passage 6 (a news item)

(Transcript 10)

18	What has Air France decided to do?	(*4 marks*)
19	What two reasons are given for this?	(*2 marks*)
20	Why can the money not be borrowed?	(*2 marks*)

Part ii)

In this part you will hear an extract from a discussion between two speakers, Natalie and Yves, about shopping. The whole passage will be played first, during which you are advised to listen without taking notes. Otherwise you may take notes when you wish. After the first hearing each section will be replayed twice. After the first announcement of the section number there is a short pause in which you may take notes or begin to answer the question or questions on that section. After the second replay there is a longer pause during which you should complete your answers on that section. When all sections have been completed the passage will be replayed in full. After this you will have a few minutes in which you may check or complete work on either Part (i) or Part (ii) of the paper.

Section 1

(Transcript 11)

21	Give two reasons why Yves prefers to shop at the market?	(*2 marks*)
22	Why does Natalie express a personal preference for supermarkets and hypermarkets?	(*3 marks*)

Section 2

(Transcript 12)

23	What criticisms does Yves make of larger shopping centres?	(*2 marks*)
24	Why does Natalie feel that her preferred form of shopping is more suited to the modern world?	(*6 marks*)

Section 3

(Transcript 13)

26	How, according to Natalie, can this problem be avoided?	(*3 marks*)

Section 4

(Transcript 14)

27	What does Natalie say about catalogues and what is her hope for the future?	(*3 marks*)

Section 5

(Transcript 15)

28	Give two examples mentioned here of ways in which technology can help the consumer.	(*4 marks*)

(AEB, Contemporary French, 1989)

NB The examination paper does not have this format. The questions are printed in a booklet and there is a space for the answer after each question.

Q4

This paper is made up of four parts; you will hear each recording twice. There will be pauses before, during and after each listening text, and the length and placing of these pauses is marked on your paper. You will have two minutes before you hear each text for the first time but you must not use your dictionaries while a text is being read out. Single 'bleeps' will be used to mark the beginnings of passages and at the beginnings and ends of pauses within passages. Double bleeps will indicate the ends of passages, and three bleeps will signal the end of the paper. The first two passages have one 30- second gap inserted in each reading; the third and fourth passages have two 30-second gaps inserted in each reading.

You may now look at the questions for section one, and the text will begin in two minutes.

Part One

Here are ten statements about the text you are going to hear. Five of them are correct; put a tick against those five, and do not put any mark against the others.

You will hear the text once with a 30-second pause within the text; you will then have two minutes in which to answer. Next you will hear the text again, and it will again be followed by a two- minute pause. Two bleeps at the end of that pause will indicate that you should turn to the questions on part two, and you will then have two minutes before the text of part two begins.

(Transcript 16)

1 Elle s'entend bien avec son père.
2 Elle est fille unique.
3 Son père est très chaleureux avec elle.
4 Elle a l'impression de ne pas connaître son père.
5 Son père a été élevé en Italie.
6 Elle est toujours au CES.
7 Elle n'habite plus chez ses parents.
8 Elle croit que son père lui en veut.
9 Elle tient à rester en contact avec sa mère.
10 Elle a fait un effort réel pour comprendre ce problème.

Part Two

Here are eight questions on the interview you are going to hear. Answer in English, but not necessarily in full sentences. You will hear the text once with a 30-second pause within the interview; you will then have three minutes in which to write. Next you will hear the text again, and it will be followed by a four-minute pause to allow you to complete your answers. Two bleeps at the end of that pause will indicate that you should turn to the questions on part three, and you will then have two minutes before the text of part three begins.

(Transcript 17)

1 What does Michel Vautraux do for a living when he is not refereeing?
2 Why, in his opinion, is it more difficult to be a referee than to be a judge?
3 Why might his refereeing hinder the progress of his full-time career?
4 How much does he earn per match?
5 Does he have to pay tax on his earnings from refereeing?
6 Describe two of the five types of referee mentioned by the journalist.
7 Why was Michel Vautraux not able to go in for sport when he was young?
8 What kind of people (to the journalist's surprise) are not becoming referees?

Part Three

Answer A and B

You will hear the text once with two 30-second pauses within the news; you will then have three minutes in which to write. Next, you will hear the text again, and it will be followed by a four- minute pause to allow you to complete your answers.

Two bleeps at the end of that pause will indicate that you should turn to the questions on part four — you will then have two minutes before the text of part four begins.

A. You will hear six separate news items. Choose six descriptive phrases from the following list of nine, and put numbers 1 − 6 against them to indicate the order in which you hear them.

(Transcript 18)

a) Students demonstrate against reform of higher education.
b) Stock Exchange news — dollar stronger.
c) News about the P.T.T.

d)   Teachers' union challenges government.
e)   Who will be the new head of the French employers' organisation?
f)   French nationals expelled from Africa.
g)   Privatisations — massive over-subscription.
h)   Pro-government demonstration in Paris.
i)   Illegal immigrants expelled from France.

B.   Give, in English or in figures, the answers to the following questions.

1   Combien valent les actions de Saint-Gobain?
2   Combien vaut le dollar en ce moment?
3   Combien de personnes ont manifesté à Paris?
4   Combien de Maliens ont été mis à la porte?

Part Four

The three women are, in general, in agreement about this topic. With which of the following opinions would they agree? Tick those five and do not mark any of the others. You will hear the discussion once (with two 30-second gaps), then there will be a 3-minute pause. You will then hear the discussion again (again with pauses) and you will then have four minutes to complete your answers. Three bleeps will signal the end of the paper.

(Transcript 19)
1   Les étudiantes anglaises sont plus féministes que les Françaises.
2   Les étudiantes anglaises ne sont pas très indépendantes vis-à-vis de la famille.
3   Les femmes mariées anglaises ne sont pas féministes.
4   'Sois belle et tais-toi' – c'est la devise de la femme libérée.
5   Les femmes mariées anglaises se font belles pour elles-mêmes.
6   Les femmes anglaises qui frisent la quarantaine se maquillent beaucoup.
7   En France, plus on vieillit, plus on fait attention à son apparence.
8   Pour les Anglaises, se maquiller, c'est se dévaloriser.
9   Si une femme se maquille c'est pour les hommes.
10 On ne peut pas être à la fois féministe et coquette.
11 On se maquille pour soi-même.

TRANSCRIPTS

Transcript 1

S.   L'hôtel Raymond se trouve à Cavalaire-sur-Mer, tout près de Saint-Tropez, et le patron est M. Meunier. M Meunier, bonjour.
M.   Bonjour.
S.   Où est-il situé, votre hôtel?
M.   On est à la sortie du village, là . . . entre les plages, à 500 mètres de la mer.
S.   Bon, je vous propose de jouer avec la chambre 27 qui est occupée, je crois, par deux personnes qui sont là depuis le 19 août, c'est exact?
M.   Oui.
S.   Donc ça fait 16 jours. Vous pouvez me donner leur nom?
M.   Oui c'est M.Failleau.
S.   Comment ça s'écrit?
M.   F-a-i-ll-i-a-u.
S.   C'est un monsieur avec son épouse, je présume?
M.   Oui.
S.   Ils sont en pension complète?
M.   Oui, c'est exact.
S.   Quel est le prix de la pension?
M.   280 francs par jour.

Transcript 2

150 personnes, répondant à l'appel de la C.F.D.T., empêchent depuis ce matin l'accès à un magasin d'électro-ménager, magasin ouvert au public malgré un accord réglementant le repos dominical. Ce magasin, situé dans un centre commercial de la banlieue de Nantes avait annoncé par des prospectus publicitaires qu'il serait ouvert ce dimanche, sans vendre mais en offrant le petit déjeuner à ses visiteurs.

You now have one minute to study questions 5 – 8 (see page 133):

Transcript 3

I.   Monsieur le maire, bonjour!

P.B. Bonjour.

I.   Merci d'être venu passer cet après-midi avec nous.

P.B. C'est un plaisir.

I.   M. le maire, dites-moi, votre définition à vous de votre rôle de maire, parce que je suppose que . . . euh . . . le maire, excusez-moi, mais c'est un petit peu le papa, la maman d'une commune à qui on dit, bon j'ai quelque chose qui va pas, je vais m'adresser au maire.

P.B. C'est une très belle définition.

I.   Votre définition, à vous . . .

P.B. Vous savez, d'abord . . . euh . . . effectivement, le problème d'un maire d'un village de 300 habitants ou d'une ville de 300,000 habitants, n'est pas tout à fait le même, mais ce sont deux maires et qui ont tous deux, je dirais, la responsabilité de leurs ouailles . . . euh . . . j'emploie . . . euh . . . peut-être à dessein un mot qui est employé dans d'autres circonstances mais parce que le bureau du maire est devenu un peu le confessional de tous les habitants de la commune et . . . euh . . . le maire doit s'occuper à la fois, bien entendu, de diriger, en premier lieu, les services municipaux, qui sont très importants, qui sont les services de la voirie, des ordures ménagères, de l'éclairage public . . . il doit s'occuper bien entendu de la sécurité mais il doit être aussi, et avant tout, je pense, l'ami de tous ses habitants, l'ami et le confident . . . et il doit être à l'écoute de toute la population.

I.   Oui, c'est une grande responsabilité . . . comment peut-on un jour se dire, j'ai envie d'être maire?

P.B. Je crois que pour ça il faut avoir une envie . . . euh . . . très . . . euh . . . très importante de s'occuper des affaires publiques, de s'occuper des autres . . . euh, j'ai l'impression que, en ce qui concerne les élus municipaux, il n'y a pas de manque de vocation puisque à chaque élection on trouve des candidats et des candidates multiples de toutes opinions . . . dans ma commune il y a 45 conseillers municipaux, c'est-à-dire que le maire a en plus 44 conseillers autour de lui et de toutes opinions politiques, puisqu'il a été introduit, lors de la dernière élection, une proportionnelle . . . une dose de proportionnelle . . . une dose qui . . . euh . . . peut aller jusqu'à 25% de . . . euh . . . d'opposants mais qui sont des opposants constructifs en général.

I.   Oui, mais je pense que dans une commune . . . euh . . . est-ce que je peux espérer que les opinions politiques passent après . . . euh.

P.B. On ne parle que très peu, je dois reconnaître dans un conseil municipal . . . euh . . . un conseil municipal, ça doit être un endroit de dialogue et où on doit arriver à un consensus entre les différentes opinions, dans l'intérêt des habitants.

I.   Ce que vous faites, j'imagine chaque jour, dans votre mairie de Levallois-Perret, euh . . . votre pouvoir sur la propreté de la ville, je pense qu'il est sûrement grand, non?

P.B. Oui, madame, il est très important et c'est même une de nos premières préoccupations dans une ville comme la nôtre, nous avons un problème, c'est que nous avons la plus forte densité de toute la région parisienne, puisque sur 240 ha. nous avons à la fois 55000 habitants et 50000 emplois — ça veut dire que nous avons 100000 personnes en même temps dans la ville chaque jour . . . euh . . . avec les stations de métro, avec les gens qui sortent du métro en jetant leurs tickets . . . euh . . . les gens qui ne visent pas très bien les corbeilles à papier et qui en mettent un petit peu partout. Eh bien . . . euh . . . figurez-vous que, en ce moment, je suis en train de me préoccuper de doubler tous les crédits concernant la propreté de la ville. Nous allons améliorer ce service puisque dans les jours à venir nous avons d'autres machines qui vont rentrer en service . . . nous avons doublé le nombre de balayeuses de trottoir, le nombre de balayeuses de chaussée, d'arroseuses, tout ça exige un matériel extrêmement lourd, extrêmement . . . euh . . . coûteux et . . . euh . . . pour vous donner une petite idée de ce que coûte le euh . . . le nettoyage de la commune, il coûte douze millions de francs.

Transcript 4

Cet exercice consiste de trois parties La première partie comprend trois flashes, la deuxième est un commentaire et la troisième est une interview.

Première partie
Fouilles archéologiques à Acy-Romance; échappement de gaz dans une usine à Joigny-sur-Meuse; et une école cambriolée aux Charmois.

D'abord les fouilles archéologiques. Les fouilles archéologiques viennent de commencer sur le site d'Acy-Romance et les jeunes gens âgés d'au moins 17 ans qui désirent y participer sont priés de s'inscrire auprès du responsable M.Lambeau, 14 rue Colbert. Ces jeunes peuvent éventuellement être nourris et hébergés gratuitement au centre de loisirs.

Fuite de gaz à Joigny-sur-Meuse. Mardi après-midi une fuite de gaz a été décelée dans les usines Force de France. Vers 17 heures un ouvrier a percé un réservoir, occasionnant une émanation importante de gaz. Ce sont les propriétaires d'un terrain de camping qui ont prévenu.

Vol et saccage à l'école des Charmois. Désagréable surprise pour le concierge de l'école des Charmois qui constata lundi matin qu'une classe et la bibliothèque de l'établissement avaient été visitées. Pour s'introduire les visiteurs avaient cassé un carreau pour avoir accès au système d'ouverture d'une fenêtre et forcé une porte. Suivant les premières constatations ce serait du matériel et des fournitures scolaires qui auraient été volés.

Deuxième partie
Pour la dernière séance de cet après-midi on va commencer avec Didier, qui va parler des radios locales en France. Didier.

Oui, Aujourd'hui je ne vais parler que des radios locales libres. Alors pourquoi vais-je en parler? Tout simplement...bon, vous allez comprendre quand je vous aurai donné deux petits renseignements. En 1981 il y avait une personne sur 15 qui écoutait les radios locales libres. En 1984 c'est-à-dire aujourd'hui même il y a une personne sur 4 donc d'une sur 15 on est passé à une sur 4 en trois ans. Ensuite le mouvement a eu tellement de succès en France que l'on compte actuellement 1 800 radios libres c'est-à-dire qu'il y en a environ 20 par département. Il s'agit donc d'un vrai phénomène et pour vous l'exposer j'ai choisi d'abord de vous faire un petit historique puis de vous donner les raisons de l'apparition des radios libres et enfin dans une dernière partie je parlerai du mouvement enfin de la situation actuelle. Mais donc que peut-on dire sur les radios libres? Alors tout d'abord peut-être une remarque générale c'est que euh l'histoire des radios libres est liée de très près à celle du monopole de l'Etat sur les mass medias.

Troisième partie
Bon mademoiselle, pourriez-vous nous parler un petit peu de votre ville?

Ah oui, ma ville, euh, elle est petite, elle a environ 30 000 habitants simplement, et c'est dans une région assez touristique. C'est une région montagneuse avec bien sûr disons des restes romains et euh certaines ruines de châteaux euh du moyen âge ou même plus vieux et ma ville est même très vieille, elle est située dans des vieux murs, il y a une enceinte de pierre qui a été conservée comme au moyen âge et une très vieille cathédrale.

Très bien, je vous remercie mademoiselle. Alors maintenant madame, vous nous parliez tout à l'heure de cette question de cité-dortoir. Est-ce que toute la population se déplace le matin pour revenir le soir ou bien y a-t-il encore quelques personnes qui restent dans cette ville?

C'est-à-dire que en fait c'est une ville qui est bâtie sur deux collines, le village est au milieu, l'ancien village, c'était un marché important au moyen âge et dont il ne reste pratiquement rien. Une commune est résidentielle, dans le sens que c'est une commune qui est habitée par des gens assez riches, les femmes restent à la maison toute la journée et les enfants vont à l'école qui se trouve pas très loin. Ils reviennent vers quatre heures, il y a quand même assez d'animation. L'autre colline est une commune pauvre principalement habitée par des ouvriers qui s'en vont le matin très tôt vers Paris et reviennent très tard le soir et en fait là il n'y a pratiquement aucune vie, les enfants étant à l'école.

Transcript 5

Lancement aujourd'hui d'une campagne pour faire baisser le nombre d'enfants qui sont tués chaque année ou gravement blessés dans les accidents de la route. C'est la première cause de mortalité des enfants qui ont plus de cinq ans. Le Ministre des Transports et son collègue, le Ministre de l'Education vont présenter aujourd'hui le slogan de leur campagne . . . `Choisissons la vie, changeons de conduite.' Cela s'adresse aux automobilistes, bien sûr, mais également aux parents qui ont parfois tendance à faire trop vite confiance à leurs enfants . . .

Transcript 6

Innovation spectaculaire! Voici le grand Atlas de la France . . . chez tous les marchandsdle journaux . . . édité en 22 luxueux volumes grand format. Le grand Atlas de la France n'a pas son pareil pour la qualité de cartographie, l'abondance des renseignements statistiques, la beauté des illustrations et des photos . . . Le grand Atlas de la France . . . vendu un mardi sur deux . . . chaque exemplaire prévoyez 85 francs.

You now have time to make notes or to begin to write your answers:

(1 minute pause)

Transcript 7

Le Parisien et *Le Quotidien de Paris* s'intéressent donc eux à l'essence sans plomb, à l'Eurosuper. 'La révolution de l'auto propre' comme titre *Le Parisien*. Commentaire dans un sous-titre du *Quotidien*: 'Les décisions de la Communauté européenne dans le domaine de la pollution risquent de coûter cher aux automobilistes.' L'essence sans plomb coûtera un franc de plus par litre, et les modifications imposées au moteur avec notamment l'introduction des pots d'échappement catalytiques entraîneront une augmentation de prix des voitures de l'ordre de six mille francs. Ces directives entreront en vigueur pour les voitures de plus de deux litres de cylindrée dès le premier octobre, c'est bientôt. *Le Quotidien* consacre deux pages à cet accord européen passé sous la pression des écologistes allemands parce que les forêts européennes sont ravagées par les pluies acides.

. . . François la Bruyère nous rappelle que les principaux accusés dans les pluies acides sont les installations industrielles, les centrales thermo-électriques, les moteurs de voitures et de camions . . . et on estime la responsabilité de l'automobile autour de 15% dans cette pollution.

Les vapeurs d'échappement sont devenues les boucs émissaires des écologistes allemands qui n'ont pas terminé leur croisade. Ils demandent en effet maintenant une limitation de la vitesse à 100km/heure sur les autoroutes et à 80 sur les routes nationales allemandes.

You now have time to make notes or to begin to write your answers:

Transcript 8

Nous, on pense au niveau des distributeurs, qu'on a beaucoup trop de brochures qui reprennent exactement les mêmes destinations, les mêmes hôtels dans certaines brochures . . . à des prix différents bien évidemment. Donc on a une perte de temps à chaque fois pour expliquer au client que c'est comme dans les Monoprix: si on vend beaucoup on a des petits prix; si on vend très peu, on a des prix qui sont plus forts et qu'en réalité le produit est le même . . . il n'y a aucune différence.

Est-ce que vous avez découvert des destinations nouvelles, des produits nouveaux?

Pour l'hiver il n'y a guère de produits nouveaux . . . il y a l'Autriche qui commence à faire des produits 'club', des stations de sports d'hiver qui s'aménagent pour plus de sports, plus d'animation le soir parce que c'est ce qui manque dans les stations sportives, en hiver et en destination soleil il n'y a pas grand-chose de nouveau.
Et pour les prix . . . qu'est-ce que vous avez à constater?
Au niveau prix . . . euh . . . la France n'est pas bon marché. Les pays limitrophes ont des tarifs qui sont bien plus performants que les nôtres pour cet hiver.

You now have time to make notes or to begin to write your answers:

Transcript 9

Je m'appelle Catherine . . . je suis institutrice et mon mari est comptable. Nous avons deux enfants: une fille de treize ans et un garçon de quinze ans. Quand les enfants étaient petits je restais à la maison mais j'avais envie de revenir à ma carrière, alors j'ai repris le travail il y a sept ans.

Mon travail pour moi c'est quelque chose d'essentiel. Je rencontre des gens, j'ai des responsabilités bien que je ne gagne pas beaucoup et que je sois toujours fatiguée. Chez nous tout le monde partage les tâches ménagères. Mon mari fait les achats, quelquefois il lui arrive de préparer un repas. C'est déjà quelque chose! Avant, il s'installait dans un fauteuil en face de la télévision. Son attitude a provoqué des drames mais je suis contente de dire qu'il comprend mieux la situation à présent, même que, de temps en temps il repasse ses chemises.

Les enfants acceptent très bien de faire des petites choses. Ils lavent la vaisselle après les repas, ils mettent le couvert et débarrassent la table. Mais on a des problèmes avec leurs chambres. J'ai du mal à leur faire ranger leurs affaires et faire les lits . . . mais enfin on s'entraide et on est content que chacun participe aux travaux de la maison.

You now have time to make notes or to begin to write your answers:

Transcript 10

Air France a besoin d'argent pour moderniser sa flotte et pour cela la compagnie aérienne a décidé de céder 15% de son capital à des actionnaires privés. Explication: Gabriel Minezi.

'Pour faire face à la concurrence et au choc de la dérégulation qui s'amorce un peu partout dans le monde, Air France doit impérativement se moderniser et notamment renouveler sa flotte; coût de l'opération: 25 milliards de francs. Comme il n'est pas question d'emprunter cet argent sous peine de mettre en danger la situation financière de l'entreprise, reste la solution de faire appel à des actionnaires privés.'

You now have time to make notes or to begin to write your answers:

Transcript 11
Nat. Moi, je préfère faire mes achats dans les grandes surfaces.
Yves Alors moi, j'aime mieux aller au marché pour acheter des légumes frais, des oeufs, des fruits. Il y a plus de possibilités de choix, et au marché les produits on les apporte frais le jour du marché.
Nat. D'accord, mais en principe faire ses achats dans les grandes surfaces c'est plus pratique, c'est plus facile aussi pour moi qui travaille.

(End of section one)

Transcript 12
Y. Mais au marché c'est plus agréable . . . on a plus de contact avec les commerçants, on peut discuter avec eux, ils donnent quelquefois une recette parce qu'on peut choisir des produits d'une qualité supérieure. Dans les grandes surfaces les fruits et les légumes sont touchés et tripotés par les gens, et c'est très impersonnel. Je préfère être reconnu et rencontrer des amis.
N. Oui, mais dans les années 80 le monde a changé. Dans les grandes surfaces les gens qui travaillent peuvent aller au même endroit pour tous leurs achats et profiter d'heures d'ouverture plus longues. En plus il y a toute une gamme de produits, on a beaucoup plus de choix. On y voit des familles entières qui vont faire leurs courses et en même temps jeter un coup d'oeil aux vêtements, aux produits électro-ménagers . . . il y a des choses comme ça.

(End of section two)

Transcript 13
Y. Voilà le plus grand problème. Dans les supermarchés on est très tenté . . . on achète un produit parce que c'est en promotion et on sort avec un chariot plein de choses dont on n'a pas besoin.

N. Oh, moi, je suis prudente, je me méfie des offres promotionnelles, je compare les prix, et surtout, je fais une liste pour éviter d'acheter plus que je n'ai besoin. D'ailleurs la dernière fois que je suis allée au marché je n'ai pas pu garer ma voiture, il pleuvait et on m'a volé mon porte-monnaie. Non, tu ne vas pas me convaincre . . . je préfère les grandes surfaces. Tout est sous un seul toit, en plus, au moins il y a le parking.

(End of section three)

Transcript 14

Y. Je n'aime pas être surveillé par une caméra, je déteste cette musique qui est destinée à endormir vos facultés mentales et je préfère le contact humain.

N. Oh! quant à moi j'ai envie de voir le jour où l'on pourra faire tous ses achats sans jamais quitter la maison.

Y. Mais tu sais que ça existe déjà.

N. Que veux-tu dire?

Y. Tu sais, il y a des catalogues, par exemple 'Les Trois Suisses', 'La Redoute' pour les achats par correspondance.

N. Oui, mais ce ne sont là que des achats limités . . . je parle du jour où l'on pourra faire son marché sans sortir.

(End of section four)

Transcript 15

Y. Ça aussi, c'est en train. Tu sais qu'avec le progrès technique on pourra bientôt faire son marché tout en restant chez soi.

N. Comment?

Y. Grâce à l'ordinateur par exemple. Il suffira bientôt de taper sur une touche pour recevoir ses courses. Mais pour les autres services par exemple . . . tu sais que tu peux déjà réserver ta place en avion et vérifier ton compte bancaire grâce au minitel.

N. Oh, vive le minitel!

(End of section five)

Transcript 16

PART ONE

Topic 1   Girl on her relationship with her father − 2 minutes.

− Euh . . . parce que, justement, à cause de mon père qui . . . on a eu . . . on s'entendait pas du tout et . . . euh . . . pour des raisons inconnues, si vous voulez, le mot n'est pas trop fort, mon père ne m'aime pas . . . enfin il a même dit qu'il me déteste, et euh . . .
Si vous voulez, donc, avec moi plus spécialement qu'avec mes autres frères, il est . . . il est très froid, il est glacial. C'est comme un inconnu, si vous voulez, pour moi . . . et je ne peux rien dire, je ne le connais pas . . . c'est comme un étranger que j'ai croisé, par exemple, Jardins du Luxembourg, c'est comme ça.
Donc, ce que j'aime en lui . . . y a rien . . . ce qu'y a, ce que j'éprouverais peut-être pour lui, c'est une espèce de . . . peut-être de la pitié − même pas, je le plains, d'en être arrivé là, parce que j'ai quand même essayé de, d'avoir des contacts mais jamais il ne m'a laissé m'exprimer, jamais . . . Toujours ce principe qui revenait − parce que j'avais tort . . . j'étais jeune aussi . . . ça aussi, ca y fait . . . (Et c'est quoi, qu'il vous reprochait surtout? les sorties?) Surtout,
surtout . . . tout était bon . . . les sorties, oui, et puis même, par exemple . . .
Comme il a été élevé en Italie, son grand principe, c'était 'la femme reste à la maison et les hommes sortent'.
    Bleep − 30-second pause − bleep
Donc, moi, vivant à l'extérieur quand même, dans mon lycée, en assistant à des cours je voyais autre chose, je voyais les autres vivre autre chose, alors je me sentais un peu frustrée, complexée, et j'ai essayé de m'en sortir en faisant le grand boum, en m'en allant, carrément. Et mon père, ça me le reproche, c'est sûr . . . Parce que lui aussi est persuadé certainement que je ne l'aime pas que . . . qu'il y a une certaine indifférence entre nous et, maintenant, c'est, c'est . . .
Mon père, c'est un homme que . . . je ne vois plus, quoi; je vois ma mère parce que . . . on fait tout pour essayer de se voir puisque . . . vu que mon père n'avait aucun contact avec moi, ma mère . . . on est très proche l'une de l'autre, quoi. C'est un peu comme un journal.

Donc, mon père . . . je peux rien vous dire vraiment de précis là-dessus . . . c'est trop flou, c'est trop . . . peut-être parce que j'y ai pas vraiment réfléchi, j'ai pas essayé de comprendre pourquoi, tout ça . . .

2 bleeps at end of passage

Transcript 17

PART TWO

Les Arbitres 2.21

1er journaliste:	Des réflexions, Michel Vautraux, le plus jeune arbitre international de football, est las d'en entendre.
M.V.:	Réflexions des élèves, réflexions des voisins, car lorsque la critique s'abat sur nous, et malheureusement trop souvent, justifiée ou non, chacun nous attend au coin du bois et nous parle du pays au retour. Et lorsque vous arrivez en classe avec euh des élèves qui sont au départ évidemment euh plus ou moins euh attentifs à tout ce que fait leur professeur . . . il est certain que parfois j'arrive la tête basse en cours, surtout lorsque les critiques sont répétées à droite ou à gauche sur toutes les ondes de radio plus ou moins complaisantes.
2ème journaliste:	C'est vraiment le rôle le plus ingrat?
M.V.:	Oui, mais c'est certain . . . il est ingrat toujours de rendre la justice, même dans les tribunaux, et sur un terrain de sport également plus, parce que nous n'avons même pas le temps de réfléchir.
	Et je suis obligé d'avoir recours surtout à la gentillesse de nos . . . mes supérieurs qui me libèrent pour pratiquer l'arbitrage. Cela pose d'énormes problèmes parce que . . . pour la suite de ma carrière professionnelle je suis marqué en rouge, on pense souvent que je suis indisponible, je suis peut-être pas éventuellement pas sérieux dans mon travail, dans la mesure où je ne suis pas toujours disponible. Et ça, on n'y pense pas. C'est . . . c'est-à-dire que l'arbitre, on l'utilise actuellement, et plus tard, lorsqu'on n'a plus besoin de lui, il se retrouve seul et éventuellement avec un grand désavantage dans sa carrière professionnelle.

30-second pause

2ème j.:	Combien vous rapporte l'arbitrage?
M.V.:	Bien, l'arbitrage euh rapporte surtout d'être connu, du point de vue indemnité il n'y a pas de cachet, dans la mesure où ce sont des tarifs publiés. Un international a une indemnité de 600 francs par match.
2ème j.:	Et le fait d'être connu, c'est une satisfaction pour vous?
M.V.:	Non, pas spécialement, mais c'est surtout de connaître beaucoup de personnes, et puis je voudrais vous dire également que ça me permet également de payer des impôts euh supplémentaires, parce que l'arbitre n'est pas oublié, lui non plus, par le fisc, même s'il n'est pas professionnel.
1er j.:	Mais qui sont donc ces hommes qui acceptent encore aujourd'hui de tels sacrifices, de prendre de telles responsabilités, de courir de tels risques? Généralement, il s'agit d'anciens joueurs qui veulent rester dans l'ambiance, de joueurs au talent limité mais qui aiment trop le sport pour tout laisser tomber, de joueurs victimes d'une blessure et qui ne peuvent pas courir le risque d'un autre accident. Il y a aussi les bénévoles, qui arbitrent pour rendre service au club, comme ils tiendraient la buvette. Enfin, il y a ceux qui n'ont jamais joué, comme Michel Vautraux que vous venez d'entendre, parce que, souffrant d'un souffle au coeur, tout effort physique lui était interdit pendant sa jeunesse. Et il y a les femmes, mais, oui, dans le secteur de l'arbitrage aussi les femmes ont gagné du terrain.

2 bleeps for end of passage.

Transcript 18

PART THREE

(Le journal de France-Inter, 18h, le 24 novembre)

1 Beaucoup de standards téléphoniques ont frisé la saturation ce matin chez les agents de change. La mise sur le marché des actions de Saint-Gobain s'est révélée un succès. On s'arrache depuis quelques heures les actions, à 310 francs la pièce, de la première firme privatisée. En Suisse, un million d'actions de Saint-Gobain proposées aux investisseurs helvètes ont déjà toutes trouvé preneurs. La demande à Genève a largement dépassé l'offre; toutes les demandes ne pourront pas être honorées.

2 A la Bourse de Paris, l'opération Saint-Gobain a donné un petit coup de fouet aux valeurs françaises. Elles ont progressé aujourd'hui de près d'un point. Le dollar, lui aussi, était en hausse. Il gagne trois centimes par rapport à vendredi. Le billet vert s'est échangé à 6,62 francs.

30-second pause.

3 La guerre des chefs. La succession d'Yvon Gatta à la tête du patronat Français maintenant largement ouverte. C'est pour l'instant François Périgaux le président d'Unilever-France, qui tient la corde face à son rival Yvon Chottard. L'ancien président du CNPF François Férax, souhaite qu'Yvon Chottard retire sa candidature. Il l'a fait savoir au cours d'une interview accordée à nos confrères d'Europe I. L'Assemblée Générale du Patronat Français tranchera courant décembre.

4 Si le gouvernement ne négocie pas, c'est une attitude suicidaire – voilà les propos de Jacques Pommateau le secrétaire général de la FEN, la Fédération de l'Education Nationale, dont la manifestation a rassemblé hier à Paris plusieurs dizaines de milliers de participants. La FEN a décidé d'engager un bras de fer avec René Monory, le ministre de l'Education Nationale, et en règle générale avec le gouvernement. La manifestation d'hier, très politisée puisqu'elle a réuni également de nombreux responsables socialistes, fait dire au P.S. qu'il s'agit là d'un avertissement sérieux pour le gouvernement.

30-second pause.

5 Dans les universités, le mouvement de grève des étudiants se développe, lui aussi, et se durcit. D'autres facultés sont gagnées par la contestation du projet Devaquet, le projet de réforme de l'enseignement supérieur. Une manifestation nationale est prévue, d'ailleurs, jeudi, le jour même où le projet sera débattu à l'Assemblée Nationale.

6 21 ressortissants africains, pour la plupart des Maliens, ont été interpellés et placés en garde-à-vue à Vitry-sur-Seine, dans le département du Val-de-Marne. La nuit dernière ils avaient essayé de pénétrer dans les bâtiments d'un foyer pour immigrés à Vitry. Les locaux ont été en partie dévastés. Cette attaque semble liée à l'expulsion de ce foyer de plusieurs dizaines d'occupants il y a deux semaines, pour la plupart des Maliens qui se seraient trouvés à la rue, en situation irrégulière et sans papiers.

2 bleeps for end of passage.

Transcript 19

PART FOUR

Spontaneous 3-way discussion 3.08 minutes

Bleep to mark beginning.

– Je viens de croiser un étudiant anglais qui m'a dit que que les f . . . les femmes anglaises étaient les plus féministes d'Europe et qu'elles avaient dix ans d'avance . . . sur les femmes en France.

– Et . . . les femmes . . . ça dépend de de leur âge . . . je pense que que les jeunes, les jeunes Anglaises, surtout lorsqu'elles sont étudiantes . . . euh sont certainement plus féministes que les Françaises dans la mesure où elles euh elles insistent sur leur sens de d'indépendance, leur désir de voyager seules ou de s'amuser seules. Elles ne dépendent pas ni . . . elles ne dépendent ni de la famille, ni ni des garçons, par exemple.

– Oui, c'est vrai. J'ai trouvé ça aussi, la volonté de . . . d'être indépendantes aussi vis-à-vis de la famille d'abord, et puis c'est certainement ça qui . . . qui les pousse à vouloir être indépendantes après vis-à-vis de . . . de leur mari ou quelqu'un quelqu'un d'autre.

Bleep, 30-second pause, then another bleep.

— Mais je pense que ça se reflète chez les jeunes, cette espèce de mentalité . . . euh . . . je ne pense pas que ce soit le cas pour les femmes mariées, ou, du moins (Oui, oui) pour les femmes qui sont mariées actuellement . . . pas pour celles qui se marieront (oui). Parce que j'ai l'impression que, ma foi . . .

— Alors moi, franchement je dirais que . . . euh . . . les femmes mariées anglaises sont certainement dans le monde occidental les moins féministes (les moins féministes) à moins qu'on redéfinisse ce que 'féminisme' euh veut dire . . . Euh certainement dans des soirées les femmes anglaises savent qu'ils euh . . . enfin ils appliquent le slogan 'Sois belle et tais-toi' . . . encore que 'Sois belle', ça doit aller dans . . . euh . . . avec l'idée de l'homme . . . on ne s'habille pas d'une façon criarde (On ne se maquille pas énorment) . . . elle s'éteint un petit peu quand elle se marie.

— Je je je mélange un peu féminisme et féminité . . . j'ai remarqué que les femmes anglaises, les femmes qui ont une trentaine . . . enfin, plutôt quarante ans se maquillent très peu, font très peu attention à à leur, à leur apparence, ne se mettent pas en valeur, alors qu'en France, au plus on vieillit, au plus, plus on a tendance à à se mettre en valeur, je pense.

Bleep, then 30-second pause, then another bleep.

— Oui, bien, c'est intéressant parce que . . . en disant euh de se maquiller, ou de bien s'habiller pour se mettre en valeur, c'est tout à fait le contraire du système anglo-saxon (C'est ça). C'est se dévaloriser (C'est ça, oui) euh parce que, bon, je suppose que c'est c'est c'est sans doute là que le puritanisme ressort euh les Françaises sont peut-être les les femmes du monde occidental, les . . . (Mais) qui résistent le plus cette idée de penser qu'on est moins féministe parce qu'on est coquette (C'est ça, c'est ça). Alors qu'il y a une censure, il y a vraiment une censure.

— En fait, il faut se débarraser de l'idée que si une femme se maquille, c'est pour les autres. Je crois que maintenant, l'idée de se faire belle pour soi-même . . . c'est . . . je dirais en France surtout, c'est c'est bien rentré dans les . . . (dans les moeurs) dans les moeurs, oui (Je pense, oui) . . . on se maquille, pas pour être un objet pour l'homme (Non) mais simplement, ma foi, parce que c'est comme ça, parce que c'est . . . on se sent mieux.

— On se sent mieux, c'est comme aller chez le coiffeur, on change de tête (Voilà . . . voilà).

Double bleep to mark end of passage, then four-minute pause, then 3 bleeps to mark end of paper.

OUTLINE ANSWER TO QUESTION 1

This outline will take you through the preliminary operations necessary for answering the questions. When you have followed them through you can complete the answers yourself.

Make sure that before you begin the test you know what its format will be. How many listenings will there be? How will the recording be divided up? You will find that the instructions to this Paper tell you that every item will be heard twice and that there will be a number of short items and one longer piece.

Make use of all the information that you are given at the beginning of the test and the pointers that the questions provide in order to anticipate what is going to be said. Try to anticipate some of the French words that you might hear. For example, Question 1 is 'Where exactly is the hotel situated?' Think of terms which indicate the position of a building (e.g. à côté de, près de, situé, derrière, à deux kilomètres de etc.). The actual words of the recording may not come into your head but this kind of thinking will help you to listen along the right lines.

It is advisable to make your notes in French. You will not have time to write very much and in fact you need only write enough to help you remember what has been said.

Notes

1   Cavalaire sur mer/Saint-Tropez
    sortie village
    entre plages
    500 mètres

2   2 personnes
    M. et Mme Failleau
3   19
    16 jours
4   pensions complète
    280
5   magasin/centre commercial
    banlieue, Nantes
6   empêcher l'accès
7   ouvert malgré accord
8   prospectus: ouvert dimanche sans vendre
    petit déjeuner
9   papa/maman
10 services: voirie
    ordures
    éclairage
    sécurité
    ami, confident/population
    (The fact that this question carried 6 marks shows that it is not enough to say that he
    is in charge of public services: it is necessary to give details of those services.)
11 44 conseillers + maire
    toutes opinions
    25% d'opposants
12 dialogue
    consensus
13 grand
    240 ha. 55000
    50000
    100000
    tickets de métro
14 doubler crédits
    d'autres machines
        balayeuses trottoir
        balayeuses chaussée × 2
        arroseuses

A STUDENT'S ANSWER TO QUESTION 2 WITH EXAMINER'S COMMENTS

Première partie

1   Archaeological activities.
2   Young people of 17.
3   Free food and lodging.
4   A gas leak.
5   A worker from factory left open an (important seal.)
6   A burglary and ransacking of building.
7   The library had been broken into – school furniture, property taken.
8   Door forced, window broken to reach catch.

> 66 Not precise enough; young people of at least 17. 99

> 66 Not precise enough, it is "a dig". 99   0
>   0
> 66 An incorrect guess. 99   1
>   1
>   1
>   1

> 66 Note-form acceptable if meaning is clear. 99

> 66 Candidate sound on numbers and dates — they need particular practice. 99

> 66 Include all relevant details — it was a library and a classroom. 99   ½
>   1

Deuxième partie

9   In 1981 1 in 15 listened to local radio but in 1984 figure was 1 in 4. There are 18 of these stations, they are free.   3
10 The history of local radio – how it has come into peoples' lives. Way radio has moved and changed over the years.   1
11 How its history comes very close to monopoly of the mass media.   0

> 66 French only partly understood. 99

> 66 Answer not clear enough. 99

“Text does not say this. Don't add words that change their meaning.”

“Some understanding but information imprecise. Relevant details omitted.”

“It is built on two hills.”

“A careless error?”

12	It is very small; has about 3,000 inhabitants; it is a tourist frequented area; it is mountainous.	2
13	Ruined castles, old town, cathedral still in use.	0
14	Does everyone leave the town in the morning and return in the evening?	2
15	Between two hills.	0
16	One community rich, women sat at home all day, children go to school. Other community poor, mainly workers who leave very early to work in Paris and come back very late.	4

A TUTOR'S ANSWER TO QUESTION 3

1   To reduce the number of children killed or seriously injured each year on the roads.
2   Because road accidents are the most frequent cause of death in children over 5
3   Because there are those parents who are sometimes too hasty in thinking that their children can be trusted to look after themselves.
4   An atlas of France.
5   a) The quality of the cartography.
5   b) The large amount of statistical information.
5   c) The beauty of the illustrations and photos.
6   Every other Tuesday; 85 francs.
7   They could be expensive for motorists.
8   a) The motorist will have to pay 1 franc more per litre for lead-free petrol.
8   b) They will put up the price of a car by about 6000 francs.
9   Because the forests of Europe are being destroyed by acid rain.
10   They are asking for a speed limit of 100 kilometres an hour on motorways and of 80 kilometres an hour on main roads.
11   There are too many which have the same destination and the same hotels but at different prices.
12   Facilities for more sports and amusement in the evenings.
13   Not cheap compared with those in neighbouring countries.
14   She is a primary school teacher; her husband is an accountant. They have a daughter of 13 and a boy of 15.
15   She meets people and has responsibility. She does not earn very much and she is always tired.
16   Previously he did nothing but sit in an armchair and watch television and his attitude caused tensions. He understands the situation better now: he does the shopping; sometimes he prepares a meal; he occasionally irons his shirts.
17   She finds it difficult to get them to put their things away and to make their beds.
18   To sell off 15% of its capital to private shareholders.
19   The company has to face up to competition and to deregulation of air fares.
20   It would endanger the financial situation of the company.
21   There is more choice. The produce is fresh.
22   It is more convenient; it is easier for her because she works.
23   People handle the fruit and vegetables and it is very impersonal.
24   Working people can go to one place for all their purchases and take advantage of longer hours of opening. There is
     a whole range of goods and more choice. The entire family can go shopping and look at clothes and household goods at the same time.
25   One is tempted by special offers into buying things one does not need.
26   By being careful and wary of special offers; by comparing prices and making a list of what one needs.
27   They are limited in what they offer for sale. She hopes to be able to do all her shopping without leaving the house.
28   Shopping can be done by tapping into a computer. You can reserve a seat on an aeroplane or check your bank account by using minitel.

Further reading

P. Pimsleur. *Le Pont Sonore*, Hachette

M. Leon. *Exercices Systématiques de Prononciation Française*, Hachette.

Cassettes Radio France (75786 Paris Cedex 16 France and some of these are available through European Schoolbooks, Croft St. Cheltenham GL53 0HX)

P. Bellemare et J. Antoine. *Histoires Vraies* vols 1 – 5. *C'est Arrivé un Jour* vols 1 – 3 (Livre de Poche Edition No. 1)

TRANSLATION INTO ENGLISH

GETTING STARTED

All other language work contributes towards the student's proficiency in translating from French into English. Practise at listening comprehension, intensive reading for building up active vocabulary, extensive reading for increasing passive vocabulary, and studying texts for reading comprehension. All these activities develop the skills which are essential for success in the translation paper.

It does not follow, however, that this is the only preparation which is required or that translation into English, simply because it involves writing in one's own language, is the easy part of the examination. The purpose of the translation paper is to test the candidate's ability to understand the foreign language and to express that understanding as accurately as possible in good, natural English. However, it is clear from examination scripts that many candidates see comprehension of the French as the main difficulty to overcome and therefore tend to neglect the accuracy and quality of the English. It is not sufficient to demonstrate general comprehension and to convey the gist of the passage or of a section of it (unless the rubric states specifically that this is all that is required); a precise translation and correct English are necessary at all times.

You should understand that practice is essential and that there are helpful techniques which can be acquired. The candidate who does exceptionally well will have mastered these techniques, will have read and listened to a great deal of French and will have a very good command of his own language (as his performance in other parts of the examination which are written in English invariably shows). It should not be forgotten that the translation paper is a test of French *and* a test of English.

When getting started on preparing this part of the examination you should map out as far as possible the ground to be covered. Consult the syllabus and as many recent papers as you can so that you know whether you will be required to translate one passage or two, how much time is allowed for the paper, how many marks it carried and what type of passage or passages you can expect. As you will see from the selection of past papers later in the chapter the French passage may be descriptive, discursive or narrative; again it may be colloquial, journalistic or literary. In examinations where two passages are set they are likely to be in contrasting registers. Know, therefore, exactly what you are preparing for and ensure that your reading programme and translation practice include passages of the appropriate type.

ESSENTIAL PRINCIPLES

THE NEED FOR GENERAL KNOWLEDGE

> Improve your general knowledge.

Choosing the right passages for reading and practice will do more than enable you to cover the relevant vocabulary areas. Different types of passage (e.g. narrative, discursive, dialogue etc.) can present their own problems and you should get used to tackling them.

The discursive or documentary text which deals with current affairs, for example, can often be more confidently understood and competently translated if your general knowledge is adequate. A text set recently for translation at A-level dealt with an aspect of the Common Market. A good many candidates would have coped much more satisfactorily if they had had some elementary knowledge of the EEC. They would not have translated *le traité de Rome* as 'the Roman treatise', *la communauté* as the 'Commonwealth' and they would have realised that *il vaudrait mieux repartir à six* meant 'it would be better to start again with six members' rather than 'it would be better to leave again at six o'clock'.

If you are familiar with the subject-matter then clearly you are in a better position to understand the passage and to choose those English terms which are appropriate within the context. If, by sampling past papers, you can see that you may be asked to translate a passage which touches on subjects such as trade unions, the French educational system, the French press, Paris, the French postal system, etc. (which have all appeared in recent translation papers) then try to make certain that your reading in French and translation practice include the kind of passage which will provide you not only with the vocabulary but with the general knowledge which will help you to produce a good translation. It is not specialist knowledge which is necessary: it is a question of sufficient general knowledge, provided quite adequately in newspapers and periodicals, which will allow things to fall into place more readily when you are working on a text which deals with a contemporary subject.

It is always valuable to have had plenty of experience of the type of passage which will be set in the examination. (Note that the type of passage may vary within a range from examination to examination. The syllabus regulations will tell you which types could be set: discursive, narrative, dialogue etc.). General knowledge of the kind discussed above may not be important if you are translating a passage of narrative or dialogue from a novel but it is still essential to understand fully the situation, so that you can know what is going on. If you choose your reading material sensibly then experience will help you to become familiar with not just narrative or descriptive vocabulary but with the way in which French writers deal with description or narrative or even the way in which dialogue is presented and punctuated on the printed page. You will also be better able to judge the tone, the formality or perhaps the humour of a passage, and to get a proper 'feel' of it, which is an essential step towards turning out a first-class translation.

CRITERIA FOR ASSESSMENT

The translation paper tests close understanding of the passage in French and ability to express its meaning in natural English.

Allowance is made in marking for the fact that there is often more than one way of translating the French phrase or sentence and for the fact that a wrong translation is often not entirely wrong.

Types of errors

The more serious errors would include the total misinterpretation of a word, an omission or unnecessary addition which distorts the meaning of the original, and grammatical errors such as the *wrong* choice of tense or the wrong use of pronouns, prepositions or adverbs. An expression which is definitely not English or a grammatical inaccuracy in the English (even though the meaning appears to be correct) would also be considered as a more serious error.

Less serious errors would include the use of a word or phrase which is not completely appropriate, a clumsy turn of phrase which nevertheless conveys the right meaning or an unnecessary addition which does not alter the meaning of the French.

The system of marking is a precise one. It reflects the importance of understanding thoroughly the original passage and the need for accuracy (and this should include punctuation and spelling) in the use of English. The translation paper, because of the way in which it is marked and the nature of the exercise itself, requires that you should give very careful attention to every word that you write.

FOUR MAJOR AREAS FOR IMPROVEMENT

THE PROBLEM OF VOCABULARY

When asked what worries them most about this paper students usually say that it is the problem of vocabulary, of simply not understanding the words or some of them. It is true that this is the most obvious cause of a poor result but it is never the only cause. Inability to understand structures, inaccurate use of English and unfamiliarity with the techniques of translation can also be major areas of weakness. You should therefore take positive steps to improve in all four areas throughout the course. If it seems that you are having to fight a battle on several fronts then console yourself with the thought that if you managed to make progress in only one direction you would still improve your chances quite significantly.

VOCABULARY

When preparing for the translation paper your objectives as far as vocabulary acquisition is concerned will be rather different from those required when working towards prose translation and the essay in French. Those two exercises depend on your active vocabulary. When you tackle the translation paper you will need to draw widely on the resources of your *passive* vocabulary which comprises that stock of words and phrases which you should be able to recognise but which you may not be able to recall spontaneously from your memory. The learner's passive vocabulary is assumed to be considerably wider than his active repertoire so you should aim at building it up throughout the course. Working on the translation set by your tutor will help but in order to ensure that your vocabulary is sufficiently wide and varied you should follow a programme of extensive reading (as opposed to the intensive reading described in chapter 11). There is advice on organising such a programme on page 110.

The more you read the more likely you are to meet new lexical items on subsequent occasions and so consolidate your recognition of them. This is important because although it may not be necessary to establish the new word as part of your active vocabulary, it is necessary nevertheless to be able to identify it accurately and to avoid the confusion which has led past candidates to read *chaussé* as *chauffé*, *honteusement* as *heureusement*, *jouir* and *jouer*, *épuisé* and *épousé*, and so on.

Of course you are bound to meet words that you do not recognise in the examination, no matter how conscientiously you have worked at extending your vocabulary. However, all is not lost if you do. The following points will help you to interpret a word which you are not sure of or even one which is totally new to you:

1 *Read the whole passage again* carefully. The context will often provide clues to the meaning of an unknown word and the surrounding sentences may even contain a synonym which you can recognise for the word which is baffling you. Generally speaking, the more important the word is to the passage you are translating, the more likely you are to accumulate evidence as to its meaning as you read on.
2 Always use your knowledge of grammar to establish whether the word is a *noun, adjective or verb*. If you can be certain of its function in the sentence then you are one step nearer to deciphering its meaning.
3 Use your knowledge of *suffixes and affixes*. They may indicate, for example, that a word is negative (e.g. *in*opportun), that it has unfavourable meaning (e.g. un *mal*faiteur) or that it probably indicates a process or an action (e.g. le ravitaille*ment*).
4 An *idiomatic expression* (that is, a lexical item consisting of several words with a meaning which cannot be deduced from the meaning of the individual words, e.g. y être pour quelque chose, en vouloir à quelqu'un, l'emporter sur quelqu'un etc. is difficult to interpret if you have not met it before. However, if you can isolate the group which the words make up and can decide that it is indeed an idiomatic expression, you may be able to deduce the meaning from the context and you will be less likely to produce a clumsy, literal translation.
5 Some expressions are *metaphorical* (e.g. des prix qui *montent en flèche*, un hôtelier qui *égorge* ses clients). You should look for this possibility if the literal translations seem unlikely. Identify the two terms of the comparison (e.g. rising prices/arrow), consider their characteristics and try to infer the meaning of the expression. You would therefore discard 'prices which rise like an arrow' and substitute 'rocketing prices'. It is likely that the English usage will require a metaphor involving different terms (e.g. not prices = arrow but prices = rocket).

6   A further difficulty sometimes arises because certain words have *more than one meaning* (e.g. toujours or toucher). Once again it is important to be prepared for this possibility and to relate the word to its context to ensure that you have chosen the right meaning.

STRUCTURES

When the structure of a sentence makes its interpretation uncertain it is again advisable to approach the problem systematically. The 'difficult' sentence is often one which confuses the student because of its length and complexity, even though the individual items of vocabulary have been recognised. The following sentences taken from past A-level papers are typical. They caused many candidates problems which could have been solved if there had been a little more reflection and method in the approach.

> *Reflection and method solve problems.*

a) Mais bon nombre d'écrivains prévoient un avenir que les progrès de la science et de la technologie rendront encore plus standardisé que le présent et où l'homme perdra progressivement sa liberté de choix.

b) Rappelant que serait célébré le mois suivant le 25ième anniversaire du traité de Rome, qui avait été indiscutablement pour quelque chose dans la prospérité qu'avait connue une Europe sortie de la guerre exsangue et ruinée, le ministre poursuivit: 'Pourquoi faut-il que cette célébration soit nuancée d'amertume?'

If you find yourself faced with a sentence like one of these and the meaning eludes you, first try reading it rapidly several times. A rapid reading of sentence (b), for example, will help you to connect *Rappelant* with the subject of the verb, *le ministre* which does not appear until the end of the sentence. After rapid reading ask yourself questions about what you think the sense might be and then read the sentence again slowly to see if there is any evidence that you were right. Reading the sentences which precede and follow should also provide clues to the meaning of the problem sentence.

If the sense still does not emerge clearly you can resort to a more systematic analysis:

1   Find the *main verbs* and try to establish what their *subjects* and *objects* are. Be prepared for the inversion of subject and verb, particularly after the relative pronoun 'que', as this is a very frequent source of confusion. There are examples of inversion in sentence (b) above.

2   Identify those *words which belong in the same semantic group or breath group*: le mois suivant, not *le mois suivant le 25ième anniversaire*; not *la guerre exsangue et ruinée* (it makes no sense to attach 'exsangue' and 'ruinée' to 'la guerre') but *une Europe . . . exsangue et ruinée*.

3   Identify the *present participles* and *past participles* and decide with what *subject* or *object* they belong. For example, 'rappelant' belongs with 'le ministre' and 'sortie' belongs with 'une Europe' in sentence (b) above.

4   If necessary, *rearrange the sentence* in a more straightforward manner, using all the grammatical clues that you can: e.g. les progrès (de la science) rendront l'avenir plus standardisé; Rappelant que le 25ième anniversaire (du traité de Rome) serait célèbre; une Europe (sortie de la guerre) avait connu la prospérité.

Under examination conditions you may be forced into inferring the meaning of words from context or into disentangling the syntax of a difficult sentence in order to draw out the sense. However, attempts at working out the meaning of a word or sentence based on the points listed above should not be reserved for the examination. Practise deducing meaning whenever you can. When you come across unknown vocabulary while reading or doing course-work translations, do not immediately open the dictionary; first see how far you can decipher the sense by using only those clues which are contained in the passage. You will be training yourself in a skill which will prove invaluable on the day of the examination.

USE OF ENGLISH

Once you have grasped the meaning of the text you are translating there remains the essential task of expressing that meaning accurately in English. Candidates are not always aware of the importance of this part of the exercise. Although they may have reached a sound, detailed understanding of the French they are not always careful enough about the way they express themselves in English.

When the English is substandard it is sometimes because the candidates simply do not have sufficient control of their own language to avoid grammatical errors and spelling mistakes. In the main it is the process of translating itself which leads them to invent words, to distort syntax and to produce stilted, non- English sentences which they would probably not write at all under normal circumstances. Of course, it is not easy to switch from reading and understanding a testing passage of French to expressing yourself fluently and accurately in English. It is certainly not a skill which can be suddenly produced on the day of the examination; it is a mental exercise which must be practised throughout the course.

When you work on a translation, try to think of more than one English version for any phrase or sentence. Ask yourself which version is closest in meaning to the original and then ask yourself whether it sounds natural within its context. When you have finished the work it is a good idea to put it aside for a day or two so that you can reread it and criticise it later as a passage of English. Better still, get somebody to read it who has not seen the original. You may have to admit that what you have written, or some of it, is stilted and reads like 'translationese' rather than genuine English, but you will know what it is that you have to improve. Try rephrasing what you have written or look for a word which is more normal in English, but always check once more to ensure that your correction satisfied the sense of the original.

It may seem rather surprising to learn that you have to work at your English when you have chosen to study French, but it will pay dividends. Faulty, imprecise or clumsy English will cause you to lose marks in the examination. As examiners' reports regularly point out, use of English is an aspect of the translation paper which many candidates seem to neglect and it contributes more significantly than many realise to success or failure in this part of the examination.

TECHNIQUES OF TRANSLATION

Here we will review a number of points which really are to do with the technique of translation under examination conditions. They are based on experience of the way in which candidates tend to perform in the translation paper and can be regarded as essential guidelines as to what should be done whenever you embark on a translation, and, more importantly, when you sit down to tackle the translation on the day of the examination.

1   *Read the French thoroughly several times.* Even if you can understand it without difficulty, it is important to get the feel of the passage. Do not aim at understanding only the words. Read into the passage so that its logic, if it contains an argument or discussion, is clear to you. If it is narrative, description or dialogue, try to picture the situation and keep it in your mind. This will ensure that you translate not just words but ideas and that whenever you translate a word or phrase you relate it to its context.

2   Although, quite obviously, you should not attempt to translate the French word by word, you should *make sure that you have taken account of every word of the original.* Candidates regularly lose marks needlessly because words have been carelessly omitted. It is easily done; the translation may make perfectly good sense in spite of one or two missing adverbs or adjectives and so mislead you into thinking that all is well. It is important to make a final check in order to compare what you have written, sentence by sentence, with the original passage.

3   When you read the French attentively in order to grasp its full meaning you will *give careful thought to all grammatical structures.* There are, however, certain aspects of grammar and syntax which cause problems more frequently than others. An analysis of 250 scripts produced in past examinations shows that particular attention should be given to the following five areas:

   a) **Use of tenses** (easily the most frequent source of error). Candidates tend to misinterpret compound tenses (e.g. elle avait régressé; il se serait accru), particularly when they are uncertain of the meaning of the verb (a 'double' difficulty is likely to lead to at least one error). They also frequently overlook a change of tense (e.g. from past to present, from simple past to pluperfect) in the original.

   b) **Relative pronouns.** Qui, que, qu', ce qui, ce qu' are very frequently confused, usually with disastrous results for the rest of the sentence.

   c) **The articles.** Many candidates are careless in distinguishing between the definite and indefinite article and sometimes between the definite article and the possessive or demonstrative adjective. To write 'a typewriter' instead of 'the typewriter', 'the letter' instead of '*this* letter', '*his* umbrella' instead of '*an* umbrella' may not alter the sense very much but it may well make enough difference for marks to be lost. It is therefore important to check details of this nature.

d) **Pronouns**. Many candidates interpret pronouns rather carelessly. Errors arise when candidates do not distinguish between direct object and indirect object pronouns (so that a sentence such as *je lui/leur présentai Jean* is translated incorrectly as 'I introduced him/them to Jean') and when they relate the pronoun to its noun (with the result that *he* is written for *she*, *he* for *it* and so on).

e) **Conjunctions**. A mistake involving a conjunction is very noticeable since it will affect the sense of the whole sentence. It is not possible to list here all the conjunctions which you should know but it can be said that the following have caused numerous problems in recent examinations: en outre, de reste, encore que, alors que, aussitôt que, à moins que. If you are uncertain of the meaning of any of these then you should certainly look up co-ordinating and subordinating conjunctions in your grammar-book and revise them. The conjunction is a keyword which will often unlock the meaning of an entire sentence.

These five 'danger areas' (a – e) do not constitute an exhaustive check-list but examining experience shows that they are major causes of difficulty and therefore they should have a place in your personal check-list.

4 Remember that you are aiming at a *precise translation* of the French. A loose translation will lose marks when words are added unnecessarily or when the sentence is recast for no good reason. When this happens the candidate's intentions are usually good; the addition of words or the rearrangement of phrases and sentences is meant to make the translation read more like English. What often happens however, is that the addition of words or recasting alters the meaning of the original. Ask yourself very carefully, therefore, whether you are adding details to the original. Be cautious about rearranging the order of sentences and phrases. Recasting a sentence should be carried out not for the sake of it but only if it is the best or only way of putting the meaning of the original into English. Wholesale recasting is seldom or never necessary. The sensible rule to follow is that if the straightforward translation conveys the meaning of the French and makes perfectly good English, do not alter it.

5 Remember that it is *often acceptable to translate a word of the original by the 'same' word in English* (e.g. *refuser* will be translated by 'to refuse', *inspecter* by 'to inspect') if it fits the context and makes good sense. This has to be pointed out because candidates sometimes distort the meaning of the original by trying, without justification, 'to get away from the French'. If a transliterated word fits perfectly well into the English sentence you may use it. If there is a more common or more natural English word which conveys the right meaning, then use that instead.

6 *When you come up against a word which you do not know* then adopt the approach described on page 151. Do not follow the example of thoses candidates who first leave a blank space, return to it later, make an uninformed guess at the word and then alter the rest of the sentence to accommodate the wrong translation.

7 When you have finished the translation read it through from beginning to end simply to *check the English*. If it does not make sense then something must be wrong and you should therefore consider the original once more.

EXAMINATION QUESTIONS

Q1

'Inconcevable', a commenté sobrement le ministre de la Justice. En s'évadant de la prison de la Santé à bord d'un hélicoptère piloté par sa femme, Michel Vautour a conquis sa place dans les annales des grandes évasions. Voleur et cambrioleur depuis l'âge de dix-sept ans, il n'en était pas à son coup d'essai: une demi-douzaine de tentatives, trois réussites, trois fois repris. Et puis, lundi dernier, une sorte de modèle du genre. L'homme ne s'était jamais résolu à rester jusqu'en 1997 derrière les barreaux. Plusieurs mois avant cet événement, l'administration pénitentiaire avait eu vent de son projet, sans pour autant empêcher sa quatrième évasion.

Au-delà des aspects extraordinaires de son exploit, une observation inquiétante demeure: il est très difficile d'empêcher un hélicoptère-pirate de survoler la capitale. Il lui suffit de quelques minutes pour aller d'un aérodrome de banlieue jusqu'au coeur de la zone interdite, c'est-à-dire Paris. Dans un délai si court, toute intervention est impossible. Démunies quand un détenu s'évade, les autorités le seraient tout autant en face de la détermination d'un 'terroriste des airs'. L'Elysée, un ministère, une ambassade: les cibles potentielles sont multiples. Et la défense inexistante.

Michel Vautour, sa femme Nadine, et leur complice le savaient. Il ne leur restait plus qu'à mettre sur pied un scénario.

Le lundi 26 mai, Nadine loue une Alouette II. A 10h 35, la tour de contrôle de l'héliport d'Issy-les-Moulineaux, responsable de la circulation aérienne sur Paris, s'étonne de cet hélicoptère qui s'apprête à franchir le periphérique, limite à ne pas dépasser. Mais le pilote reste sourd aux appels, et l'Alouette se retrouve en quelques minutes à la verticale de la Santé, en vol stationnaire.

(AEB, 1988 from *La Fille de l'air*, by Francois Rousselle, *Le Point* 1986)

Q2

Dans la presqu'ile de Quiberon: un beau terrain de camping, vraiment. La densité de population y est très forte en juillet et août. Et pourtant, beaucoup de ceux qui passent ici leurs vacances y viennent depuis de longues années, avec un plaisir qui ne semble pas s'émousser.

A bien les écouter, on comprend qu'ils trouvent là plus qu'un temps de loisir: une autre façon de vivre. Pour manger la soupe de poisson ou le poulet des grands soirs, ils sont jusqu'à cinquante ou soixante à aligner leurs tables les unes à la suite des autres. Les comportements expriment une volonté implicite de faire disparaître les barrières que le mode de vie actuel multiplie dans la vie courante. Tout le monde parle à tout le monde, y compris à l'inconnu qui vient d'arriver, tout est occasion d'entr'aide. Les enfants, en particulier, sont partout chez eux, non seulement acceptés, mais choyés comme rarement ailleurs.

L'étonnant est qu'il n'y ait pas saturation, au bout d'un moment, et que cette belle entente réussisse à tenir jusqu'au bout des vacances.

(ULSEB, 1982. *'Mille Petites Républiques Paisibles'*, by M.C.Betbeder, *Le Monde* 10.8.80)

Q3

Le lundi qui suivit l'enterrement de son voisin, Mathilde entendit des pas dans sa cour. C'était Clémonçon, le facteur, avec ses jambières qui le protegaient des chiens. Elle en eut un coup au coeur. Peut-être lui apportait-il une lettre . . . Elle n'avait l'habitude de le voir qu'aux échéances de sa pension. Autrement, personne ne lui écrivait. Car elle ne comptait pas pour lettres ces billets de Jour de l'An qu'elle recevait de ses lointains neveux et nièces, avec des nouvelles de toute l'année écoulée et des voeux de cérémonie.

Elle regarda ses mains, pour deviner ce qu'il apportait.

— Eh bonjour! fit-il.

Elle sentait sa gorge sèche et n'eut pas même assez de salive pour répondre.

— C'est un journal. Votre voisin était abonné au journal. Ça veut dire qu'il recevait *La Montagne* tous les jours. Et même il venait juste de renouveler l'abonnement. Vous voyez?

Il lui montra le journal, enveloppé de sa bande, avec le nom imprimé du destinataire.

— Alors, continua le facteur, qu'est-ce que j'en fais?

— C'est pas moi qui vais vous le dire, mon pauvre Clémonçon.

— Et si je vous le laissais, à vous, ce journal?

— A moi? Et qu'est-ce que j'en ferai?

— Vous le lirez. Ça vous passera un moment. Et puis, ça vous fournira du papier.

(ULSEB 1988)

Q4

A l'entrée de la rue Servandoni Anne se heurta à un barrage d'agents. Deux voitures de pompiers stationnaient au bord du trottoir. De larges flaques d'eau brillaient sur la chaussée. Elle leva les yeux sur la facade du bâtiment et faillit crier de saisissement. Les murs étaient noircis, toutes les vitres avaient sauté. Sur le trottoir s'amoncelaient des débris de meubles et des pièces de bois carbonisé.

Anne demanda — Que s'est-il passé?

Dix personnes lui répondirent. Selon les premières constatations, le feu avait pris, après la fermeture des bureaux, dans la réserve du sous-sol, au milieu d'un amas de vieux papiers, et s'était propagé très vite dans les étages supérieurs. Le concierge, réveillé en pleine nuit, avait alerté les pompiers qui étaient arrivés aussitôt sur les lieux mais n'avaient pu maitriser l'incendie qu'à l'aube. Heureusement il n'y avait pas de victimes. En revanche les dégats materiels étaient considérables. Ce que les flammes avaient épargné, les pompiers l'avaient noyé sous des trombes d'eau. Le propriétaire parlait de catastrophe sans nom.

– C'est sûrement quelqu'un de la maison qui a fait le coup!   (ULSEB 1989)

Q5

On l'appelait 'La montagne maudite'. On admirait son dôme inviolé. Personne ne s'y risquait. Les rares qui l'avaient affrontée n'étaient jamais revenus. Le Mont Blanc faisait peur. Deux hommes, Michel Paccard, médecin, et Jacques Balmat, guide, s'élancent à sa conquête. De la vallée on suit leur progression au téléscope. Enfin, les deux silhouettes chargées de couvertures, vivres, eau-de-vie, bois pour se chauffer, atteignent la cime. C'est le 8 août 1786. Il y a deux siècles.

C'est cette première victoire sur le Mont Blanc que l'on a célébrée avec faste. Deux guides en tenue de l'époque ont emprunté la voie tracée par Paccard et Balmat, indiquée par deux cent cinquante points lumineux rouge et argent. Un son et lumière, commenté par le guide-écrivaint Roger Frison-Roche, a illuminé la montagne en fête. Les sommets des aiguilles de Chamonix ont été embrasés par un feu d'artifice. Depuis cette période historique, le Mont Blanc a vu cinq cent vingt fois surgir au sommet de ses parois les plus dangereuses les visages triomphants de ses vainqueurs. Pourtant, récemment encore, douze alpinistes ont trouvé la mort et une vingtaine ont été blessés. Mais ses colères ont été vaines et Yannide Seigneur, Walter Bonatti, entre autres, ont contribué à la légende de la montagne maudite, aujourd'hui exorcisée. Bonatti a écrit, dans son ouvrage *Magie du Mont Blanc*: 'En ces lieux, les alpinistes sont comme des oiseaux de passage qui s'en vont avec l'été. Je me sens confondu dans l'univers.'

(AEB 1989, Jean Noli, *Le Point* 11.8.86)

Q6

Judith, 20 ans, travaille au Bon Marché pendant les grandes vacances.

– Au début, j'avais postulé un emploi de caissière. A la fin du premier jour, j'étais morte. Bien que tenir une caisse ne soit pas difficile, l'attitude des gens donne des frissons dans le dos. Il y a les pressés, qui trouvent que ça ne va pas assez vite et bousculent tout le monde dans la file d'attente; il y a les méprisants, qui ne disent jamais un mot; les méfiants, qui recalculent les sommes du ticket. Mon pire souvenir: une dame d'un certain âge, très chic, mais complètement hystérique, a renversé le contenu de son porte-monnaie dans ma caisse. Il a fallu fermer la caisse pour tout recompter. Ce jour-là, ç'en était trop. J'ai demandé à faire autre chose.

– J'ai commencé par me tromper de rayon. J'avais été affectée aux sacs (dans mon esprit la maroquinerie), et je me suis retrouvée à vendre des sacs de poubelles sur le trottoir. Remarquez, ça valait mieux que le sort de mon copain François, parachuté au rayon alimentation et qui, coiffé d'un incroyable chapeau de paille, était investi de la délicate mission de faire goûter les vins de Cahors. Certains soirs, il sortait vraiment euphorique!

(ULSEB 1990)

OUTLINE ANSWERS TO QUESTIONS 2 AND 3

Translate Questions 2 and 3. Read through the notes before beginning to translate. Each passage is followed by an English translation with which you may compare your own version.

Question 2

a) This is an example of the kind of passage which tests your ability to express yourself in English as much as the ability to understand the French. The difficulty is to find expressions and construct sentences which read naturally. What will you do, for example, with those sentences which are rather elliptical (there seems to be a verb missing!) in construction?

- Dans la presqu'île de Quiberon: un beau terrain de camping, vraiment!
- A bien les écouter, on comprend qu'ils trouvent là plus qu'un temps de loisir: une autre façon de vivre.

Here it may be necessary to remodel the sentence, perhaps by adding a verb, until it sounds like English. But do not lose sight of the original.

b) There are probably certain words that you do not recognise, such as *s'émousser, les comportements, entraide, choyés, entente*. However, you should be able to infer their meaning when you have the context clear in your mind.

   - S'émousser: there are a great many people on the campsite, people have been coming for years but their enjoyment never_____(?)
   - Choyés: children can feel at home everywhere, they are accepted, but more than that they are_____(?)

Remember to use all the clues provided by the sentence or surrounding sentences:

   - Les comportements: Les comportements expriment une volonté implicite. *Implicite* (implicit, unspoken) will throw some light on *comportements*. If a desire is not expressed in words, how is it likely to be expressed? By actions, attitudes, behaviour, sign-language, facial expression? Obviously certain possibilities are more likely than others.

c) Be careful of those phrases which are easy enough to understand — densité de population, un temps de loisir, la densité est . . . forte, au bout d'un moment, etc. — but which you will not be able to translate literally. 'The density is . . . strong', 'at the end of a moment', etc. would not, of course, be acceptable.

d) It will be helpful to try to picture what is described: Pour la manger la soupe de poisson ou le poulet des grands soirs, ils sont jusqu'à cinquante ou soixante à aligner leurs tables les unes à la suite des autres. If fifty or sixty people are eating together outside what are they likely to do with their tables?

e) Look at the structure of the more complex sentences. Try reading them quickly and then more slowly. Find the object and subject of the verb *multiplie* in 'Les comportements expriment une volonté implicite de faire disparaître les barrières que le mode de vie actuel multiplie dans la vie courante'. Make sure that you grasp the overall structure of 'L'étonnant est qu'il n'y ait pas saturation, au bout d'un moment, et que cette belle entente réussisse à tenir jusqu'au bout des vacances'. The two subjunctives will help you to understand that both clauses are introduced by *L'étonnant est qu'/que*.

Question 3

a) This passage is a mixture of narrative and dialogue. When dealing with narrative you should pay particular attention to the tenses of the original: distinguish between the narrative tense (the past historic in this passage) and the descriptive tense (the imperfect). Be careful of the way you translate the imperfect. The English continuous tense, 'was doing', 'was writing' etc. is not always appropriate. Think about these two sentences from the passage.

   - Peut-être lui apportait-il une lettre
   - Car elle ne comptait pas pour lettres ces billets de Jour de l'An

The tense is the same in each sentence in French (apportait, comptait) but is it the same in English? This is an example of how understanding the context and thinking your way into the situation which is being described can help you to translate accurately.

If you have the situation or the scene clear in your mind you are less likely to make mistakes over choosing 'his' or 'her' when translating *son, sa, ses*. Which is it in these sentences?

   - Elle regarda ses mains
   - Le lundi qui suivit l'enterrement de son voisin
   - Elle sentait sa gorge sèche

b) When translating dialogue it is again important to understand the situation, to be clear about who says what and to picture the scene so that you can be sure that each word and sentence is appropriate in its context.

It is important to reproduce as far as possible the natural speech patterns of English. 'Does it sound natural?', 'Would one say or hear that?' are the questions you must put to yourself as you translate. A literal translation is not likely to work. How are you going to deal with the following sentence?

- C'est pas moi qui vais vous le dire, mon pauvre Clémonçon.

You would not say

- It is isn't me who is going to tell you it, my poor Clémonçon.

The question of register is important. It does not follow necessarily that the language is familiar because it is the language of a conversation. The speakers may be speaking formally and carefully. However, you are obviously more likely to meet familiar or even slang terms in a passage of dialogue. Be prepared therefore to produce a colloquial rendering, but only if the original justifies it.

c) There will be words and idioms in this passage which you do not know. Probably, enterrement, jambières, échéances de pension, écoulée, voeux de cérémonie, abonné, abonnement. If you look at the word carefully and then consider the context you should be able to make an informed guess, e.g.

- enterrement — terre

- jambières – jambe; qui le protégaient des chiens

- échéances de pension — more difficult, but you can understand that it is a question of something that the postman brings on certain occasions.

Be careful with idiomatic expressions such as *Elle en eut un coup au coeur*. There are expressions in English involving the word 'heart' but they are not all appropriate here: 'her heart leapt', 'her heart sank', 'she had a heart attack', 'her heart missed a beat'. Which is it?

Translation — Question 2

In the Quiberon peninsula there is indeed a beautiful campsite. The number of people there is very high in July and August. And yet those who spend their holidays here have been coming for many years with a pleasure which never seems to diminish.

If you really listen to them you can see that what they find there is something more than a period of leisure time: they find a different way of living. When they eat the fish soup or chicken which they have on special evenings, as many as fifty or sixty of them will arrange their tables next to each other in a long row. People's behaviour expresses an unspoken desire to do away with the barriers which the way we live today makes increasingly numerous in everyday life. Everyone speaks to everyone else, including the newcomer, everything provides an opportunity for people to help one another. The children in particular are welcome everywhere, not just accepted but made a fuss of as they rarely are elsewhere.

What is astonishing is that people do not soon feel they have had too much of it and that this splendid spirit of understanding can last until the end of the holidays.

Translation — Question 3

On the Monday after her neighbour's burial, Mathilde heard footsteps in her yard. It was Clémonçon, the postman, wearing the leggings which protected him from the dogs. Her heart missed a beat. Perhaps he was bringing her a letter . . . She was only used to seeing him when her pension was due. Apart from that nobody ever wrote to her. For she did not regard as letters those New Year's greetings which she received from her distant nephews and nieces, with news of the whole of the past year and the traditional good wishes.

She looked at his hands to try to guess what he was bringing her.

— Good day to you! he said.

Her throat felt dry and she didn't even have enough saliva to answer.

— It's a newspaper. Your neighbour had taken out a subscription for the newspaper. That is to say that he used to get *La Montagne* every day. And what's more he had only just renewed the subscription. You see?

He showed her the newspaper in its wrapper, with the name of the person to whom it was addressed printed on it.

— So, went on the postman, what am I to do with it?

— My dear Clémonçon, I'm not the one to tell you what to do.

— Suppose I was to leave the paper for you?

— For me? And what shall I do with it?

— You'll read it. It will help you to pass the time. And then, it will provide you with paper.

A TUTOR'S ANSWER TO QUESTIONS 1, 5 AND 6

Question 1

'Inconceivable' was the sober comment of the Minister of Justice. By escaping from the prison de la Santé aboard a helicopter flown by his wife, Michel Vautour has won a place for himself in the annals of great escapes. It was not the first attempt for this man who had been a thief and a burglar since the age of seventeen: he had tried to escape half a dozen times before, had succeeded three times and had been caught three times. And then came last Monday's attempt which was a model of its kind. The man had never resigned himself to remaining behind bars until 1997. The prison administration had got wind of his plan several months before the event but without foiling his fourth escape.

If one goes beyond the extraordinary aspects of his exploit there is one disturbing observation to be made: it is very difficult to stop a pirate helicopter from flying over the capital. It needs only a few minutes to fly from an airfield in the suburbs to the heart of the prohibited area, that is to say Paris. At such short notice any intervention is impossible. If the authorities are powerless when a prisoner makes an escape, then they would be just as powerless when faced with the determination of an 'airborne terrorist'. It could be the Elysée, a ministry, an embassy: there are very many potential targets. And the means of defence are non-existant.

Michel Vautour, his wife Nadine and their accomplice knew this. They had only to set up a scenario.

On Monday the 26th of May, Nadine hired an Alouette II. At 10.35 the control-tower at the Issy-les-Moulineaux heliport which is responsible for air traffic over Paris was astonished to see this helicopter preparing to cross the ring road which marks the limits of the prohibited area. But the pilot did not listen to their radio calls and within a few minutes the Alouette was hovering directly over the Santé.

Question 5

They called it the 'accursed mountain'. They admired its unscaled summit. Nobody ventured there. The few who had tackled it had never returned. Mont Blanc inspired people with fear. Two men, Michel Paccard, a doctor, and Jacques Balmat, a guide, went forth to conquer it. Down in the valley people followed their progress by telescope. Finally, the two figures loaded with blankets, food, brandy and firewood reached the summit. It was the 8th of August 1786. That was two centuries ago.

It is that first conquest of Mont Blanc which has been celebrated with much ceremony. Two guides dressed in the costume of the period took the route established by Paccard and Balmat, which was marked out with 250 red and silver beacons. A 'son et lumière' display, accompanied by a commentary from Roger Frison-Roche, the writer and guide, lit up the festive mountain. The sharp peaks of Chamonix were illuminated by a firework display. Since that historic time Mont Blanc has seen the triumphant faces of its conquerors climb up over the top of its most dangerous rock-faces five hundred and twenty times. nevertheless, even recently, twelve mountaineers have died and about twenty have been injured. But its anger has been to no avail and Yannide Seigneur and Walter Bonatti, among others, have contributed to the legend of the accursed mountain, which has now been exorcised. Bonatti wrote in his book *'The Magic of Mont Blanc'*: 'Here the mountaineers are like birds of passage which depart with summer. I feel that I have lost myself in the universe.'

Question 6

Judith, who is 20 years old, works at Bon Marché during the summer holidays.

— At first I had applied for a job on the tills. At the end of the first day I was all in. Although being in charge of a till is not difficult, people's attitudes make you shudder. There are the ones who are in a hurry who think that things are not moving fast enough and jostle everybody in the queue; then there are the arrogant ones who never say a word; and the mistrustful who check the additions on the receipt. My worst memory is of a middle-aged lady who was very smart but completely hysterical, who spilt the contents of her purse into my till. We had to close down the till and count everything again. That day I had enough. I asked to do something else. I started off by going to the wrong department. I had been put on bags (to me that meant leather goods) and I found myself selling dustbin bags outside on the pavement. Mind you, that was better than the fate of my friend François who was sent off to the food department and with an incredible straw hat on his head was entrusted with the delicate mission of handing out samples of Cahors wines. On some evenings he used to come out really merry.

A STUDENT'S ANSWER TO QUESTION 4 WITH EXAMINER'S COMMENTS

> Re-phrase; not normal English. Mistranslation.

> Always best to keep French names in French.

> The street does not have a floor; think of the context.

> Not the right word to go with "policemen".

At the entrance of Servandoni Road Anne found herself at a barrage of policemen. Two fire-engines were parked at the edge of the pavement. Large puddles of water were shining on the floor. She looked up at the front of the building and failed to cry out in horror. The walls were blackened, all the windows had gone. On the pavement the remains of furniture and pieces of burnt wood were amounting.

> The pronominal verb describes a state, so the tense is wrong. The verb "to amount" is also misused.

> Acceptable to change the position of this phrase to give a more English word order.

> Wrong term.

'What has happened?' asked Anne. Ten people replied. According to the first reports the fire had started after the offices had been closed down, in the reserves of the basement, in the middle of a heap of old papers, and it propagated very quickly to the floors above. The caretaker, woken in the middle of the night, had alerted the fire-bridgade who arrived at once but had not been able to put out the fire until down. Fortunately there were no victims. On the other hand the material damage was considerable. That which the flames had burnt the firemen had drowned it with their hosepipes. The owner was talking about a catastrophe without naming it.
— It's certainly someone from within the firm who had done the deed.

> Indicates final closure — not the case here.

> The French does not say "éteindre".

> Phrase missed out — always check.

> Sounds very stilted.

> Mistranslation.

> The right meaning but is it what he would have said?

> Look at every word but do not translate literally.

> Not very likely — think again.

> A good try but not accurate enough.

Translation — Question 4

As she entered rue Servandoni Anne came up against a police road block. Two fire-engines were parked at the edge of the pavement. Great puddles of water were gleaming on the surface of the road. She looked up at the front of the building and nearly cried out with shock. The walls were blackened and all the window panes had gone. On the pavement the remains of furniture and pieces of charred wood lay in heaps.
— What has happened? asked Anne.
Ten people answered her. According to the first indications, the fire had started after the offices had closed, in the basement store room, in the middle of a heap of old papers, and had spread very quickly to the upper floors. The caretaker, woken in the middle of the night, had alerted the fire-brigade which had arrived on the scene immediately but had only been able to get the fire under control at dawn. Fortunately, there were no victims. On the other hand the damage to property was considerable. What the flames had spared the firemen had drowned with jets of water. The owner was talking of it as an unspeakable disaster.
— It's certainly someone from within the firm who is responsible!

14

ORAL WORK

GETTING STARTED

Oral examinations in modern languages have undergone considerable change, mainly because it is recognised that ability to speak the foreign language in everyday situations is the skill which is most likely to be of practical use to the learner outside the classroom. The changes which have been made mean that more emphasis is placed on oral communication. A greater percentage of the marks may now be allotted to this section of the examination (up to 20% of the total for some A-level syllabuses and as much as 40% for certain AS-level syllabuses) and oral examinations are generally becoming more broad-ranging and more life-related. They demand more of the candidate in the examination room and they require more specific preparation but they also give you the opportunity to follow up your own interests through the medium of the foreign language, to become more involved personally and to feel that communicating in French is a useful, 'real life' activity.

However, before getting involved you should find out precise details of what your oral examination will consist of. Use the syllabus regulations to answer the following questions:

- How long does the oral examination take?
- What proportion of the total subject mark is allocated to it?
- Is the examination divided into parts with a separate mark for each?
- What exactly will you be required to do for each part of the examination?
- Is there specific preparation which should be completed before the day of the examination (e.g. prescribed reading, compilation of a dossier, preparation of a chosen topic etc.)
- How much preparation time (if any) is allowed immediately before the oral?
- Is the use of a dictionary allowed during preparation?
- Will the oral be recorded? (The tape- recorder puts some candidates off if they are not prepared for it).
- Will the oral be conducted by an external examiner or by your own teacher?

The oral, because it requires you to put on a performance in a live situation face-to-face with an examiner, can make the most confident candidate feel nervous. However, it will help you to overcome nerves and to concentrate on the task in hand if you know exactly what is going to happen and have had a few practice runs under examination conditions.

WHAT IS THE EXAMINER LOOKING FOR?

PRONUNCIATION

FLUENCY

ACCURACY

RANGE

POSSIBLE ELEMENTS

IN THE EXAMINATION ROOM

VISITING FRANCE

ESSENTIAL PRINCIPLES

WHAT IS THE EXAMINER LOOKING FOR?

Above all, the examiner will set out to judge your ability to communicate naturally in French. In order to do this he will consider a number of factors. One of them will certainly be the accuracy with which you use the spoken language but you should be reassured to know that this is not the only factor and that the examiner will not be concentrating exclusively on your mistakes and simply be waiting to pounce on the first wrong gender, wrong verb ending or mispronunciation. If you are engaging him in conversation and getting him interested in your ideas and opinions he is likely to ignore errors which do not seriously get in the way of understanding and indeed he is not likely to notice every slip that you make.

Of course, he will reward accuracy but he will also consider your fluency, your ability to 'keep going' and the range of vocabulary and structures that you can handle spontaneously.

He will also be influenced by your willingness to talk and to take the initiative, and your ability to follow up points and add comments in a natural way. It is as important to try to be lively and outgoing and to have something that you really want to say as it is to form grammatically correct sentences.

In most oral examinations the examiner will use a grid to help assess the candidate's ability to take part in a conversation or discussion. The grid shown here is typical of those used in A- and AS-level orals.

OVERALL ASSESSMENT	PRONUNCIATION AND INTONATION	FLUENCY	ACCURACY	RANGE
Very poor	Hardly comprehensible.	Responds with only 2/3 words.	So incorrect that communication is not possible.	Cannot produce full sentences; very anglicised.
Poor	Very anglicised (e.g. English "r", "l", English vowel sounds).	Poor comprehension. Halting. Understands basic questions.	Much basic error (e.g. in tenses and verb forms).	Only simple sentences; vocabulary limited.
Adequate	Nasals and most vowels correct but phrases disjointed, intonation un-French.	Can produce a sentence or two at a time but needs prompting.	Basic structures correct but attempts at complex language produce error.	Beginning to use more complex sentences. A little idiom.
Good	Intonation reasonably French. Phrasing better. Some mispronunciation.	Little hesitancy; keeps going over several sentences; can take the initiative.	Mostly accurate (e.g. genders, verb forms). Simple language very accurate.	Can vary structures. Wider vocabulary; uses subordinate clauses, range of tenses.
Very good	Sounds genuinely French but with occasional mistakes in pronunciation and intonation.	Almost no problems of comprehension; capable of continuous flow; ready to lead the conversation.	Very few errors even in quite complex language.	Knowledge of idiom; wider use of adjectives, adverbs; more complex sentences.

Typical examiner's grid: A-level and AS-level orals

Of course, there is no point in trying to have such a grid in mind when you are talking to the examiner but it is useful to refer to it when you are trying to find ways of improving your oral performance. It will show you that if you are to create a good impression in the exam you must provide evidence of your ability to speak. You should not limit yourself to brief, simple answers and then wait in silence for the next question. You should endeavour to put several sentences together at a time in order to elaborate on a statement, to add an alternative point or a personal opinion or even to ask the examiner for his. You should show that you can 'think out loud' and move on to an associated idea as one does in a more natural conversation. Give the examiner something for which he can reward you. He must have something to go on; even if he knew that you were a native speaker he could not give high marks if you were generally uncommunicative, no matter how authentically you shrugged your shoulders and told him 'Bof! Je n'sais pas, moi.'

APPLIED PRINCIPLES

Whether you are aiming to improve pronunciation, intonation, fluency, accuracy or range of language you should spend a good deal of time listening to spoken French. The advice given in chapter 12 will help you to improve your ability to listen and will give you some ideas about what you should listen to. Listening to interviews, discussions, talks, radio 'phone-ins' and (preferably unscripted) recorded dialogues will provide you with models of natural speech which you will consciously and even unconsciously imitate.

By listening to French spoken spontaneously in a wide variety of everyday situations you will not only become familiar with the stress, rhythms and intonation of native French speakers you will also learn to identify and reproduce those phrases which serve as a support or framework to practically any conversation or discussion. For example, those space-filling phrases which do not mean very much but give the speaker time to think and organise what he is going to say: Alors . . .; Bon alors . . .; Moi, ce que je pense, c'est que . . .;Attendez voir . . .;Euh, c'est-à-dire que . . .; De toutes façons, il n'était pas là tout à l'heure, vous savez. You will learn how to pause, hesitate, correct yourself or ask to have something repeated or clarified while still keeping the conversation going.

PRONUNCIATION

> If your pronunciation is good then errors in your French often pass unnoticed.

You will probably have mastered the basic sounds and patterns of stress and intonation if you are embarking on an advanced course, but it is unlikely that your pronunciation, your French accent has no further room for improvement. It is as well to put it to the test before the day of the exam. You should enlist the help of the French 'assistant' or some other native speaker to help you identify persistent errors and particularly those which stand in the way of communication. The correction of just one or two recurring errors (e.g. interference of English 'r' or 'l', failure to stress the final syllable of a word or word group, failure to nasalise nasal vowels) can raise the level of performance considerably.

Many students have improved the Frenchness of their accents when they have been made aware of some of the general characteristics of French pronunciation. For example, that the production of French vowel sounds requires a certain muscular tension in the speech-organs and that the rounding of the lips plays a much greater part than in the pronunciation of English. Some students improve their delivery by 'thinking towards the lips' when they are speaking French or even by keeping in mind the way in which a French speaker forms his words when he is speaking English with a French accent.

When you have diagnosed your pronunciation errors the use of a course in French pronunciation (such as French pronunciation by Martineau and McGivney) will provide exercises and explanations which will help you to put them right. If you have access to a language laboratory with a tape library it is likely that various types of pronunciation exercises will be available on tape.

Alternatively, it is useful to make use of material which has been recorded for Listening Comprehension. A recorded text is 'exploded', that is it is re-recorded with blank intervals on the tape so that the student can listen and then imitate and record manageable sections of the text. The exercise is best done in a language lab but can also be simulated with a cassette recorder which has a pause button. If, after listening and repeating, you read and record the entire passage you will help to prepare for the reading aloud which forms part of a number of advanced oral examinations.

FLUENCY

> If you can show enthusiasm and enter into the spirit of the situation, you are more likely to impress the examiner.

You will show the oral examiner that you have fluency if you are able to sustain the flow of the conversation, responding where necessary with continuous stretches of speech. The candidate who can 'keep the momentum going' clearly performs much better than someone who can 'manage only a word or phrase in response to prompting'. Succeeding in this area comes partly from motivating yourself to communicate, from being determined to say something and partly from your ability to produce continuous French, to string sentences together.

The best way of improving performance is by performing, by putting yourself into situations where you have to make the effort to produce spoken French in order to communicate. If you have no opportunity to converse with a native speaker then practise with a friend or use a cassette recorder to record your own ad-lib accounts of everyday situations, events and routines. The important thing is to develop strategies for finding your way round difficulties, such as resorting to simpler constructions and paraphrasing. It is also useful to record yourself ad-libbing on a given subject, allowing your thoughts to be directed by the French phrases and vocabulary which come to mind, simply for the practice of putting sentences together to produce continuous discourse.

There are useful exercises which can be practised in the language lab (or with a cassette recorder) which will improve fluency:

■ Listen to a dialogue or recorded interview which is short enough to be memorised. Record the dialogue further on the tape but with one of the voices erased. The exercise is to fill in the missing side of the dialogue. The dialogues in *Guide Pratique de la Communication* (see the Further Reading section at the end of the chapter) are excellent for this purpose.

■ Use a cassette player with a pause button. Listen and re-listen to a passage of recorded French until you understand it clearly then, using the pause button, replay it in short sections. Replay a group of words and repeat them; replay the following groups of words and then repeat from memory the first group followed by the second group; replay a third group and repeat groups 1, 2 and 3, and so on. It is possible to repeat quite lengthy stretches of speech in this way. You will improve your aural memory and your fluency.

■ If you have access to a language lab with a tape library listen to a story, anecdote or news bulletin. Make brief notes and then attempt to reproduce and record the story or account using only your notes.

■ In the language lab listen to a spoken text then rewind and speak and record the text on the student track as you listen to the master track, using it to 'cue' yourself.

You should also make use of the exercises in your course-book to help you build sentences. The structural exercises in *Faisons le Point* (see the Further Reading section at the end of the chapter), for example, which are in semi-dialogue form, are ideal for such practice, particularly if you can work with a partner. Pattern practice such as the following will help you to build sentences and improve fluency:

Exemple: C'était le manteau du professeur qui était accroché là?
Reponse: Je ne sais pas si c'était le manteau du professeur, mais c'était bien un
  manteau d'homme.

There then follow cue sentences to which you supply the response, e.g:

Q.: C'était le bruit de l'avion de Londres qui vous a réveillé?
A.: Je ne sais pas si c'était l'avion de Londres, mais c'était bien un avion.

or

Exemple: Vous avez accepté de faire cette course?
Réponse: Oui, non que je la fasse volontiers.
Q: Elle a accepté de faire le ménage?
A: Oui, non qu'elle le fasse volontiers.
Q: Il a accepté de remplir les fiches?
A: Oui, non qu'il les remplisse volontiers.

You can record the cues on a cassette recorder and practise the exercises orally or you can practise them as mini-dialogues with a partner. The format of 'cue plus response' provides good practice for the oral.

ACCURACY

It is important in the oral to produce spoken French which is grammatically and syntactically accurate as the examiner will base his assessment partly on your competence in this area but accuracy does not have the same importance in the oral as it does in the essay in French or in the prose. The reasons for this are that the examiner does not (and cannot) concentrate on grammatical accuracy alone as he is testing your overall ability to communicate, and secondly, the grammar of the spoken language is different because many of the grammatical changes which operate in the written language are not apparent in speech. This should help you to feel less inhibited when you are speaking French.

FREQUENT ERRORS

Examiners' comments show that errors most frequently involve: tenses and verb forms (e.g. the candidate gives all verbs the same ending or simply uses the infinitive), adjective agreements which cause a sound change (particularly adjectives such as important/importante, intelligent/intelligente, intéressant/intéressante, etc.), genders, prepositions and the agreement and order of pronouns. It is wise to make sure that you are accurate in these areas but it is also important to find out what your own weaknesses are. It is, of course, the recurring errors, those which are going to help create an overall impression, which should be given priority treatment. Isolated mistakes, unless they interfere with comprehension are more likely to pass unnoticed or be forgotten.

There is, however, the problem of finding out where your weaknesses are when you never see your mistakes underlined in red. Some teachers tackle the problem by running a tape-recorder during a conversation class. The recording is then transferred to the language lab and recorded on the master track but with blank spaces provided so that students can record a corrected or improved version of faulty or clumsy sentences. The exercise is useful because it identifies errors and makes learners aware of the gap between what they want to say and what they can say.

> **Try to integrate written work and oral work.**

You can, of course, record yourself ad-libbing on a chosen topic, giving an account of the day's events, describing a sequence of pictures, producing an oral version of an essay which has been set, and then replay it and correct yourself.

When you have discovered what your repeated errors are you can work on selected language-lab drills to put them right. If you do not have access to a language-lab tape library you can find material for practice in a workbook such as *French Revisions Drills* (see the Further Reading section at the end of the chapter) which contains drills for individual practice to be used with or without a tape-recorder.

RANGE

When the examiner marks your oral performance for range he will be looking for variety of expression, evidence that your linguistic knowledge does not restrict you to one or two simple sentence patterns, and for depth of vocabulary.

If you display linguistic range you will show that you have the terms to make *comparisons* and contrasts, judgements, suppositions and hypotheses. You will be able to add conditions, restrictions or examples to statements that you make and express personal opinion. You will have knowledge of idiomatic expressions. You will show that you are able to communicate at a more advanced level because you can develop your thoughts, elaborate on points and get more deeply into the subject. The candidate who scores a low mark under the heading of 'range' will produce only simple sentences, perhaps nothing more than half sentences or phrases. Vocabulary will be limited and possibly repetitive.

In a recent oral examination different candidates made the following replies to the question: Est-ce qu'il est important que les enfants lisent beaucoup?

```
a) Je crois que oui, enfin, j'en suis convaincue. Les enfants aiment
   bien les livres, c'est-à-dire les histoires. A mon avis la
   lecture est un moyen de développer l'intelligence d'un enfant.
   Son imagination aussi, ses sentiments. C'est pourquoi les
   parents doivent faire lire les enfants. Pas seulement l'école,
   les professeurs, mais les parents.
b) Oui, très, très important. C'est important pour les enfants dans
   l'école primaire. Les enfants apprennent. Ils apprennent
   beaucoup de choses. Il peut . . . ils apprennent la vie. Des
   choses nouvelles. Ils aiment lire des livres.
```

Candidate (a) had greater range. She had more freedom to develop her thoughts and express an opinion. Candidate (b) did not have the confidence to choose other sentence patterns and therefore, although he communicated quite adequately, what he had to say was more limited and less interesting.

All your other language activities, listening comprehension, intensive and extensive reading, essay-writing, will improve your linguistic range but it is also a question of confidence, practice and being able to involve yourself fully in a conversation so that you feel that you really have something that you want to communicate.

POSSIBLE ELEMENTS

Most oral examinations are structured to contain more than just general conversation although part of the time is nearly always devoted to this. Other elements are likely to be:

a) Reading aloud

The candidate reads a short, unprepared passage or part of one which has been studied beforehand. The aim is twofold. It is a fairly mechanical exercise which helps the candidate settle and it is a test of intonation, phrasing and pronunciation. If it is part of your examination remember that it is worth practising. The reading takes place first and is therefore your opportunity to create a favorable first impression. Lack of practice shows. Candidates are unable to 'get their tongues round' certain sounds (e.g. nasal vowels; the French 'r'; the sound u in pour, cours etc.; the sound y in r*u*e, conc*u*rrence) − they read in a monotone and do not phrase the words in groups in order to make the meaning clear.

b) Discussion based on a stimulus

> There are examples in the examination questions later in this chapter.

One stage in the oral is likely to be discussion based on the passage read aloud, on work prescribed for other areas of the exam (e.g. set texts or background topics), on a topic or dossier prepared by the candidate specially for the oral or on visual material such as maps, graphs, diagrams, statistics or photographs provided by the examiner. It is important to know beforehand what the procedure will be and to have practised with similar material. If you have prepared a selected topic the examiner will assume that you have chosen it because you have a particular interest in the subject and that you have spent time on it. Do not disappoint him by being unresponsive and uninformed.

c) Role-play

A-level and AS-level oral examinations often include a role-play. A task (which usually involves giving or eliciting information) is set within a given situation, involving two participants. It is described to the candidate beforehand. The candidate enacts one role, the examiner the other. Typical examples are:

i) You have accompanied a school sports team to France to act as interpreter. The leader of the French team (played by the examiner) has organised a list of activities which the French are very keen to take part in. You and your team are not interested in some of them and have certain other suggestions (you are given a list). It is your task to discuss the arrangements with the French leader and to come to an agreement.

ii) You have obtained a summer job on the reception desk of the Diners' Club. The managing director of a French company has heard about the Diners' Club and phones you to find out more about it. You read a text (in English) which gives you information about the Diners' Club so that you are prepared for answering the questions the managing director will put to you.

iii) You work in a London publishing house. You receive a visit from your opposite number in a French company who wants you to handle one of their books. In the course of the discussion you are required to find out certain information (notes in English tell you what to find out).

In the oral, whether it is in a role-play or in a discussion or in general conversation you will find it necessary to carry out a number of language functions which arise out of an 'interview situation'. For example, you may find it necessary to

- defend a point of view
- introduce yourself
- express agreement/disagreement
- express a personal opinion
- make a judgement
- engage someone in conversation
- terminate a conversation
- ask for/give information
- make requests.

It is therefore worthwhile listening to recorded interviews as part of your listening comprehension programme in order to note the way in which French speakers carry out these functions (both the phrases which they use and the intonation and pronunciation of the phrases).

Guide Practique de la Communication has a repertoire of conversational phrases and vocabulary organised according to function under headings such as Remercier/rèpondre aux remerciements; Demandes d'informations pratiques; Exprimer une opinion/demander son avis à quelqu'un etc. which can be very usefully studied as part of your preparation for the oral.

IN THE EXAMINATION ROOM

1   Make sure that you know exactly what you are expected to do. Where do you wait? What preparation is there immediately before the interview? Will you be allowed to use a dictionary to do it? Will you be allowed to take any notes into the interview room?

2   make good use of the preparation time. Keep calm and work steadily even if the tasks seem difficult at first. If you have to prepare a reading passage, read it out loud to yourself. If note-taking is allowed, make only brief useful notes.

3   Be prepared for exam nerves. Few candidates are really unaffected by them, even when the examiner is their own teacher. However, examiners do their best to put you at your ease.

4   Remember that the interview is intended to be natural conversation or discussion and therefore one would expect the 'accidents' of normal spoken communication. If you do not understand something ask for further explanation; if you feel that you have expressed yourself badly then try again, using simpler terms. It is not a question of 'make or break' every time you open your mouth.

5   Look the examiner in the face and speak clearly. Do not mistake speed for fluency, take your time. Be confident but don't overdo it (like the candidate who on being shown a picture of a bird, leaned back with his hands in his pockets and said 'C'est un oswo, obvieusement!'). Remember, too, that although you may communicate in a natural and relaxed manner, the situation is quite a formal one. It would therefore be out of place to use slang or familiar expressions.

6   Do not be content with monosyllabic answers to the examiner's questions. Try to take the initiative and develop the conversation. The examiner will be ready to prompt you but he will also be quite pleased if you do not make him work too hard. On the other hand it is not a good idea to respond over- enthusiastically to the introduction of a topic that you know little about; you will not be able to answer the supplementary questions. Instead, take the initiative and try to turn to a different subject.

VISITING FRANCE

> Trying out your French on the French.

An important further step which most students are keen to take is to go and try out their French on French people. Going on holiday to France is one possibility but it can be a limited linguistic experience, particularly if you go as a member of an English-speaking group. It is more useful to take part in some purposeful activity which will bring you into contact with French people and possibly enable you to earn some money.

It will require a certain amount of resourcefulness to find vacation employment in France but there are two books published by the Central Bureau (for educational visits and exchanges) which are helpful and obtainable from most bookshops. In *Home from Home* and *Working Holidays* you will find details of visits which can be made to France and ideas for working holidays, together with addresses and useful advice.

If you are interested in working as an animateur or animatrice in a centre de vacances (helping to look after French children between the ages of six and sixteen − you choose your age-group − and organising activities for them), further information can be obtained from the Cultural Attaché at the French Embassy in London.

EXAMINATION QUESTIONS

Q1 (role-play)

Whilst in France, you see an advert for a job as a Youth Leader in a camp near La Rochelle (see Fig. 14.1). You have previously telephoned, giving your *own* details (name, age etc.). You are not attending interview.

You are very keen to get this job. You need the money and want the experience!

FRANCOCAMP

Camp pour enfants 8–15 ans
Nous cherchons un

moniteur de vacances

pour six semaines
salaire et conditions à négocier
tel. (29) 06.86.78

Fig. 14.1

Remember

1   You like children and have some relevant experience. (What?)
2   You may mention sports/activities/hobbies/skills that you can offer. (What?)
3   You are free immediately.

Possible difficulties

1   You start a job in Wales on 5 September.
2   You need to cover your travel (about £70) and would like some pocket money.
3   You do not like sharing rooms.

You should try to cover all this information and be prepared to insist politely, negotiate and agree and make decisions.   (WJEC Specimen Paper 1988)

Q2 (role-play)

Whilst staying in your French friend's house you break a large and expensive-looking vase. Go to your friend's parent (played by the examiner) and tell him/her what you have done and how the accident happened. Try to persuade him/her to accept some form of compensation. Make clear that you are very sorry for what you have done. (The parent will address you as *tu*; address him/her as *vous*.)   (JMB AS-level Specimen Paper 1987)

Q3 (role-play)

While taking part in an exchange visit to France you are introduced to some young French people of your age, one of whom (played by the examiner) says that he/she would hate to do an exchange. You try to persuade him/her of the advantages as you see them. (You will be addressed as *tu*; address your new French friend as *tu*).

(JMB AS-level Specimen Paper 1987)

Q4 (role-play)

You have bought a watch in a Paris shop. The day before your holiday is due to end the watch stops working. Take it back to the shop and ask in a polite but firm way for a replacement or for your money to be refunded. Explain that you cannot wait for it to be repaired as you are going home tomorrow.   (JMB 1988)

Q5 (role-play)

Brief: You have applied for a summer job as a hotel porter (or camp-site courier) in Switzerland and have been invited for interview in London.
Task: a) Explain why you want the job (at least 3 reasons) and why you think you are well suited for the work involved.
         b) Ask about the conditions (hours, pay etc.) the arrangements for travel, meals, accommodation, and try to persuade the interviewer to let you start a week later than the advertised date.   (COSSEC AS-level Specimen Paper 1988)

Q6 (role-play)

Brief: You are on a motoring holiday in Europe with your family. After a long drive from Italy, you reach your hotel in Chamonix rather late, only to find that the rooms you had reserved have been let.

Task: a) Apologise for your late arrival and explain the reasons why you were delayed.

b) Protest strongly when informed that your rooms are no longer available and remind the proprietor that you had sent a deposit to confirm your telephone booking.

c) Persuade him/her to find you alternative accommodation in the town and specify your requirements (facilities, maximum cost, location).

(COSSEC Specimen Paper 1988)

Q7 (discussion based on stimulus material provided by the Board)

Examine carefully the advertisement for a hotel and restaurant database below and be prepared to discuss its content. (AEB A-level 1988)

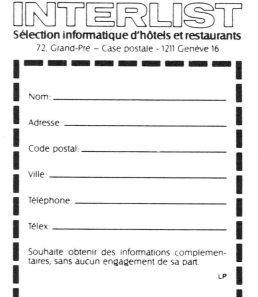

Fig. 14.2

Q8 (discussion based on stimulus material provided by the Board)
Examine carefully the following advertisement and be prepared to discuss its content.

ici tout est résidentiel

Imaginez aux portes de Paris
– 8 km par la Porte de Choisy –
proche du parc de Sceaux,
près du club de Loisirs
de Créteil, une ville résidentielle.
Dans cette ville, un quartier
calme et verdoyant,
dans ce quartier une belle maison
la vôtre.

Une belle maison (6 pièces)
vaste et bien conçue,
individuelle, entourée
d'un jardin privé, habitable
tout de suite, vous accueille.

**Elle sera votre maison
de famille.**
Vous y vivrez agréablement,
près des écoles, du lycée,
de tous les commerces et

des centres commerciaux
(Créteil, Belle Epine à 3 km),
au milieu d'un îlot protégé
de verdure.

**A Thiais, vous vivrez
différemment** sans vous couper
de Paris tout proche
par la porte de Choisy et
à 10' de la gare d'Austerlitz
par le RER de Choisy-le-Roi.

Venez mesurer tout cela sur place,
venez donc rendre visite
à votre maison, nous vous
attendons au hameau-
témoin décoré
lundi, jeudi, vendredi
de 14h à 19h, samedi et dimanche
de 10h à 12h30 et de 14h à 19h

Rue Maximilien Robespierre 94230 THIAIS Tél. 48.90.98.55

PB PUBLICITÉ **BATI SERVICE**

Fig. 14.3

A STUDENT'S ANSWER TO QUESTION 6 WITH EXAMINER'S COMMENTS

The following is a transcript of an extract from an A-level candidate's mock oral examination. He has been asked to take part in the role-play outlined in Question 6.

Examiner:	Bonsoir monsieur!
Candidate:	Bonsoir monsieur. Je m'appelle, monsieur Hemmings. Je vous ai écrit une lettre et, euh, dans la lettre j'ai demandé deux chambres . . . c'est pour moi et mes enfants, deux enfants.
Examiner:	Ah oui, Monsieur Hemmings. Malheureusement, Monsieur, il y a une petite difficulté.
Candidate:	Une petite difficulté? Ah oui, je m'excuse d'arriver si, euh, tellement en retard mais j'ai eu un accident dans la voiture.
Examiner:	Un accident de voiture!
Candidate:	Oui, euh, pas exactement un accident mais un roue a éclaté, a crevé en Italie, un roue de ma voiture, et j'ai eu beaucoup de problèmes. C'est pourquoi je suis tard.
Examiner:	Monsieur, je suis désolé: l'hôtel est déjà complet.
Candidate:	Ce n'est pas vrai!
Examiner:	Si Monsieur, je n'ai plus de chambres. Je suis désolé.
Candidate:	Mais j'ai réservé, j'ai réservé deux chambres. Ce n'est pas possible!
Examiner:	A neuf heures vous n'étiez toujours pas arrivé; j'ai loué les deux chambres à un autre monsieur. L'hôtel est complet.
Candidate:	Mais c'est-ce une disgrace. Ce n'est pas ma faute, c'est . . . euh . . . j'avais un accident.
Examiner:	Mais qu'est-ce que vous voulez Monsieur, moi je ne pouvais pas savoir que vous aviez eu un accident. Je croyais que vous aviez décidé de ne plus venir.
Candidate:	Non! C'est ridicule. J'ai écrit une lettre et j'ai payé un deposite, une somme d'argent. Puisque vous avez reçu mon argent il faut absolument que vous me donnez une chambre . . . je suis très fatigué et mes enfants aussi. Vous n'avez pas le droit de prendre mes chambres parce que j'avais . . . je vous avais envoyé de l'argent.
Examiner:	Je veux bien vous rembourser ce que vous avez payé. Je peux vous rendre votre chèque qui n'a pas encaissé.
Candidate:	Non, Monsieur, je ne suis pas d'accord, ce n'est pas raisonnable, parce que moi, euh, moi je n'ai toujours pas de chambre. Je ne peux pas rester dans la voiture pendant toute la nuit.
Examiner:	L'hôtel est complet, Monsieur, toutes les chambres sont prises.
Candidate:	Dans ce cas vous allez me trouver un autre hôtel.
Examiner:	Je pourrais téléphoner à l'Hôtel de la Paix qui n'est pas loin d'ici.
Candidate:	C'est bon. N'oubliez pas que je veux deux chambres avec salle de bans . . . petit déjeuner. C'est un hôtel à trois étoiles?
Examiner:	Oui, Monsieur.
Candidate:	Bon, ça va, mais je ne veux pas payer plus de 200 Francs . . . le même prix que cet hôtel.
Examiner:	Très bien, Monsieur. Excusez-moi, je vais téléphoner tout de suite. Je suis sûr que tout peut s'arranger.

Margin notes:

" Un accident de voiture — corrected by the examiner. "

" En retard — a slip; the candidate had the right phrase earlier on. "

" Good, convincing reactions. "

" Should be "un pneu". "

" Anglicism — say; "c'est scandaleux". "

" J'ai eu un . . . "

" An invention, say "j'ai versé des arrhes". Candidate does not know the precise terms but does well to find his way the difficulty. "

" Donniez — subjunctive after il faut que. "

" Good, fluent response. "

" Good. "

Examiner's comment

This was a good performance. The candidate responded well to the role-play and entered enthusiasticaly into the part. There was a good level of fluency and accuracy and the candidate was generally able to think his way round difficulties in order to sustain his part in the dialogue. There was some invention and un-French expression but this was compensated for by good pronunciation and intonation. The level of communication was high. The candidate was able to protest, persuade, insist and ask questions in a convincing manner. A high mark was awarded for this section of the oral.

Further reading

R.Martineau and J.M.McGivney. *French Pronunciation*, O.U.P.
Alan Chamberlain and Ross Steel. *Guide Pratique de la Communication*, Didier.
Eric Astington. *Faisons le Point — A Course in Advanced French*, Heinemann.
J.J.Walling. *French Revision Drills*, Interlang Ltd.

LITERATURE

GETTING STARTED

Many examination syllabuses, particularly at A-level, give candidates the opportunity to study literature, and in some cases this is compulsory. If you are studying for your examination at a school or college, it is likely that your tutor will already have chosen your set texts for you, bearing in mind the overall needs of the class. If, however, you are preparing for the examination as a private candidate or if you need for some other reason to choose your own set texts, you should check carefully the printed syllabus of the appropriate Examination Board. Remember that the syllabus must bear the date *when you expect to take the examination* and not the date on which you start your course of study. Usually candidates are required to study about four texts chosen from quite a long list and covering different literary genres (plays, novels, short stories and poetry) and historical periods (usually the seventeenth century onwards).

It is most important that your choice should meet the Board's requirements. If you are retaking your examination, you cannot assume automatically that the books you studied before are still on a list. You must check this carefully — a quick glance at the list is not enough. Remember that it is not unusual for set book lists to change very slightly from year to year and lists which may appear identical at first sight can in fact contain minor changes.

ESSENTIAL PRINCIPLES

THE TEXT

Unless you already have quite an extensive knowledge of French literature, you will need some help and advice when deciding on your set books. If most of your study will be undertaken privately, you will probably be wise to choose either twentieth-century prose works or texts for which you know that good annotated editions or helpful critical commentaries are available. Candidates preparing for the examination at a school or college often have their texts provided for them, but even so it is helpful to have your own personal copies if you can afford them. This will enable you to write notes on the text itself — reminders of the meaning of difficult words, underlining of useful quotations and brief comments on particularly significant parts of the work being studied. One of the most efficient ways of revising is the careful re-reading of texts which you have thoroughly annotated yourself. A word of warning, however, about notes which may have been made on a text by a previous user. As far as possible these should be ignored. They are unlikely to have the same significance for you as for the original writer. At best they may prove to be a distraction and at worst they may actually be wrong.

TRANSLATIONS

Since many of the texts which appear in set book lists are major works of literature, it is inevitable that a considerable number of them will exist in English translation. Attitudes towards the use of translations vary greatly, but all teachers would agree that they can *never* be a substitute for the original text. Ideally all works of literature should be studied directly in the original language; therefore, if you do decide to make use of a translation, it should only be because you feel that this will genuinely help you to understand and appreciate the French text. The following are the most likely reasons for which a translation may validly be used:

1 To obtain a rapid overview of a number of books, in order to select the one(s) which you would most like to study as a set text.
2 As a means of getting started on a text which you are finding difficult. Some candidates choose to read an entire work in translation before embarking on detailed study of the French text, but this can seriously impair your enjoyment and appreciation of the original which can no longer be read with spontaneity.
3 To check the meaning of individual words and phrases which you find obscure.

If, however, you can manage without a translation, you will be wise to do so. Certainly it should be no more than an initial aid and your main study, as well as all your revision, should be based on the original text only. The reasons for this are obvious. Firstly, examiners are very experienced at spotting candidates who are unfamiliar with their French texts. (It is not only those candidates who are unwise enough to quote in English in their examination answers who give themselves away!)

More importantly, however, you will have missed many of the satisfactions of studying literature in a foreign language. The purposes of the literature section of the syllabus are twofold and interdependent — they are to enable you to extend your own knowledge of the foreign language by detailed study of works in which it is admirably used, and to use this extended knowledge to read ever more widely and appreciatively. You are missing a great deal — not only in examination terms — if you do not acquire a thorough knowledge of the original text. This may be a struggle at first, but it will be worth it.

> " **Purposes of the literature section.** "

STUDYING FOR THE EXAMINATION

EARLY READING MATERIAL

Earlier in this book you were advised that the best way to extend your French language skills was to use them as widely as possible and not simply to concentrate on the specific exercises required for your examination. Similar advice holds good for your work in literature. You will appreciate your set books more and will study them more satisfactorily if you have acquired good general reading skills. It is possible that you already have experience of reading fairly extensively in French and know the satisfaction and progress which comes with reading your first full-length book in a foreign language. However, it is also possible that you are not yet at this stage and need help with getting started. You would do well to begin with fairly short items which are not too daunting — newspaper or magazine articles and short stories. These need not be 'literary' in style, but be sure that you choose items which are well written, with good sentence structures and vocabulary which is free from jargon. From this you can progress to novels — again do not choose anything which appears forbidding to begin with. Choose a work which is not too long, in language which appears reasonably accessible at first glance. It does not matter if the content is 'light', as long as the work is well written. Of course there are also established works of literature which are relatively simple in style and can be taken as your starting-point. Stories by Maupassant and novels such as *L'Etranger* by Camus or *Bonjour Tristesse* by Francoise Sagan can be appreciated even by a relatively inexperienced reader.

APPROACHING THE SET TEXTS	The way in which you approach the study of the set texts themselves will naturally depend on the advice given by your tutor. Where possible it can be helpful to have read the *entire* work straight through before you begin studying it in detail in class, but there are some circumstances when this may not be appropriate. Some teachers find it advisable, particularly near the beginning of the course, to give their students special help with the opening sections of a book, especially if the structure of the work is in any way complicated — for instance if it includes a flashback or if the relationship between the characters is not immediately obvious.

POETRY

If poetry is included among your texts or if you are studying a relatively early work, you are also likely to need help at first. In order to read French poetry or verse drama appreciatively and with ease, you must become familiar with the basic conventions of versification, since these differ considerably from the traditional forms you have probably already encountered in English. Of course, *metrical structure* is no more than the bare framework of poetry, but without some knowledge of it you will not be able to appreciate fully the qualities of a poem and the skills which have gone into its construction. At a more practical level, you will also find it harder to quote accurately in your examination if you do not understand the metre being used. Examiners frequently spot errors in quotations in the first instance because they are metrically incorrect. You need not become obsessed about the niceties of versification — examination questions do not require you to go into intricate detail or to be able to use complex terminology — but you do need to understand the basic principles.

Similarly, if you are to study one of the great seventeenth- century dramatists (the work of Corneille or Racine or some of the plays of Molière), you must understand the verse structures used — and in particular *the alexandrine* or *12-syllable line* — if you are to hear the rhythm of the speeches correctly. Needless to say, you are expected to set these out as *verse* and not as prose when you quote them in your examination answers. You need not be daunted by the prospect of studying seventeenth-century authors provided that you have some initial help. The text can look forbidding at first sight, but the language of classical drama is much less difficult than you might suppose and can be easily grasped by the modern reader with a little practice. It is the experience of many examiners that seventeenth-century plays make stimulating examination texts and candidates not infrequently write well on them, sometimes producing their best answers. Nevertheless they are not to everyone's taste and the class tutor is probably the best person to decide on their suitability. Works written before the seventeenth century are much more difficult to study and considerable knowledge of French is required before they can be read with ease. Hence they only appear on some post A-level syllabuses.

Whether or not you have read the whole of a set work before beginning to study it in class or with your tutor, you should *always* prepare carefully for each lesson, going carefully through the appropriate parts of the text. 'Passive learning', whereby you simply wait for your tutor to tell you what each part of the text means and do not tackle the difficulties yourself, will only slow down your progress. Obviously you will make notes in the course of your lessons and you may also be given some sets of notes by your tutor. Such sets of notes can be very helpful provided you use them sensibly. They may just be factual (giving details of the author's life or essential background information) or they may

> " Passive learning = slow learning. "

be more concerned with literary criticism (for example with matters such as style or characterisation). Notes of this latter kind can be useful if they serve to stimulate your own ideas, but you should be wary of learning them by rote. In an examination you should always express ideas which *you* have thought out for yourself and which you can substantiate. In the same way works of criticism and the introductions to annotated editions can be very helpful in suggesting lines of thought and ways of interpreting a text, but you should never simply 'learn' another person's opinions. Think about them and take them seriously because reputable critics will know much more about your set authors than you do, but do not accept an argument with which you do not agree. And if you do not agree with something or, more importantly, if you do not understand it, do not learn it.

MAKING NOTES AND REFERENCES

When you have completed the detailed textual study of each set work and can read it with ease, you should set about making careful notes on it in preparation for your eventual revision. It may seem self-evident to say that you must know each text in its entirety, but in fact not all candidates allocate their study time with sufficient care, and it is the experience of examiners that quotations and references are often drawn from the early parts of set works, the later stages being much less well known. Be sure that this does not happen to you. It is a problem which can arise in connection with any book, but is most likely to occur if you are studying a collection of short stories or poems. Remember that you must allow time to study and revise them all. In your examination answers you cannot of course refer to every part of a set collection and you will need to be selective. If you are answering a general question on a collection of stories or poems (for instance on Maupassant's use of humour or the main characteristics of Verlaine's style), you must refer to several of them to illustrate your arguments. Be sure that you are adequately prepared so that you can make your choice wisely — if you try to deal with them all your answers will run the risk of becoming scrappy and superficial, but a very limited range of examples will restrict the scope of your discussion. So know each text thoroughly.

While making notes you would do well to compile a list of useful quotations, indicating briefly the reasons for your choice. Where applicable you may like to collect quotations under different headings (such as what they show about various characters or the author's style or ideas). Be discriminating in your selection and make sure the quotations are not too long, since you will need to learn them accurately by heart. It is possible that your tutor will indicate some of the key quotations to you, but add to these any which strike you personally as interesting — these are the quotations which you are most likely to remember and an examiner will find it refreshing not always to encounter 'stock' examples.

In your notes you cannot hope to cover every aspect of your text which could possibly be the specific subject of an examination question, but you should attempt to deal with all the major features. These will vary from one text to another, but careful thought should reveal them to you. They are likely to include some or all of the following points:

1 The main *themes* of the work and the ways in which they are treated. These could include such topics as friendship, honour, hypocrisy, avarice and so on.
2 *Characterisation*. Think about each character in turn and consider which adjectives you could use to describe them and how these could be substantiated from the text. Be prepared to compare and contrast characters and to discuss the relationships between them and their influence on one another.
3 The *role or function of each character*. What do they contribute to the novel or play? Are they important in the plot, for shedding light on other characters, for expressing the author's ideas, for contributing humorous elements, and so on?
4 The *motives and reactions of characters* and the extent to which they are responsible for what takes place. The role of fate may be included here.
5 The *title* of the work. Does it have any special significance? Would any other title be appropriate?
6 The *structure* of the work. How is the plot handled? Does it contain flashbacks? Is it in diary form? How is tension created? If you are studying a play, how effective would it be on the stage?
7 The *setting*. Does the work have a regional, geographical or historical setting which enhances its effectiveness?
8 The *author's ideas*. These may include social satire (as in the work of Beaumarchais or Voltaire for instance) or may be more philosophical (as in the work of Sartre or

Camus). If your set author is also a philosopher you will need to have some understanding of his/her ideas and to be able to explain them clearly in your own words. Technical terminology can be useful if correctly used, but is not essential and should certainly never be used to mask lack of real comprehension.

9   The *author's style*. This can include the quality of the description and the narrative method chosen, such as use of the first person and its effectiveness.

10   The *major qualities of the work*. What are its merits? Why is it an important work of literature?

Obviously the above list is not exhaustive nor does all of it apply to every work, but it should suggest ideas for the planning of your own notes. Do not learn these slavishly and insist on forcing every quotation into an examination answer or on making a set of pre-learned notes fit another topic. In the examination room you must *think* about each question and *select* the material which you can use.

In addition to studying the texts themselves, you may well want to read the opinions of critics as well as other works by your set authors. These will help to develop your judgement and critical awareness, but remember that in the examination room it is the prescribed texts themselves that you will be questioned on.

TYPES OF EXAMINATION QUESTIONS

These are usually of two main types:

1   *Context questions* in which an extract from the text is given, together with questions arising from it.
2   Questions requiring an answer in *essay form*.

CONTEXT QUESTIONS

The main purpose of these is to ensure that you have studied the text closely and with understanding, although it is unlikely that you will be asked to translate parts of the extract given. You should always read the questions which accompany the extract with great care in order that you may understand their implications fully. Usually you will be asked to do some or all of the following:

a) Identify the point in the text where the extract occurs. This does not necessarily mean that you have to give the precise number of the scene or chapter. What is important is to be able to describe briefly and clearly, without undue narration of the plot, exactly where the given passage comes from. You should of course be able to say if the passage occurs at a crucial point in the structure of the work — for example if it is the opening or final scene of a particular act in a play.

b) Explain the significance of specific sentences or phrases.

c) Comment on certain aspects of the content of the extract, such as what is its importance in the plot, what it reveals about the characters involved, how it contributes to our understanding of the author's ideas, and so on.

d) Comment on the context of the extract in relation to the work as a whole.

The following examples of context questions will help you to understand these points more clearly.

EXAMINATION QUESTIONS (CONTEXT)

Q1 Beaumarchais: *Le Mariage de Figaro*

(For those who have not read this play, the situation is as follows: Suzanne, the Countess's maid, is to be married to Figaro, the Count's valet. However the Count, weary of the wife he once loved, has designs on Suzanne and the intrigue hinges on his being outwitted. The scene quoted below — Act II scene 24 — occurs after a series of farcical incidents in the Countess's apartment. The young page, Chérubin, was being dressed in Suzanne's clothes in order to take her place at a rendezvous with the Count, when the latter arrived unexpectedly on the strength of an anonymous note from Figaro falsely warning him that his wife had an admirer. After remaining in hiding during scenes of complicated activity, Chérubin managed to jump through the window, watched only by Suzanne, but his escape

arrival of the gardener complaining of damage to his plants. Eventually all is well and Suzanne and the Countess remain alone.)

i) Situate the following passage in its context, explaining the significance of the phrases and sentences underlined.

ii) Show what the scene reveals of the relationship between Suzanne, la Comtesse and le Comte.

Suzanne, La Comtesse

La Comtesse: Vous voyez, Suzanne, la jolie scène que votre étourdi m'a value avec son *(dans sa bergère)* billet.

Suzanne: Ah! Madame, quand je suis rentrée du cabinet, <u>si vous aviez vu votre visage</u>! il s'est terni tout à coup; mais ce n'a été qu'un nuage, et par degrés, vous êtes devenue rouge, rouge, rouge!

La Comtesse: <u>Il a donc sauté par la fenêtre?</u>

Suzanne: Sans hésiter, le charmant enfant! Léger . . . comme une abeille.

La Comtesse: Ah! <u>ce fatal jardinier!</u> Tout cela m'a remuée au point . . . que je ne pouvais rassembler deux idées.

Suzanne: Ah! Madame, au contraire; et c'est là que j'ai vu combien l'usage du grand monde donne d'aisance aux dames comme il faut, pour mentir sans qu'il y paraisse.

La Comtesse: Crois-tu que le Comte en soit la dupe? et s'il trouvait cet enfant au château!

Suzanne: Je vais recommander de le cacher si bien . . .

La Comtesse: Il faut qu'il parte. Après ce qui vient d'arriver, vous croyez bien que je ne suis pas tentée de l'envoyer au jardin à votre place.

Suzanne: Il est certain que je n'irai pas non plus. Voilà donc mon mariage encore une fois . . .

La Comtesse: Attends . . . Au lieu d'un autre, ou de toi <u>si j'y allais moi-même?</u> *(se leve)*

Suzanne: Vous, Madame?

La Comtesse: Il n'y aurait personne d'exposé . . . Le Comte alors ne pourrait nier . . . Avoir puni sa jalousie, et lui prouver son infidelité, cela serait . . . Allons: le bonheur d'un premier hasard m'enhardit à tenter le second. Fais-lui savoir promptement que tu te rendras au jardin. Mais, surtout, que personne . . .

Suzanne: Ah! Figaro.

La Comtesse: Non, non. Il voudrait mettre ici du sien . . . Mon masque de velours et ma canne, que j'aille y rêver sur la terrasse.

(Suzanne entre dans le cabinet de toilette)   (JMB 1985)

The questions on this passage require you to fulfil all the tasks listed under (a), (b) and (c) above. However you will also notice that you cannot adequately deal with the question which requires you to show what the scene reveals of the relationship between Suzanne, la Comtesse and le Comte *unless* you also know and can refer back to the relationship between these characters in the earlier part of the play. Hence the task listed under (d) is also partly required of you, even though it is not specifically expressed in the wording of the question. (Of course this does not mean that you are required to *narrate* what has happened earlier.) Notice also that the sections underlined are not linguistically complex, but it is necessary to understand the events and characters to which they refer if they are to have any real meaning.

Q2 Mauriac: *Thérèse Desqueyroux*
(For those who have not read this book, the passage occurs near the beginning of the novel when Thérèse, accompanied by her father, is travelling home from court after the case against her — that she tried to poison her husband — has been dismissed for lack of conclusive evidence.)

What is the situation at this point in the novel? In your opinion, how does Mauriac wish the reader to react to this description of Thérèse? Examine the methods used to obtain this reaction, and show how these are typical of Mauriac's methods in the novel as a whole.

Elle enlève son chapeau, appuie contre le cuir odorant sa petite tête blême et ballottée, livre son corps aux cahots. Elle avait vécu, jusqu'à ce soir, d'être traquée; maintenant que la voilà sauve, elle mesure son épuisement. Joues creuses, pommettes, lèvres aspirées, et ce large front, magnifique, composent une figure de condamnée — oui, bien que les hommes ne l'aient pas reconnue coupable — condamnée à la solitude éternelle. Son charme, que le monde naguère disait irrésistible, tous ces êtres le possèdent dont le visage trahirait un tourment secret, l'élancement d'une plaie intérieure, s'ils ne s'épuisaient à donner le change. Au fond de cette calèche cahotante, sur cette route frayée dans l'épaisseur obscure des pins, une jeune femme démasquée caresse doucement avec la main droite sa face de brûlée vive. (Cambridge, 1983. *Thérèse Desqueyroux* by Mauriac, Bernard Grasset)

The questions on this extract differ from those in extract one in that although you are again asked to locate the passage in the text, no comment on specific words or phrases is asked for. However, very close examination of the text is necessary in order to deal with the reader's reaction to this description of Thérèse and the methods used to obtain it. Notice also that the final question is much more general in application than any of the questions in extract 1 and will particularly require consideration of later parts of the novel.

Q3 Camus: *L'Etranger*
(This extract is easier to follow without previous knowledge of the text than are the two other examples. The work is written in the first person by a young French Algerian named Meursault. In the first part of the book, from which this extract comes, he describes events in his daily life which culminate in the shooting of an Arab. Part two of the book tells of his trial.)
  i) Relate the following passage to its context.
  ii) Show what it reveals of the relationship between Meursault and Marie.
  iii) To what extent does it help the reader to understand Meursault's character?
  iv) What significance do you attach to Meursault's comment on Paris at the end of the passage?

Le soir, Marie est venue me chercher et m'a demandé si je voulais me marier avec elle. J'ai dit que cela m'était égal et que nous pourrions le faire si elle le voulait. Elle a voulu savoir alors si je l'aimais. J'ai répondu comme je l'avais déjà fait une fois, que cela ne signifiait rien mais que sans doute je ne l'aimais pas. 'Pourquoi m'épouser alors?' a-t-elle dit. Je lui ai expliqué que cela n'avait aucune importance et que si elle le désirait, nous pouvions nous marier. D'ailleurs, c'était elle qui le demandait et moi je me contentais de dire oui. Elle a observé alors que le mariage était une chose grave. J'ai répondu: 'Non.' Elle s'est tue un moment et elle m'a regardé en silence. Puis elle a parlé. Elle voulait simplement savoir si j'aurais accepté la même proposition venant d'une autre femme, à qui je serais attaché de la même façon. J'ai dit 'Naturellement.' Elle s'est demandé alors si elle m'aimait et moi, je ne pouvais rien savoir sur ce point. Après un autre moment de silence, elle a murmuré que j'étais bizarre, qu'elle m'aimait sans doute à cause de cela mais que peut-être un jour je la dégoûterais pour les mêmes raisons. Comme je me taisais, n'ayant rien à ajouter, elle m'a pris le bras en souriant et elle a déclaré qu'elle voulait se marier avec moi. J'ai répondu que nous le ferions dès qu'elle le voudrait. Je lui ai parlé alors de la proposition du patron et Marie m'a dit qu'elle aimerait connaître Paris. Je lui ai appris que j'y avais vécu dans un temps et elle m'a demandé comment c'était. Je lui ai dit: 'C'est sale. Il y a des pigeons et des cours noires. Les gens ont la peau blanche.'

(JMB 1985. *L'Etranger*, by Camus, Gallimard)

This set of questions is obviously different from the set in example two, since you are not asked specifically about either the style or the book in general. Careful examination will reveal them to be quite close in type to those in example one, even though their layout appears different at first sight. In considering questions ii) and iii) you will see that inferences about both relationships and character have to be drawn from the extract given, and sound general knowledge of the text is required for this to be done satisfactorily. This is particularly so in the case of the question on Meursault's character which implies wider knowledge of his personality on which this extract may shed some light. Although no phrases are underlined as they were in example one, the final remark about Paris needs commentary (question iv). However, in this case, you are not asked so much to explain a reference to another incident in the text as to examine the implications of Meursault's comments about Paris. As in the Beaumarchais question, the words themselves are easy to understand. Here it is the *interpretation* of them which is testing.

EXAMINATION QUESTIONS REQUIRING AN ANSWER IN ESSAY FORM

You have already been given advice on the writing of literature essays. You may find it helpful to go back over that advice before considering the following examples of examination questions. Remember that the length of examination answers is not in itself important and should never be regarded as a criterion of excellence. It is the quality of the content which counts. Essays should always be illustrated with precise references to the text and brief, apt quotations, whether or not this requirement is specifically stated in every question. In the following list questions have been based on those in some recent past A-level papers and are intended to illustrate some of the points above on which it was suggested that you should make notes.

Q1
Prévert: *Paroles*. 'A major theme of *Paroles* is compassion for the less privileged members of society.' Discuss this statement.

Q2
Corneille: *Le Cid*. Compare and contrast the characters of Rodrigue and don Diègue. To what extent do they have the same values?

Q3
Pagnol: *Le Château de ma Mère*. What were the most important influences on Marcel's development during childhood?

Q4
Anouilh: *Becket*. Choose three characters other than Becket and the King and discuss their function in the play.

Q5
Racine: *Britannicus*. Examine the motives which underlie Néron's behaviour in this play.

Q6
Camus: *L'Etranger*. Give an account of Meursault's reactions and emotions at his trial. To what extent can the reader sympathise with him at this point?

Q7
Molière: *L'Ecole des Femmes*. To what extent do you think that Arnolphe brings about his own downfall?

Q8
Gide: *La Symphonie Pastorale*. Examine the significance of the title of this book.

Q9
Troyat: *Grandeur Nature*. Discuss the structure of this novel and comment on the way in which Troyat has introduced parallel characters and situations.

Q10
Alain-Fournier: *Le Grand Meaulnes*. Examine the ways in which Alain-Fournier creates the atmosphere of mystery surrounding 'la fête étrange'.

Q11
Beaumarchais: *Le Mariage de Figaro*. Discuss the importance of costume, props, settings and physical action in this play.

Q12
Prévost: *Manon Lescaut*. What picture of eighteenth-century life is given in this novel?

Q13
Sartre: *Les Mouches*. Show how this play exemplifies Sartre's existentialist view of life.

Q14
Verlaine: *Romances sans Paroles*. Discuss the way in which Verlaine treats landscape in the poems in this collection.

STUDENT'S ANSWER

Obviously it is impossible to give the one perfect answer to a question about literature, for much will depend on the personal style and approach of the writer and examiners often award high marks for very different essays on the same topic. In any case it is unwise to model your own style of writing on that of another person; you will do much better if you polish and improve a style which is natural to you. Nevertheless you will need to have some examples of what constitutes an acceptable standard. The following essays were written in examination conditions, with a time allocation of 45 minutes, by *students* who had just finished their A-level courses. They represent a standard which examiners would find very satisfactory and which should not be beyond the reach of most serious students.

Question 1

Balzac: *Eugénie Grandet*

(Set in Saumur in the early nineteenth century, this novel tells of the restricted and impoverished life of Eugénie, the only child of a rich miser, and of her hopeless love for her irresponsible Parisian cousin Charles.)

Question: Do you agree that the main interest in this novel is the study of the way in which avarice destroys human relationships? Support your discussion with precise references to the text. (London, 1985)

In his novel *Eugénie Grandet* Balzac depicts two kinds of society, the provincial and the Parisian. In both money occupies the thoughts of nearly all the characters and it is their greed for it which leads to their frequent disregard for moral standards.

In Monsieur Grandet Balzac has created a miser whose obsessions are monstrous. He resides in the provinces, at Saumur, where he is the richest man in the area, and because money buys respect in provincial society, he is held in high esteem by the local people. Balzac writes of the lawyer, Monsieur Cruchot, and the banker, Monsieur des Grassins: 'Ils témoignaient publiquement à Monsieur Grandet un si grand respect . . . ' In fact these two families from the town of Saumur do their very best to gain favour with Grandet, in order to win for one of their members the hand in marriage of his daughter Eugénie. The Cruchots and the des Grassins are attracted to the idea of marrying Eugénie into their families solely because they would be marrying her wealth and all the respect and dominance it brings with it. Hence their outward friendliness towards Grandet is merely a superficial facade; any desire for friendship with him is based entirely upon gaining his money, and we are shown how a simple human quality such as friendship is destroyed and remoulded around greed.

Grandet, as the main embodiment of the avarice that is rife in the provinces, is presented by Balzac as being an extreme and not an exception in his lust for money which has become an obsession. He himself admits: 'La vie est une affaire.' Business deals come before everything else and he has lost all perspective on life. He is devious and cunning. 'Financièrement parlant, Monsieur Grandet tenait du tigre et du boa.' Money corrupts his relationships with fellow businessmen. He stutters when making a deal in order to cause confusion, and he gains pleasure in exploiting others. Grandet's lust for money has destroyed any possible sympathy he might have felt for other people, to the extent that his only use for others is as a means to gain money.

Grandet's family life is sad and almost unbelievably restricted. His care for Eugénie stems from the fact that she will be his heiress and therefore will be entrusted with his fortune. Hence, when she asks for his deathbed blessing, he can only say: 'Aie bien soin de tout. Tu me rendras compte de ça là-bas.' Previously Grandet's thoughts had stayed in the present and he would act upon his desire for money without thinking of the consequences. Balzac reminds us that all misers think this way: 'Les avares ne croient point à une vie à venir, le présent est tout pour eux.' Grandet cares little about the effects of his behaviour on his family. He cannot even show his daughter natural fatherly affection. The only time when he appears to do this, calling her 'fifille', is when he has completed a successful business deal. When Charles weeps for the death of his ruined father — the miser's own brother — Grandet can only say: 'Ce jeune homme n'est bon à rien, il s'occupe plus des morts que de l'argent.' As his wife lies dying, Grandet refuses to call a doctor, whom he would have to pay. He changes his mind when he is informed that if his wife dies he will have to part with much more money because of Eugénie's inheritance rights. This is a sad reflection upon his attitude to life. He cannot show his daughter fatherly affection, he has no respect for his dead brother, and he holds his wife in such low esteem that his beloved money has become more important than love for her.

Balzac's interest in the theme of a desire for money destroying human relationships is evident also in the way in which he depicts Parisian society. Paris and the provinces are portrayed as different in matters of fashion and finesse, but a consuming desire to gain money is apparent in both. In Paris, as in the provinces, money has corrupted friendship. Balzac writes: 'Là, pour voir juste, il faut peser chaque matin la bourse d'un ami.' Friendship has become superficial because it is based on the money in a friend's pocket, rather than the feeling in his heart. Charles Grandet is the product of such a society. After his father's bankruptcy and suicide he knows only too well how his former friends would treat him. 'Il connaissait assez la société de Paris pour savoir que dans sa position il n'y eût trouvé que des coeurs indifférents ou froids.' He is sadly aware of the rebuff that would await him if he returned penniless to Paris: 'Ni mon âme ni mon visage ne sont faits à supporter les affronts, la froideur, le dédain qui attendent l'homme ruiné.' But although Charles is aware how he and his society have replaced love and true feelings with interest in one another's wealth, it is a situation which he accepts. In Paris we hear of 'double corruption, mais corruption élégante et fine, de bon goût'.

Charles is briefly awakened to the sincere and self-sacrificing love of Eugénie. She, along with her mother and their servant La Grande Nanon, is depicted by Balzac as being pure and innocent. She is 'l'Ange de Pureté', untouched by the corrupting power of money. Thus her love for Charles is based on true human feeling; but Charles, though momentarily struck by the natural charm of such a relationship, stops returning Eugénie's love when he is once again drawn into the world of money. He joins the slave trade and leads a debauched life, devoid of morals, and his love for Eugénie is immediately abandoned.

Thus Balzac illustrates for us the corrupting influence of a desire for money. We have seen how Grandet mistrusts everyone and has no true feelings for his family; and Charles, a product of a society dominated by money, abandons his love for Eugénie to return to his corrupt world. Therefore, because Balzac shows us the power of money to destroy wherever the action of the novel takes place, it can be seen as the most prominent and persistent theme in the book.

Notice that this student has a clear essay plan, which the introduction does indeed *introduce*, and that the conclusion follows naturally from the content of the essay. The question has been answered in a direct way, with no padding, irrelevance or unnecessary narration, and the arguments are well illustrated with brief, apt quotations.

Question 2
Colette: *Le Blé en Herbe*, Flammarion
(Written in 1923, this book tells of the painful development of an adolescent relationship between two childhood friends, Phil and Vinca, who every year have spent the summer holidays in a villa shared by their families on the coast of Brittany.)

Question: Examine the picture of family life which Colette presents in this novel. Your answer should be supported with precise references to the text. (London 1985)

One of the most striking features of *Le Blé en Herbe* is undoubtedly Colette's insight into the confused emotions and strained relationships of adolescence. The novel is written through the eyes of the adolescent characters Phil and Vinca, and in particular the action of the story stays in constant touch with Phil; therfore every event, character and detail of the environment is presented frm the viewpoint of the adolescent. In *Le Blé en Herbe* family life has a very imortant role; it forms a secure, comforting presence at the edge of Phil and Vinca's perceptions, yet for the most part it is portrayed very hazily. This is because the children make a constant attempt to divorce themselves from the influence of their parents and from their childhood, represented by their parents' presence and even by the holiday villa itself.

While family life is centred in and around the villa, the domain of Phil and Vinca is to be found beyond such boundaries; they escape to the coast whenever possible and seem intimately connected with the natural environment. Their perception of other members of their family is very cloudy; the parents are referred to as 'les pâles ombres' and seem 'à peine présentes'. Phil and Vinca are very much wrapped up in their own emotions and in their feelings for one another, and it seems that, as adolescents, they are seeking to liberate themselves from the constraints and influences of family life: 'Ils goûtèrent une solitude parfaite, entre des parents qu'ils frôlaient à toute heure et ne voyaient presque pas.' However, they cannot entirely escape from the influence of the family, for their interests and aspirations have obviously been shaped by their parents. Vinca speaks of her mother's plans that she should take over the care of the household and of her younger sister Lisette in the future, while Phil describes the years ahead as 'ces années où il faut avoir l'air, devant papa et maman, d'aimer une carrière pour ne pas les désoler'.

There are continual reminders in the novel both of the childhood which Phil and Vinca have lost and of their aspirations to form a family themselves. Watching Vinca and Lisette on the picnic, Phil dreams of filling a paternal role in this scene and fantasises about forming a family with Vinca:

Il fut en même temps un Phil très ancien et sauvage, dénué de tout, mais originairement comblé, puisqu'il possédait une femme . . . Un enfant . . . C'est juste, nous avons un enfant . . .

Clearly then, Phil has been influenced by the family life of which he is a part, even though he often feels misunderstood.

The parents appear in few chapters of the novel; they are seen mostly within the villa, at mealtimes and in the evening, and they are described as 'les ombres familières, devenues presque invisibles' who are treated by the adolescents with indifference or even with vague scorn. Yet the scenes which involve all the family are important in that they provide the secure background against which the relationship between Phil and Vinca develops. Colette describes two middle-class families with the same concerns for their

children, the same interests and topics of gentle, everyday
conversation. The relaxed relationships between the parents serve
to emphasise the agonised, tormented love which Phil and Vinca often
experience, and there are occasions when the adolescents seem to
respect and admire their parents' maturity and calm attitudes:

> Ils envièrent . . . leur facilité au rire, leur foi dans un avenir
> paisible.

For the most part, however, Phil and Vinca feel a slight disdain for
their parents, and seem to believe it impossible that these figures
— these 'parents-fantômes' — could ever have experienced the agony
of adolescent passion. When, at a moment of secret distress, Phil
sees his father approaching, he seems no more than 'une apparence
humaine agréable, un peu cotonneuse, à contours flous'.

Both Phil and Vinca look forward eagerly and impatiently to their
own maturity, and their romantic idealism is in sharp contrast to
their parents' straightforward realism — when Monsieur Ferret talks
romantically of the moon, it seems incongruous within the adult
conversation. In one sense family life exerts a restricting
influence on Phil and Vinca and they seem unable to find adult
identities in their parents' presence. For example Phil's father
rebukes his son's silliness thus: 'Ce n'est pas seize ans, c'est six
ans qu'il a!' At the same time, however, the adults' peaceful,
simple outlook on life, epitomised in Monsieur Audebert's
description of his own pleasures — 'Le pays, la maison. Et puis les
Ferret . . Tu verras comme c'est rare, des amis avec qui on passe
l'été tous les ans, sans se faire de mal' — provides a comforting
image, and suggests in a quiet and attractive way the future of the
tormented adolescents in the novel.

Notice how in the opening paragraph this student has been careful to tie in general remarks about the book with the specific question asked. The main body of the essay is well constructed with ideas flowing on naturally from one another, and appreciation of Colette's writing is evident. The use of quotation is good and in particular provides a skilful conclusion.

Doubtless, having read this chapter, you will have a final question to ask: How will your literature answers be marked? Of course the precise methods used vary from one Examining Board to another, but the following basic principles hold good no matter which examination you are taking:

1 Does your essay answer the question set?
2 Has precise, relevant knowledge of the text been shown?

If the answer to both these questions is yes, you can rest assured that your work will be adequate.

Further reading

J.Cruickshank (ed). *French Literature and its Background vols 2 – 4*, O.U.P.
A.Lagarde et L.Michard. *Les Grands Auteurs Francais du Programme 17e, 18e, 19e, 20e Siècles*, Bordas.
The following series contain critical commentaries on many A-level set texts:

Studies in French Literature, Edward Arnold
Profil d'une Oeuvre, Hatier
Lire Aujourd'hui, Hachette
Théâtre et Mises en Scène, Hatier

INDEX